MW00904391

The Mighty

Man Manual

Victory and Freedom From Lust

and Pornographic Addictions

Edition II

By Jon Snyder

The Mighty Man Manual, Edition II
©2014 by Jon Snyder

References to "The Mighty Man Manual" Edition I,
©2009 by Jon Snyder

All rights reserved. Published by Jon Snyder and Mighty Man Ministries, PO Box 314 Edgemont, PA 19073. Cover art and design ©2008 Matrix Design, Inc. www.matrixdesign.us
Unless otherwise noted, Scripture quotations are taken from the New King James Version, © 1979, 1980, 1982, 1984 by Thomas Nelson, Inc. All right reserved.

www.MightyManManual.com
info@MightyManManual.com

ISBN-13: 978-1500269029
ISBN-10:1500269026

Printed in the United States of America

Thanks, praise, glory and all accolades to my Lord, my Savior, my confidant, my tutor who made me, loves me unconditionally, draws me to His presence, changes my heart daily and inclines my ear to hear His voice, who taught me line upon line, truth upon truth. Who is like the Lord our God? And words of thanks ineffable to my loving wife who believes in me and has labored in love and prayer for my freedom. Thank you for making me a better man.

CONTENTS

PART IV - FINDING REAL FREEDOM

The Good News...

Many of you who have found your way to this book have been searching for answers. What seemed like innocent entertainment at first has become a lifestyle of shame and bondage. Many of you have probably tried many times to give up pornography and are worn out from trying.

Jesus says to you, "Come to Me, all you who labor and are heavy laden, and I will give you rest... for I am gentle and lowly in heart, and you will find rest for your souls (Matthew 11:28,29)." There are many places to find treatment for addictions, but I can say with confidence, Jesus is the ONLY source of true freedom. If you want to be totally free and restored in your mind and heart, Jesus in not AN answer... He is THE answer.

Two thousand years ago, He claimed to have come to give salvation for sinners, to heal the broken hearted, to set people free who are in spiritual captivity and to give liberty to people bound in oppression (Luke 4:18). Two thousand years later, His mission hasn't changed! If you want to be free, Jesus died, conquered sin and death and lives today so that you can be!

He isn't waiting for you to get it all right before He helps you. *"God demonstrates His own love toward us, in that while we were still sinners, Christ died for us (Romans 5:8)."* He has borne our sins and carried our sorrow. He wants to give us freedom that only He can give. He wants to forgive your sins and give you a fresh start if you'll let Him.

If you have not known Jesus as your savior, as the healer of your heart and as the One who will set you free, you can know Him today. You are not too far gone for Him to save you. The Bible says He is able to save to the uttermost those who come to God through Him. There was no person on earth when Jesus lived who He was unwilling to save and love if they'd come to Him — and there is no person today who He is unwilling or unable to save. There is no depth of bondage that He can't free you from. He did it for me and He will do it for you too, if you'll put your faith in Him.

He offers salvation and eternal life to people who put their faith and future in His hands. The Bible says it is an unbreakable promise: in hope of eternal life which God, who cannot lie, promised before time began, (Titus 1:2).

If you have become addicted to pornography, nobody needs to tell you that sin enslaves and leads to death. You know this better than most people. All God's ways lead to life and freedom. You don't have to work for this freedom. It is God's gift to those who trust in Him. You receive that gift by confessing your sins to God, turning from them, asking Him to forgive you and to give you His free gift of eternal life.

If you would like to know Jesus as your savior, use the prayer below as a model, but make the words your own:

SALVATION PRAYER:

Father God. Forgive me for the sins and bad choices I've made that have hurt you, others and myself. I'm sorry and I want to be saved. I believe that you love me despite my sin and even sent Jesus, Your Son, to die in my place for my sin. Jesus, please take the place for my sin right now and make me clean and whole. I turn from my life of sin now and ask You to help me live for You and what is right. Thank you for saving me. In Jesus name I pray, Amen.

HEALING PRAYER FROM BONDAGE:

Father, I confess that I have a problem with pornography and sexual addiction. Please forgive me and right now, start working in my heart and life to set me totally free. Please give me mercy if I should mess up and grace to overcome when temptations arise. I confess that I belong to God and not to sin. Please cleanse my body, my soul and my imagination from every former act and let even the memories of the way I was fade away. Please also use the lessons of this book to teach me how to overcome and to know You better every day. Amen.

If you made Jesus your savior, you are on your way to freedom from the bondages of lust and pornographic addiction. God says that in Christ we are more than conquerors and can do all things through Him who strengthens us. So let us begin this journey out of bondage together. Better things are to come.

The Making of a Mighty Man...

IT DOESN'T TAKE A 'SPIRITUAL GIANT' TO SLAY GIANTS.

...Sibbechai the Hushathite killed Sippai, who was one of the sons of the giant. And they were subdued.

... Elhanan the son of Jair killed Lahmi the brother of Goliath the Gittite, the shaft of whose spear was like a weaver's beam.

...Yet again there was war at Gath, where there was a man of great stature, with twenty-four fingers and toes, six on each hand and six on each foot; and he also was born to the giant. So when he defied Israel, Jonathan the son of Shimea, David's brother, killed him.

... These were born to the giant in Gath, and they fell by the hand of David and by the hand of his servants.

1 Chronicles 20: 4-8

Most of us have heard about David and Goliath... One giant defies a nation and one boy with faith in a great God defies the giant... then against all natural odds, the boy defeats an enemy that men of greater stature could have never defeated. The thing I love about the passage above is that this story of slaying giants didn't end with David and one giant. His actions inspired others with the message, if God can do that with him, God can do that with me. Israel continued to be tormented by giants, but one man's actions changed everything.

Throughout Israel, men began to stand up and slay their own giants. I love these stories found in 2 Samuel and 1 Chronicles. It tells me that even the people who weren't spiritual giants at first and allowed their giants to rise up, can themselves become more than conquerors. They tell me that a "little old me" can slay giants - but not because I am great. Rather because the One true Mighty Man, the Lord Jesus Christ lives in me and operates through me. I may not be a David. I may have been one of the Israelites that hid on the sidelines. But many of those in hiding, after seeing God deliver one man, stood up, took a stand, were transformed into mighty men of faith and valor and started slaying giants.

Why does this epic mythology of the mighty man resonate with us so deeply? Why do we love stories and movies about heroic men who do the impossible? I think maybe it is because in our heart we know that each one of us is destined to do great things – not because we're so great – but because an amazing God has put His Spirit in us and the possibilities are endless. We may not all have the strength of Samson or the wisdom of Solomon; but I think within each one of us is a realization that through God, we can do mighty things.

THE MIGHTY MAN PITFALL

Mighty men through history have had their fatal flaw: lust. It is a story we see over and over. The Beowulf's of history can outmatch any man on the battlefield, but succumb to the beautiful maids. Samson had his Delilah. David had his Bathsheba. Solomon had his, well, all of them… and the list goes down through the ages.

My giant too was lust and pornography. It ruled over me for years. And I'm not alone. The statistics are shocking if not staggering how rampant this problem has become in Christian circles. Nearly every survey I've seen indicates that pornography is a problem for over 75% of Christian men. I even recently heard a study where 95% of Christian men admitted to struggling with lust and pornography. Just as Israel had its giants in the land, Christians today have theirs too. We are living a modern Beowulf saga, tormented by the seeds of lust spawned by our own weaknesses.

This book is the story of one "little-old-me" who God strengthened to slay his Goliath. This is my story of transformation from meek to mighty in

God. Chapter after chapter represents lesson after lesson that God taught me to walk out of my addiction and overcome. Like the men who saw another man slay a giant, may all who read this become Mighty Men of Valor, slay their giants and take back the Promised Land.

Getting the Most out of this Book

This book is about the struggle that we face with pornography from a Christian, Biblical perspective. But we will still be addressing "unchristian" concepts and talking openly in some parts about pornography or worldly influences. Even reading about pornography will make the struggle more difficult for some men. But in the end, I believe you will find great freedom through these lessons.

Through the course of these lessons we will retrain our mind, body and spirit how to think, act and react to the influences that bring struggle.

MIGHTY MAN TRAINING AND APPLICATION SECTIONS

Many chapters will have a section at the end for notes, prayer and action that should be taken. I think this is an important aspect to this book; because whereas stories and lessons may be very applicable, each person must make the lesson their own – take ownership, if you will – and allow God to do the work that only He can in order to get true freedom.

For this reason, this is more of a manual or workbook than a piece of literature to be read without responding to it. Take action! Ask God to speak to you through each chapter and help you understand how my lesson can relate to your struggle.

Understand that many of the lessons in here took time to be formed in my heart. You may need to go back and read a portion that seems really applicable to your areas of struggle while God works that lesson deep into your heart. I don't think that this manual is a template A-B-C formula for freedom. Every person is different and is in bondage for a different reason. That is why I believe this interactive, Spirit led approach is so important.

So prepare for your training. God wants to set you free and make you a Mighty Man of Valor…

Book Overview

PART I: MY STORY

This is my account of how I became addicted to pornography, saw it escalate in my life, and how I began my journey out. This section isn't intended to be deep or doctrinal. I get into teaching and application later. My story is just that… my story. If there is anything that I want it to teach is that God can heal any man… no matter how stuck in sin he may be. I'm not proud of the things I've done, but praise God who works all things together for good! I hope what I have come through can help bring freedom to many other men.

PART II: FOUNDATIONAL TRUTHS

This section includes lessons that are so important, so completely foundational, that every other lesson is meaningless without them. They provide the backbone for every man's freedom. You may be tempted to see chapters about grace or love and casually glance over them. Don't. Most people think they know about grace. But it is more deep and more profound than any of us can ever fully grasp.

PART III: FIGHTING BATTLES

Coming out of this sin WILL NOT be easy. I don't believe the intense struggle has to last forever. There is real freedom in Christ over our battles. But in the time between now and true heart change, you will have your share of battles to fight.

Lust is difficult to overcome because it is one temptation that can have roots in the fleshly dimension, mind and soul and in the spiritual. I don't know of any other books on this topic that take the time to really address all three areas of temptation with practical teaching and tactics. This part of the book has tough lessons that focus on how to train your mind and heart so that you are equipped to win the struggle "next time" and every time.

PART IV: FINDING FREEDOM

Many other teachings and workshops on the topic of lust depict a grim picture of "victory." I don't accept that victory is merely the ability to whip my flesh into shape. I believe that true heart change is both possible and taught in the Bible. While I believe learning how to fight our battles and temptation is essential to ultimate victory, simply knowing how to win a battle doesn't translate into "freedom." To be free, the heart must change. This is the work that only God can do and is addressed in the fourth and final section of the book.

The purpose of this book isn't to help you manage your sin. I'm not into "solutions" that don't bring about a true change of heart. This book's purpose is to bring you *through* the struggles into a place of true intimacy with God. From that place of true love and intimacy, we find the thing our souls really longed for in the first place and healing for the heart issues that keep us stuck in sin.

With God's help and guidance, every one of us will be able to say one day, "I don't struggle with lust or pornography." That is true freedom and the only solution I accept as valid.

GOING DEEPER:

This part of the book contains additional information and resources that can help you take the lessons of the Mighty Man Manual to the next level in your own life or to the next man you encounter who needs this. As you find freedom, help your brothers find freedom also.

As iron sharpens iron, So a man sharpens the countenance of his friend.
- Proverbs 27:17

~ Part I ~
My Story

This account isn't for the faint of heart. I was an addict. My struggle with pornography and my search for godly freedom may shock some people. I'm certainly not proud of the things I've done. But praise God who is still in the business of saving and restoring sinners.

I'm not trying to establish doctrine from my story. It is simply that: my story. We will get into some heavy teaching in the following parts of the book that talk about the lessons I learned on the way out. But for now, here's how the journey begins...

CHAPTER 1

The Journey In

It is a story and a sin that too many Christian men share: pornography. My fascination with it started... well, as early as I can remember. I can remember sneaking around even as a very young boy to try to find revealing pictures of women. This continued into adolescence and only got worse. My friends and I were so nonchalant about it. We'd talk about it, share magazines and movies and always conspire new ways to get our hands on more of it. When the internet came along and it got easier to find massive amounts of porn at the click of a button any time of night or day, that's when things started getting bad, but I didn't even know it at the time.

Amazing grace! Despite all my sins and shortcomings, God got a hold of my life along the way. I became a Christian and got saved in college. My fixation with pornography didn't stop, however once I was a Christian. I discovered that my Christian friends and I now shared pornography in a different way: as a secret addiction that couldn't be shaken. I was stuck with a habit that I hated and despite my best efforts I was stuck. **And I stayed stuck for years.**

I wish I could say that my journey out had a quick solution, some magic pill that any man can take and instantly the desire and struggle with this be gone. But that wasn't my story. Maybe there is a grand solution for some men stuck with this addiction, but they're probably not the ones reading a book like this. I think for most of us, the reality is that something that took years to get where it is doesn't go away overnight despite the most sincere prayers, pleas and tears.

"SOLUTIONS" THAT DIDN'T WORK.

It isn't that I didn't want to be free. I tried all the "solutions" that people and the Christian books I was reading claimed would work. I installed internet filters and cyber sitters. These could keep me from certain sites, for a time. But then the internet got smarter than the filters and some sites would still get through. And in times of desperation, rather than surf easily from site to site, I just surfed to see what sites and images I could find that wouldn't be blocked by the filter. I was getting frustrated. I was still an addict. I was just an addict with an internet filter. Eventually I learned a little more about computers and how to disable these filters even if I didn't have the password and I found myself right back in the addiction again with full force.

I realized that by putting a filter on my computer, I was just putting a wall between my wicked flesh and my wicked ways. A cyber sitter didn't change me, it just changed my circumstances. And I suppose these things have their place, but I wanted more. I wanted freedom – real freedom – not a band-aid. **I wanted a higher standard - a higher truth - to make my decision because I love God, not have my decision made for me by some program.**

I do think an internet filter is absolutely essential in a house with children - and extremely useful in avoiding accidental exposure to offensive content. So I'm not telling you to remove one if you've got it on your computer... yet. But like a child must remove the training wheels on a bike to know if they can really ride it, the acid test of your victory will be to see if you are free when there are no external restrictions in place. So there should come a time when you are the administrator of your own internet filter and can set your own passwords and disable them - to be bound by nothing but your convictions. You aren't free until freedom comes from within.

I can honestly say that today I am walking in freedom. I don't need an accountability group or a cyber filter. I have no restrictions on me and I still walk in freedom. That is where we are going... but right now, this is a story about where I was. And so my search for freedom continued...

Next I tried accountability. I do think that accountability groups have their place and can be one important step for many men. I'm not convinced, however, that they are an answer by their own merit. My experience with them was just OK. A bunch of Christian guys confessing our sins to each other in a small format men's Bible study group. All six of us in the group struggled with the same sin - lust and pornography. And so the dynamic was interesting. We all started strong. But after a couple weeks, in any given meeting at least a couple of us messed up that week. And while it was shameful at first, after a while it was almost a given that most of us would have messed up and the power was gone. It is hard to be tough with someone who messed up that week when you either messed up yourself or spent the whole week wanting to.

There was no shame or embarrassment in acting shamefully. It just became normal for us to be messing up. And after a while, it was more of us falling in a week than standing strong. Some weeks there was not one of us who didn't mess up. And so our accountability group turned into just a group... Maybe we weren't hard enough on each other. Maybe we should have really laid on the condemnation so that we really felt more crappy about ourselves when we screwed up. Maybe we should have laid the guilt on thick, or verbally berated each other to make the shame worse. But is any of that the way that it is supposed to work? Why does the loving kindness of God lead men to repentance (Rm. 2:4), but shame groups are supposed to do the job in Christian circles?

I've heard of accountability groups getting more creative. Some groups require someone who falls to buy dinner or simply fine each other for each slip up – some as much as $1000 per offense. And I think to myself, is that the answer? Do we trade our love of lust for the love of money and call ourselves free? Or have we just replaced one godless desire for another?

I was quickly disillusioned. This tool of accountability that so many Christian men swear by was not doing what I had hoped. But even if it did, is that the "freedom" I was hungry for? Did I want to be free simply because I'd be afraid of the shame of telling someone else? If shame is the only reason I keep my hands clean, I haven't conquered my sin, I've just found something I like more... pride.

I was still hungry for real freedom: to do what is right because I love God. Period. Don't get me wrong... accountability is good and has its place - I'm not telling ANYONE to stop fellowship or accountability. But an accountability group will never be anyone's savior... nor can the input of men affect the heart change that can only come from God. Accountability alone can't be what makes it happen for you. Victory comes from freedom within, not fellowship without.

Eventually that group fell by the wayside. But I met a wonderful girl and started dating her. We began praying with each other regularly and I thought, "Maybe this is my answer. She doesn't share my struggle. I'll have her as my accountability partner. Then I'll really be too ashamed to mess up." And so I confessed my struggle with her. And she confessed her issues with me, and we prayed for each other regularly and I confessed my sins to her when I'd mess up. And she kept dating me and forgiving me and I got used to her stuff and she got used to mine and eventually the sting was gone from that arrangement too. And I was back to my old habits. And eventually, accountability was more of an afterthought with us.

She married me and kept on forgiving me and loving me… but I didn't get better. Maybe she should have been tough on me and refused to marry me until I was better. Maybe she should have thrown a fit over my sin to make it a big problem. Maybe she should have threatened to divorce me for marital unfaithfulness with these fantasy girls online. But none of that happened. But if it had, would I be free, or would I again have to choose between something that I wanted and something I wanted. Carnal solutions to carnal problems are just more carnality in the end.

What I really wanted was to choose God over my sin. I wanted to love God more than my lust. I wanted to honor Him with my body, soul and spirit. Even though I would have been happy for any of these other approaches to work, they really were not what I wanted deep down.

I was crying out for FREEDOM. Real freedom.

I heard about deliverance from demonic strongholds. I thought that would be my answer. Any man who has struggled with this sin for long enough comes to realize there are spiritual things happening beyond ourselves in regard to this – perhaps removing these creatures from the equation would result in the freedom I was hoping for. Now, I actually have had amazing success in some areas of my life through deliverance. And this may be the answer for some people – I don't presume that the answer for me was the answer for everyone.

So I met with a pastor at my church and we talked and he prayed and laid hands on me and told these devils to leave. And I felt pretty good about it. I didn't feel any different, but I was taking that as my answer by faith. And a few days went by and I was OK and then I started to struggle again. It was horrible to have the realization set in that after deliverance, I was still struggling this hard. I had now tried just about everything you could imagine and I still wasn't free. I have come to realize that deliverance is one spiritual solution. However, lust can be triggered by the flesh, the mind and soul or the spirit. So even if you get rid of the spiritual tormentors, you can still be chained in your flesh and soul.

I turned the counseling up a notch and tried some third party "mega-counselors." These people went through family history and broke generational curses, broke soul-ties with everything that could be remotely tied to this thing, looked under every rock and spiritual corner, even tried theophostic-type prayer. Some of this gave me some measure of temporary victory and I'd re-attack this vice with renewed zeal and fervor.

Sooner or later, however, all the willpower and determination of man will fail. I'd come to realize later that it isn't willpower that wins this war but that a man's heart MUST be healed and truly rooted and grounded in the love of God in order to fight with something stronger than mere willpower. So I was stuck riding a rollercoaster of spiritual and emotional highs and lows. Over time, the lows kept getting lower and darker and longer. Again and again I'd fall, eventually pick my soul off the floor, and vow that I'd never fall again... only to discover that I was wrong, weeks, days or hours later. Through all these efforts and failures, despair and a disgusting feeling crept in that there was no hope for me.

I guess that's when it started to get really bad.

CHAPTER 2

The Journey Deeper

Pornography became a lifestyle for me. It wasn't an occasional slip-up. It was a daily event – sometimes multiple times every day and for hours on end I would sit and gratify this sin. I hated it and I hated myself for doing it. But I was stuck.

This became one of those self-perpetuating cycles: your self-esteem is in the toilet because of your addiction, but your addiction takes your mind off the fact that you hate yourself and so you run back to it. You feel like dirt... or like sludge on the underside of dirty dirt... so you wallow in grief and self-pity for a while and then run right back to your tormentor for another quick fix.

I'd cry out to God over and over, "Save me! Help me! Deliver me! Forgive me! Don't forsake me!" But the longer this cycle continued, the more I feared that God really did forsake me. I was afraid that I just got too dirty for Him to use. I assumed He certainly couldn't like me or accept me the way I was... after all, I couldn't like me or accept me the way I was and I'm not a holy god. But often, I'd have these wonderful times with God and it seemed like I was growing in other areas of my life and walk. So it seemed like I could keep these areas of my life separate. On the surface I was Jon, the growing Christian man that people respected... at home I was the miserable porn addict.

In church, I'd be fired up for God and certain that I would never go back to porn ever... but the temptation would come and I'd be right back into it. Every breakthrough that I had in God, I was sure would be the crucial component that would guarantee my freedom. My logic was, "If God hated my sin as much as I did, wouldn't it be the first thing on His list to 'fix' on me so that He could actually love me and so that I could love myself?"

They say that insanity can be defined as doing the same thing over and over but expecting different results. If that is an accurate definition of insanity, I'd say that I was certifiable. I can't tell you the number of times I'd tell God, "that was the last time." And I'd repent as hard as I could and feel good for a day or two and then be right back in it again. Sometimes I'd pick myself up right away and other times I'd go into a self-esteem spiral and on a porn bender for days.

I got bad enough that I literally couldn't be left alone. If I had any time without people around, it was almost a guarantee that I'd be in front of the computer getting a fix. I'd probably want to cry if I actually calculated the cumulative hours and number of years of my life that were wasted gratifying this sin... But that wasn't the part that frightened me the most.

THE LAW OF ESCALATION:

Every good junkie will tell you, they started small and their habit became an addiction and their addiction a prison. Pornography is no different. The law of escalation will affect EVERY person who thinks they can play with sin. If you have been struggling with pornography for any length of time, my guess is that you now watch more hardcore things than you used to. This is the path that I also was on. And it scared me.

I was in a hotel lobby and a TV in the corner was interviewing a felon in jail. He was convicted for child molestation. When they asked him how he got started, it may shock some people that he started with a well known franchise famous for, "innocent" softcore porn. Of course, this well known enterprise doesn't have a secret, underground, child porn branch, nor will every person who looks at pornography become a child molester or violent criminal. However, **porn, by its very nature induces an escalating addiction.** An addiction to softcore will turn into addictions to hardcore and so on... the only way it can go is to grow. Lust and perversion can never fill the void in the heart that it promises to fill. No addiction can. But this guy kept feeding his demons and his addiction grew and grew and turned vile. Rapists will often have the same story: escalation. I've heard the same thing from every branch of sexual pervert and sex offender.

Perversion of sexual orientation is another common way addiction causes escalation. I have counseled many men and heard testimonies from many others who started with heterosexual pornography and never had any bent toward homosexuality. But as their addiction spun out of control, the need for something more perverse and forbidden took them to a place they didn't want to go to get the same height of excitement. I even saw this happen firsthand with a close friend of mine in college. Nice guy. Nice girlfriend. Not so nice porn addiction. A friend and I found out about this one day when we decided to pull a prank on him – nothing harmful - we just thought it would be funny to move all his furniture around in his dorm room when he was away for a couple minutes. We started to move his bed and quickly discovered that the full length of the bed underneath had boxes full of porn. We quickly moved the bed back to its original location. We went to move the arm chair in the corner only to find stacks of boxes filled with porn behind it as well. We went to move a smaller chair only to find the same thing, a box of porn underneath that. Out of curiosity, we opened his closet and, sure enough, there was box after box of porn in there too. We quietly left his room, our prank foiled by not wanting to expose his intense addiction. A couple years later and a couple girlfriends later, he "came out of the closet." But his path to homosexuality started with porn. His porn collections when we saw them were "straight" porn, he didn't start out gay, but years of searing his conscience to sexual sins and escalation led him down a path of perversion that he couldn't escape. Even recently, a pastor in the news who was caught with a transsexual prostitute shared this same testimony – a "straight" porn addiction escalated into a perversion that was insatiable.

The human soul is not designed to find satisfaction apart from God. When we try to meet our needs with something that can never do the trick, we must increase our "dosage" to continue to fill whatever need we are trying to meet. Escalation doesn't happen overnight. But it happens. Perversion takes hold and escalates the problem. Then, when the next level of the addiction doesn't fill the hole either, our soul searches for more perverse ways to "fill the hole." You can only play with fire for too long before you start to get burned.

This was the part that really scared me. I remember seeing a couple scenes that originally shocked me. Later, however, I wanted to go back and see them again and others like them. This time the shock of what had at one time

9

been too "hardcore" now had a perverse fascination for me. My conscience was just a little more seared.

I realized that this is how the horror stories start and if I didn't get a handle on this, in 10 years, I could be another violent criminal whose story sounded like the others… "It all started innocently enough."

Deeper in my addiction than ever, but with a new fear in my heart, I began what I could call the first stages of the journey out…

CHAPTER 3

The Journey Out...

My freedom didn't come overnight or with one swift deliverance. But over a period of more than two years, one truth at a time God led me out. It is my hope that with the lessons from this manual, God can lead you out in a much quicker time.

You've heard it said that a journey begins with a single step. My first step was to understand that I was in too deep to get out alone and to get help from the person who knew me the most. So with a new conviction that I had to be free, I approached my wife with my problem. I needed to come clean with her and ask for her help and forgiveness in a bigger way.

"I need you to pray for me." I said. "Pray hard. Pray every day. Pray as often as you think about me. I've been struggling with pornography. More than I told you before. I'm addicted and not a day goes by, hardly, that I'm not messing up. I don't know how it got this bad, but **I need to believe that I can be free.**"

She was hurt but supportive and we prayed that night that God would free me and set me on a right path. We set a plan to pray together regularly and follow up. As the days and weeks passed, we continued to intensely pray that God would lead me out of this addiction and give me faith for freedom.

This was a type of accountability partner that I probably needed all along: one who would pray, pray and pray some more. Prayer changed me in a way that just confessing sins through accountability never did. We had a purpose together beyond simply holding me accountable: she was fighting for me. We were in it to win it this time... together. She would encourage me and I would stir myself up. Nothing changed overnight. I was still messing up almost constantly. But in about a month or so, one thing had changed. I started to believe that I could be free.

This was a huge step. My first real step. For years, I honestly didn't ever think I was going to be free. I went from slip up to slip up hardly fighting. But just to believe again and have hope was like catching a glimmer of light from a dark place or a cool breeze in a sweltering attic.

I went from thinking "I can someday be free from this" to believing it, to having strong conviction that I was going to kick this and that God was fighting with us. I think this was an important first step. It started bringing me into an attitude of faith and agreement with God. Hebrews 11:6 gives us an important insight: without faith it is impossible to please Him, for he who comes to God must believe that He is, and that He is a rewarder of those who diligently seek Him. We must come to God with this attitude of faith. Faith is like a key that unlocks what God is doing.

During Jesus' earthly ministry, even though He was God in the flesh, God wouldn't overstep His bounds and go beyond people's participation of faith. When Jesus went to His home town, the Bible tells us He couldn't do many mighty acts there because of their unbelief. Then in Matthew 9 when the father of the epileptic child came to Jesus, He zeroed in on the man's unbelief in Jesus as Lord saying, "All things are possible for him who believes." It then says that immediately the man cried out "Lord, I believe... help my unbelief!" He confessed his unbelief and put his mustard seed of faith in Jesus. Jesus then did what He does best: He brought freedom.

Jesus wants to bring us the freedom He paid for with His life. I had cried out to Him so many times and didn't see answers that I had begun to doubt His willingness to help me. But there were heart issues that He needed to heal before I could be set free. I came to realize during my journey out that my deliverance was layer upon layer of heart healing. It takes time to heal a broken heart. And God has never been holding anything back. He wants my freedom and your freedom even more than you do. He wants to bring you into a deeper relationship with Him even more than you do. He wanted it enough to die for it. If He already gave up His only Son and most precious possession to buy your freedom, how much more will He also give you the inner healing to bring you up out of this and set you on a rock to make you the mighty man of valor you are called to be in Him?

Your freedom is inevitable if you are pursuing God with all your heart. "Be confident of this, that He who has begun a good work in you will complete it (Php. 1:6)." God didn't draw you to Himself to leave you high and dry. He won't leave you or forsake you. He won't brush you aside. Jesus tells us He came to heal the broken hearted and to set the captives free (Lk. 4). He didn't just come for salvation. He came to give an abundant life of freedom.

The journey out starts with a single step. I had just taken my first step. I would find that there were many more layers of bondage and wounding that I would have to go through. This book follows my order of progression to be set free. You may have to learn these lessons in a different order, in which case you may want to re-read this a second time. Or you may have lessons that you need to learn that aren't in this book. But God will take you through them and set you free. He has promised it. Believe that you can be free. Ask God to give you the faith for your freedom and let the promises of scripture speak to you. Trust that God willing to fight for you and that you aren't in this alone. Stand on His word and His character. All things are possible to him who believes.

Time for your Mighty Man training... get ready for battle.

~ Part II ~
Foundations
of Freedom

As God led me out, these lessons became integral to every other lesson. Don't casually glance over these "familiar" concepts. Rather learn their lessons as a fresh start and perspective. Apart from these foundational truths, every other lesson found after them is virtually meaningless...

These will serve as a backbone of theology and form basic understanding of terms and concepts throughout the rest of this text.

CHAPTER 4

More Than You Can Bear...

UNLOCKING THE POWER OF GRACE

Before we get into practical teaching on how to fight and win our daily battles, we have to get one thing straight. **This is the most important thing you can ever learn: your victory isn't about you, your will, your endurance or mastering your temptations - ALL glory must go to God alone!** The real lesson is this: it is by grace only that you stand. All real strength, real virtue, all willpower, all ability to walk in the Spirit is from God alone.

Grace is bigger than we realize. Ninety-nine percent of the teaching and understanding of it focuses on its role in forgiveness and salvation – but this is just the tip of the iceberg, the entry point into God's grace. The beauty and majesty of God's grace that brought us into His Kingdom as sons grows deeper and more beautiful and more powerful if we allow it to keep operating in our lives. This is the same grace that Jesus needed for His earthly ministry in Luke 2:40 – not the salvation from sin, but the grace to destroy the works of the devil and receive from heaven the power that He, living as a man in a man's body, as a model for us all, could exhibit through grace. When you lay a hold of THIS grace, EVERYTHING changes. The years of struggle in the power of your own will and flesh come into context; and the things that *should* have worked now take on a new life and power. Glory to God alone!

I've heard testimonies from people who claim to get free from this, but their story is all about them. And I have heard these same teachers then condemn people still stuck in the very thing they used to struggle with. And I wonder, "The same God who gave me all the help, revelation, grace, mercy and strength to overcome - was this the same God that helped them?" Brethren, this is important: only God holds the keys to your victory; only God heals the heart; and so only God can get the credit for your victory. To think anything else is pure pride. This lesson is so foundational; and until you really get this, you'll never walk in victory because God opposes the proud but gives grace to the humble (Jas. 4:6). God will literally oppose your victory until you begin to grasp how very desperately you need His guidance through each and every moment and temptation.

The Bible teaches that God won't ALLOW us to be tempted beyond what we can bear (1 Cor. 10:13)... now understand the implications of that statement: **no matter how strong you are, there are temptations stronger than you!** You see, if by walking with God, HE keeps away temptations beyond what you can bear, then it logically follows that when you are not walking with God, there WILL be temptations that you are not able to bear. You are not your own keeper. YOU aren't the one who overcomes temptations. There are spiritual forces at work that you haven't ever contemplated and levels of temptation that you will never face because God has decided in His grace to shelter you.

The enemy is smarter than you and has been successfully tempting people for thousands of years. Apart from the active work of the Spirit of God, this isn't a fair fight. If it is just you and the devil... I'm sorry, but you are in way over your head. Thankfully God does shelter us according to His sovereign wisdom. **This is a function of grace.** You don't deserve this protection - you receive it by grace. Since God alone can keep you from temptation that goes over your head, none of us can boast in our strength or overcoming virtue. By the grace of God we walk and by grace alone we stand.

But Jon, you say, I've been in battles over my head and lost time and again. That's why I'm reading this book. True, but there is another function of grace that you also must discover: the enabling power of God through you. Winning this battle has nothing to do with you and your strength; for the Bible says that victory is not by might and not by power but by God's Spirit (Zec. 4:6). **You will NEVER stop sinning by trying to stop sinning.** Your carnal mind, carnal flesh and carnal will cannot stop carnality. This is why you've tried and tried with no success. Once you are born again, you are a new creation. God isn't trying to teach you how to not be a sinner, but how to be a son. He isn't teaching you how to NOT walk in the flesh but how TO walk in the Spirit. By the Spirit we put to death the desires of the flesh; and we learn to walk in the Spirit by grace.

Does grace mean we just sit back and don't fight when we are being tempted? Not at all. When you read through Romans, Paul admonishes us in chapters 5 and 6 to fight our battles, present our bodies as slaves to righteousness, etc., etc. But then in Romans 7, he talks about the fact that even though he knows the good he's supposed to do, he finds that he doesn't have the ability to do it and he keeps on sinning. He doesn't downplay the fact that we still have to fight sin. Just don't think for a minute that grace will make the journey out of this sin easy. What does this mean to us then? **It means there is a higher law than "try harder."** It means there is deeper truth to be found.

Paul continues his dissertation on overcoming sin throughout the rest of Romans with teachings about victory through setting our mind on the spirit, walking in the spirit, and taking on the mind of Christ. That is basically to say the same thing as Galatians 5:16, *"I say then: Walk in the Spirit, and you shall not fulfill the lust of the flesh."*

Our victory has everything to do with the Spirit and very little to do with our own strength. We must fight the battles we face - and this takes heart, preparation and endurance - but God's grace places us in battles that are not too great for us and by unlocking the power of grace, we receive what we need to walk in the Spirit and have victory in the midst of those battles. Despite all your preparations and fighting – mentally, emotionally and circumstantially – only God can keep you from falling. Proverbs says, *"The horse is prepared for the day of battle, But victory is of the Lord"* (Pr. 21:31). There is not one of us so great or so powerful in the Spirit that we can endure and stand strong if God were to allow the devil full access to us. We are protected at all times and sheltered from the brunt of attack. Just as the devil had to ask permission of God to afflict Job and Peter, he also has boundaries that he can't cross in our lives.

This is why Jesus prayed, *"And do not lead us into temptation, But deliver us from the evil one. For Yours is the kingdom and the power and the glory forever"* (Mt. 6:13). Jesus knew that ALL the power is from God and if God were to lead us to a place where the temptations were greater than we could bear, there is no man that could survive a full frontal attack from all the forces of hell.

What about when we do fail? If God's Word says we will not carry out the desires of the flesh if we are in the Spirit, then it stands to reason that the times we fall should cause us to step back and say, "Where did I stray from walking in the Spirit?" I propose to you that the times we feel like we couldn't stand up under the weight of the temptation we were facing, we had pride creep into our hearts and steal the grace that would allow us to stand – steal the truth of who we really are in Christ. God will still allow the battle to get intense... so intense, in fact, that it may even seem that it is more than you can bear. However through humility, you will receive the grace to escape your temptations.

The reality is this: we should pray every day that God, in His grace would help us to be humble enough to give Him all the glory for our victories, deliver us from all the attacks of the devil and not allow us to have a temptation that is more than we can bear. We will still have to fight and struggle, but we will have no illusions about who gets the real victory for the win. The strength to fight is even an act of grace, because real strength is from God, even as Paul admonishes in Ephesians 6:10, *"Finally, my brethren, be strong in the Lord and in the power of HIS might."*

HOW TO RESPOND TO FAILURE

Do you ever beat yourself up after messing up? It is common to have an attitude of, "I can't believe I did that... I'm such a jerk... I'm the scum that jerks wash off"... that is actually pride speaking and not humility. You heard me correctly. It doesn't SEEM like pride when we are beating ourselves into the mud, but think about this. **If YOU are disappointed that YOU failed, it was YOUR strength that you were relying upon.** You put hope in the power of your faithfulness to God as opposed to trusting in the power of God's faithfulness to you. That self-effacing, berating mentality says, "I'm disappointed in my own lack of strength... I thought I was stronger than that." God isn't surprised by our lack of strength. Why should we be? It is evidence that we had an exaggerated opinion of our strength (pride) and we just got knocked down a peg. If you beat yourself up after sin, you've got a pride issue and need to learn the law of grace.

I've gotten to the place before where "I was doing so well" at staying free from sin, that I literally thought I'd beaten it forever. And then I got hammered with temptation that I just couldn't fight. It was a wake-up call. I wasn't the strong one. I simply had figured out how to beat the level of temptation that I had known. There were higher levels of temptation that I simply wasn't ready for. My pride went before my fall.

Peter warns in his first epistle, *"Humble yourself in the sight of God casting all your cares upon Him"* (v.5:7). We tend to think that humility is "carrying our cross" and we've got to bear our own burden. That is actually the *opposite* of humility. We can't bear our own burden. That's why Christ had to take our heavy yoke in exchange for His light one. When we take up our own cares, we are doing the opposite of humbling ourselves. There is no person who is strong enough to stand against the devil if God were to remove His protection. So why do we feel as if we are so responsible for our success? That is the attitude of pride that opens the door for us to sin. That pride chokes out grace.

We are sinners. We *deserve* no good thing from God. We deserve the wages of our sin, but Jesus gave us the wages of His righteousness. Grace is our ONLY strength. Some people look at themselves and are proud of a strong self-will or their intellect or spiritual gifts. But who can take credit for the way God sovereignly chose to make and equip them? Our gifts and equipping are a function of sovereign grace.

If you are realizing the power of grace right now, it is because God has given you the grace for your spiritual eyes to be opened. You can't even take credit for learning about grace because the Bible teaches that God allows the curse of spiritual blindness on all people to be lifted by His mercy! So even what you know, you know by grace. We need grace even to get grace! Without grace, we are spiritually deaf, dumb, blind, helpless, hopeless and stuck on a highway to hell.

Grace allows you forgiveness. Grace allows you access to God. Grace enables you to learn spiritual truth. Grace allows you to walk in the Spirit. Grace keeps the devil from full access to you. Grace. Grace. Grace. It all comes down to grace.

You are God's workmanship. He is the potter. We are the clay. Hands off the pottery! The sooner you settle that you can take credit for nothing and give God ALL the glory for your victory, the quicker God can work.

My attitude must not be to say that I've attained because of something I've done or trust in my strength. We need grace first and imparted strength second. Grace places us in the right battle and then God imparts strength to win through grace. I must by faith access the grace to overcome by giving all the glory to God.

It is no coincidence that Peter writes to us about humbling ourselves. He struggled with pride to a great extent. Peter was a strong man in his own ability and resolve... so much so that when Christ told him he'd fall that night in the garden, he told God He was wrong! It was that same pride in his own strength and not the grace of God that opened the door for him to fall and deny Jesus. What if Peter had fallen on his knees and confessed that he was just a man and asked, not for greater strength... but for the grace not to fall. Would the story have gone differently?

I've noticed in my own life, the times I was asking for strength, I didn't notice a discernible help. But when I've asked for grace – grace not to be tempted beyond what I can bear and the grace to walk in the Spirit, to put on the new man, to see myself as I truly am in Christ, I believe God, then has helped me greatly. In this way we also don't have the space to make excuses for our sin. Some use grace as a license to sin, thinking that if they fall, "Oh well... God's grace will cover me." That is an abuse of grace and a cheapening of what we have available to us.

The truth of our identity in Christ is that we HAVE been made a new creation, we ARE now the righteousness of Christ, we HAVE been set free from the power of the enemy, we HAVE EVERY spiritual blessing already in Christ, our old man HAS been killed and crucified with Christ, we ALWAYS are victorious in Christ. When we get the grace to actually believe these truths from the Bible, it changes everything. As you read this book, God will establish these things in your heart more and more and heal you of many heart wounds. But through grace we don't have to wait until "some day" to walk in freedom – we are free today and in the Spirit we have access to everything we need to win every battle.

People who have tried time and again, and I was one of them, often have a difficult time believing that they can really be free. The truth is that you already are – your soul just hasn't figured it out yet. But know this: your starting point will dictate your end place. If you start, believing that you are in bondage, helpless and hopeless, then you have little to look forward to because Christ isn't going to die again for you. But if you start this knowing that Christ HAS made you free, then there can be no doubt as to whether you will find freedom. The answer is yes and amen in God!

The difference begins in relating to God through grace and enjoying the total paradigm shift from trying to walk out freedom in YOUR strength versus by the Spirit. It is grace that allows us to not be tempted beyond what we can bear. As soon as man's strength (pride) enters that equation, it chokes the grace and we indeed experience temptation beyond what we can bear. Aren't you glad God isn't telling you to try harder! He began a good work in you and He will complete it. Let us access this grace today and discover that it will change EVERYTHING!

~Mighty Man Training & Application~

If you have never tapped into God's grace for your life you can start today! Take the words of the sample prayer below and make them your own.

God, forgive me for living by my own strength and arrogance. Please change the devil's boundary lines and give me greater grace - space to come right. ALL the provision to overcome sin was paid for in Jesus. He makes me able to have victory.

I repent for identifying more with the old man who is dead than with the new man you have made me to be in Christ. Give me the grace to walk in the Spirit and to put on the new man today. Give me the grace to see myself as a son and not as a sinner.

I pray that I would not be tempted beyond what I can bear today, tomorrow and this week. Show me how to overcome temptations as they arise and give me the strength in Your Grace to fight as I should. But let me not think in pride that I have done this by my strength. All glory to you for my victories. Amen

CHAPTER 5

The Lesson of Love

It is a frustrating thing to want to be free, believe you can be free and fight harder than you've ever fought and still be messing up regularly. I was fighting now... struggling daily for freedom... and that was a big step from messing up and just accepting that as normal. But I was only keeping clean for a week or so at a time and then I just lost the power to fight. The constant battles, the dreams... it all wore me down until I just couldn't fight any more and I'd give in and go sin (sometimes throwing off all restraint for days before I'd get "back on the wagon").

Frustrating isn't the right word for it. Heartbreaking. Demoralizing. Awful. Those are maybe more accurate terms. I'm sure you know how this feels. Feeling battered down, I heard about a counseling program from a friend that had a great reputation, so I decided to get some professional help.

The morning of the counseling session, something amazing happened... but not with the counselors. As I was getting out of bed, God gave me a vision. There's no other way to describe it. I was sitting up on the edge of my bed, not sleeping or dreaming and I started to see a scene as though I were dreaming.

The following took place:

I was on the ground in a sort of pit with a highway overpass up above me. The color was that sand colored concrete that they make those overpass slabs out of. And I could see two lanes or roads up above. And so I was jumping to get out of my pit, trying to grab a hold of one of the concrete slabs which started this highway above me. I was jumping and jumping, but couldn't reach it. So I thought I'd try to reach the other lane (which was just as high) and I started jumping for that one. But I couldn't reach that one either. And so I desperately kept jumping and trying to reach these platforms, going back and forth between the one on the left and the one on the right until I was exhausted. It was once I realized I could NEVER reach those platforms that I looked to my left and saw a doorway out of this pit. The door was on the ground and I could have easily walked out. But there was an interesting twist. In my vision, I had been jumping for so long, that I couldn't STOP jumping. I was like a human pogo stick. I pogoed my way over to the door and discovered that the door was only high enough to walk through. As I would jump, my head would crest the top of the doorway and I couldn't go through it. In my vision I began to cry and called out to God, "God I don't know how to stop jumping so that I can walk out this door?... I'm so tired."

The vision stopped and I went to the shower and just fell down on the floor of the shower crying. I still didn't understand all that God was trying to tell me in the vision. As I sat there, I asked for the interpretation. This is what God told me. The two roads or platforms symbolize the ways that I thought I'd have more love and acceptance from God. The one road was the things that I was going to not do (i.e.: sin and lust and porn, etc.). The other road was things I was going to do (i.e.: be pure, write books, do ministries, win souls, etc.). I subconsciously thought I'd have more of God's love and approval if I did all these good things and less of it if I did all these bad things. I realized from that vision that I was trying to *earn* God's love, approval and acceptance *because I didn't really love myself* or understand how fully God loves me.

My self esteem had been so hurt and continued to be so demolished by the porn addiction that I didn't feel acceptable to God. I saw myself as a tarnished, dirty vessel. The way I felt about myself was such that I could never love myself as long as this sin was in my life... so I assumed that God felt that way too. It wasn't a conscious thought, but in my heart I was believing, "If I can only stop sinning like this, then God will love and accept me more. If I can only walk in purity and do great things for God, He'll have a reason to give me favor and approval." I was trying to jump for God's approval and love. The doorway on the ground represented the easy availability of God's love for me.

But as long as I was trying to earn it by doing this and not doing that, I could never walk through that door and experience it.

Can you love and accept yourself today even though you have this sin in your life? Say, "I love myself and who I am" out loud right now. If that is difficult to say and believe, you are seeing yourself through what you do rather than as who you are in Christ. This lesson is for you.

KNOWING THE UNFAILING, UNCONDITIONAL LOVE OF GOD IS ESSENTIAL TO YOUR FREEDOM

What I was beginning to learn was a cornerstone revelation that would be the foundation for my inner healing and growth. Let me say something shocking: God will minimize His help for you to overcome your sin until you start to see yourself as lovable and as something of great worth. "God demonstrates His own love toward us, in that while we were still sinners, Christ died for us (Rom. 5:8)." Until you learn this lesson, God actually *has* to oppose your freedom, because to set you free with this in your heart would literally reinforce the notion that you are unacceptable now and more acceptable when you are "good." To reinforce these beliefs would desperately entrench your heart in idolatry.

What idolatry, you ask? The idol of Perfect You. When we feel as though we *have* to get it right and as though God is *waiting* for us to get it right, we are trusting in ourselves for acceptability and strength instead of God. We are saying, "When I'm perfect, I'll be acceptable and lovable. When I have it all right, God will certainly love me then." So we're putting our faith in a potential-future-you rather than in the truth. We can't trust our commitment to God more than God's commitment to us. There is no comparison.

The idol of Perfect You further reinforces a vicious cycle of shame. Though we may seldom even be consciously aware of this idol in our hearts, the devil likes to taunt us with these notions of all the things we aren't - not just in regard to our sexual integrity, but in every area of life. We have the ideas of what the perfect Christian should be, the perfect spouse, the perfect career, parent, etc. We compare ourselves to our ideals and fall short every time. This breeds shame, resentment, anger, frustration - all the things that often serve to trigger our desire to escape, self-gratify and find an outlet in sexual acting out.

24

The acting out breeds more shame and further reinforces how far we are from our mark… and the cycle continues.

A key indicator which lets us know when we have this idol in our lives is how we respond when we mess up. If you beat yourself up and get depressed when you've messed up, you have an idol in your heart. The Bible tells us there is a difference between godly sorrow and worldly sorrow; between godly repentance and worldly repentance. "For godly sorrow produces repentance leading to salvation, not to be regretted; but the sorrow of the world produces death (2 Corinthians 7: 10)." It then goes on to describe the characteristics of godly repentance and sorrow: diligence to clear yourself, vehement desire, zeal, vindication, etc.

Conversely, what most of us do when we mess up is we start to beat ourselves up, "I can't believe I did that again. I'm such an idiot. Why can't I just get it right? I'm scum… I'm the scum that scum doesn't even like, etc., etc., etc." What are we doing when we think this way? We are comparing ourselves to our idol of potential-future-self rather than seeing ourselves as the Bible tells us we are. We are trusting in our works rather than in God's grace.

We are allowing that devil to cut us down. Why? Here's the interesting bit of psychology behind it all: humans don't like to feel bad about themselves. If we create a scenario where we feel bad and thereby punish ourselves for what we've done, we're creating a reinforcement tool to not do it again. If we don't like to feel bad about ourselves, we'll try hard to not do the thing that makes us feel bad any longer. We are trying to create an environment where we can save ourselves out of our sin through self-chastisement rather than use the Bible's principles to save us and define our self-image.

God CAN'T set you free when you are operating in this mindset! If He were to do so, He would be affirming your idol as truth. If God were to give you freedom and fellowship while you actually believe in your heart that you have to earn it, He would create a monster 1000 times worse than you struggling with porn. Most of us don't consciously believe in our mind that we can earn God's love. We "know better." But if you struggle with self-deprecating thoughts after sinning or if you find it hard to run to God in prayer IMMEDIATELY after sinning, a good psychologist will tell you that in your heart, you think that God will accept you more if you've stopped sinning. I'd guarantee if this is the case, this idol is in your heart. It has to go before the sin does.

GET GOD'S PERSPECTIVE

The reality is that our sin doesn't change the way God feels about us. *"Who shall separate us from the love of Christ? Shall tribulation, or distress, or persecution, or famine, or nakedness, or peril, or sword? For I am persuaded that neither death nor life, nor angels nor principalities nor powers, nor things present nor things to come, nor height nor depth, nor any other created thing, shall be able to separate us from the love of God which is in Christ Jesus our Lord* (Romans 8:35, 38-39)." Your sin doesn't separate you from God's love. He loved you even before He saved you; and He saved you even knowing you would blow it over and over after salvation.

Nothing changes His love. Somehow we get the idea that God is up there with His arms folded and a frown on His face waiting for us to get it right. Nothing could be farther from the truth. God understands our weaknesses. That's why He gave us grace in the first place. Jesus knows what it is like to be a man.

"We do not have a High Priest who cannot sympathize with our weaknesses, but was in all points tempted as we are, yet without sin. Let us therefore come boldly to the throne of grace, that we may obtain mercy and find grace to help in time of need (Heb. 4:15, 16)." This same High Priest *"is also able to save to the uttermost those who come to God through Him, since He always lives to make intercession for them* (Heb. 7:25)."

I hope you catch the depth of this: Jesus, **always, continuously, without ceasing** lives to make intercession for you because He loves you and understands what you are going through. If you could run into heaven right after messing up, you'd see Jesus doing this very thing: interceding for you. You'd hear Him saying the same thing He did on the cross, "Father forgive him… he doesn't know what he's doing."

The Bible says there is no condemnation for those in Christ (Rom. 8:1). That means He's never holding you at arm's reach. God wants us to be able to run to Him when we feel dirtiest, not once we've cleaned up our act. We can't clean ourselves. Only the blood of Jesus can. So therefore, run where the blood is immediately and learn to access His love and grace instead of finding guilt and shame. Jesus took your guilt and hung naked and ashamed for you, so you'd never have to bear it again. He took your sin and its punishment so you'd never have to take it again. He gave you His righteousness, a righteousness that you'll never deserve. And when we walk in worldly sorrow, we agree with the devil instead of choosing to see ourselves as righteous.

How You See Affects How You Act

Have you ever offered someone something to eat but had them refuse because they "just brushed their teeth."? Or have you ever seen someone spill something on themselves and hear them say, "I just washed this shirt!"? If they had a dirty mouth or a dirty shirt it wouldn't have been a big deal to get it dirtier.

If you see yourself as pure, you won't want to get dirty. It's like a spot of dirt on a clean car... it bothers us so much more than if the car is filthy. So when we see ourselves as dirty, it's like, "Who cares... I may as well go sin." But when we see ourselves as God sees us, we will have something worth fighting for. Purity doesn't come by our actions - it came by Jesus' actions on our behalf. If we begin to build our self-esteem through the intense love of God rather than self-effort, we will be less susceptible to the devil's lies and will have less desire to project our own negative self-worth on the women in porn (this is one of the dynamics that takes place in pornography).

We don't truly understand how deep God's love is for us. I don't think I can say it better than Jesus did in John 15:9. "As the Father loved Me, I also have loved you." YOU HAVE TO GET THIS: Jesus says, "I love you as much as God loves me." But that's not all! In John 17:23, He prays that we would come to know that the Father loves us as much as He loves Jesus. Can you fathom that? The Father and Jesus want you to know this: **there is as much love in heaven toward you as there is for Jesus.** The Father loves you as much as He loves His perfect son! Jesus loves you as much as the Father loves Him! You are that important to them. Who can fathom that much love for sinners like us? But it is there. And we must learn to trust this love and run to God with our sin instead of away from Him. God loves and accepts me with all my junk and all my stuff.

Only when we begin to understand that we are truly loved like this can God have the freedom to set us free. When we understand that He won't love us any more when we're sin free than He does now, powerful forces will be set in motion and it won't be long until you are free indeed.

You may have been waiting for God to smack you on the head with a two-by-four, but the only one you'll find Him use is Romans 2:4, "the loving kindness of God leads us to repentance." Why? Why is this the path? Why isn't it a ten-step program or the next big conference? The Bible teaches that we receive strength in our inner man when we are rooted and grounded in love - that as we know this love of Christ, we are filled to the fullness of God (Eph. 3:16-19)! Love is God's launching platform.

When we begin to fathom the love that sent Jesus to the cross for us, the love whereby He loves us as much as the Father loves Him, it can finally go from head knowledge to heart knowledge that His work on the cross is a finished work. He already purchased our freedom. He already purchased the healing of our hearts. He already made us acceptable. He gave everything. There is nothing left to give or to be done. I lived my whole life as though something were "missing" - as though I had something left to get from God. When it came to spiritual matters, my cup was always half empty rather than half full. Actually it was more like I saw it as all empty rather than all full. Having a revelation of God's love enabled me to stop seeing all the things I'm not and embrace all the things I am in Christ.

When you start to realize that you have a spiritual inheritance, that you are spiritually rich, that you are now a son of God, your identity will begin to be more than just a Biblical concept. It will become a truth that governs how you think and act. You'll begin to access the grace to receive and walk in the truths that are already a Kingdom reality in your life. You will have something to protect rather than feeling that you have nothing to lose by giving away your inheritance. You will begin to see your self-worth and immense value to God. You'll be able to cast away that idol that says, "You'll be acceptable when…" These are the FOUNDATIONS of real freedom.

When we have tried and failed, it is because the foundation is faulty in our hearts. It REQUIRES something of us to fight temptation. If our "spiritual reserve tank" is empty because the devil has sucked it dry through shame, we will have nothing from which to draw in order to resist the devil. Furthermore, if we have no foundation - if we are not "rooted and grounded" in love, all of our self-efforts and attempts at faith will eventually fail because the scriptures teach that faith works through love is what avails in Christ (Ga.5:6).

Learning to walk in love is 99% of this battle. Really. I didn't understand it myself for so long. For years I cried out for answers and God would minister His love to me… and I'd resist it because I felt too dirty and didn't love myself. I had an intellectual knowledge of God's love for me without the experiential knowledge of it. But make no mistake about it, the Bible says that, "But whoever keeps His word, truly the love of God is perfected in him (1 Jn. 2:5)."

Did you get that? If you are able to walk in God's ways and keep His word, it means that the LOVE of God has been perfected in you. We've emphasized so many things in Christianity. People think that pursuing holiness is more important than pursuing love. But love is the key to it all because God is love. All His ways work through love and come alive and make sense in love. God needs you to know His unfailing love more than He wants you to stop sinning. Really. But if you learn this love you will also stop sinning. But you will not stop sinning if you think you need to in order to receive His unfailing love. His love is so much bigger than your sin. It always has been. It always will be. At your worst, God's love is at its best: indomitable, unchangeable, infallible, unfailing, unfathomable... and plainly wonderful.

Love is the key, my friend. It unlocks our spiritual inheritance. It unlocks a healthy self-image. It unlocks relationship with God. It gives a foundation from which we fight. It gives us emotion and spiritual reserve. If you want to know what you have been searching for in lust and pornography, look no farther than love - real love - the love of God. He is ready to heal your heart and pour out the love that you have been dying for. Don't listen to the voice of the devil that says it can't be for you. Listen to the voice of the Spirit and let Him fan the flame of His love for you.

THE POWER OF LOVE

Let me ask you a question: if you had never sinned and if this sin was not in your life, how differently would you think and relate to God? How would your expectations differ from the Lord? THIS is how you need to begin to think and relate to God now because it is an insult to the sacrifice that Jesus made to live any other way as a Christian. He gave everything and took what you deserve so that you could be free and get what He deserves. You, therefore deserve the right to relate to God with the same confidence that Jesus has before the Father.

Let me ask you another question: what do you really think that getting over this sin will add to Christ's work for you? Ouch. You've probably never looked at this sin that way before have you? But that is what we are doing when we make this sin out to be something more than it is: one of many works of sanctification that God will do in your life that have nothing to do with your position before God. Your relationship with God exists because of Christ's works, not yours. Your blessing is the blessing of Christ. Many have been taught to think that God will bless us more if we are good. But the Bible is clear that God has already given us EVERY blessing, has given us ALL things that pertain to life and Godliness and with Christ will withhold no blessing (Eph. 1:3, 1 Pet. 1:3, Ro. 8:32). What else is there? Will you earn for yourself more blessing than the "ALL THINGS" that God has given us in Christ. What more do you hope to gain that Christ hasn't earned on your behalf?

Your freedom is Christ's freedom. How, by getting over some stinking sin, do you hope to improve upon perfection? Will you earn for yourself more acceptance or love than the perfect love and acceptance that Christ has earned for you? It is time to cast off our illusions and simply embrace the simplicity of the gospel of grace. You are loved more than you can imagine today. THIS love is the power for change.

The devil has perverted Christianity and the gospel of grace to remove Jesus from the center and in His place give us a works-based treadmill. The pursuit of life for most Christians isn't relationship with God but what they are doing and aren't doing "for God." They are trading the unconditional love of the Father for a performance based acceptance that no one can live up to. And this isn't to say that freedom from sin isn't possible. It is! But it flows FROM relationship that God has already paid for. We must stop trying to get to a place of right relationship and receive by faith that we already have it.

God, in one mighty blow, through the cross, has settled the sin issue as it relates to our position as sons once and for all. God isn't giving you power to stop sinning any more than He is giving you the power to kill the corpse of your long-dead great, great, great grandfather. Both your sin nature and old gramps, as far as God is concerned, are dead men. WE, not God keep resurrecting the old dead man rather than reckoning him dead as the Bible tells us to do. God IS, however, giving you power to love – to freely receive His love with no strings attached; to love yourself and who He made you to be; to love Him who first loved us with the measure of love that He gives; and to love others through this miracle of love. Stopping sin will be the BYPRODUCT of that radical heart change. Again, the Bible says that if anyone keeps God's word, truly the LOVE of God has been perfected in him (1 Jn. 2:5).

Love is the power of God. Ephesians 3:16-21 are some of the most powerful scriptures in the New Testament and regularly used by pastors world-over in their benedictions: *"that He would grant you, according to the riches of His glory, to be strengthened with might through His Spirit in the inner man, that Christ may dwell in your hearts through faith; that you, being rooted and grounded in love, may be able to comprehend with all the saints what is the width and length and depth and height to know the love of Christ which passes knowledge; that you may be filled with all the fullness of God. Now to Him who is able to do exceedingly abundantly above all that we ask or think, according to the power that works in us, to Him be glory in the church by Christ Jesus to all generations, forever and ever. Amen."*

We want God to do exceedingly, abundantly above what we can ask in delivering us from this sin, right? Well what is the POWER that works in us? The POWER of God in us is LOVE! It is not force of will. The power of God is not self-control. Self-control is a FRUIT of the Holy Spirit, not of our will (Gal. 5:23). Love will take you father in obedience than your will ever could. Love will give you the power to see yourself as someone of great worth; and therefore not someone to debase with worthless lust. Love will give you the power to change the way you see the people selling themselves into pornography or that girl flaunting what she has. Love will compel you to love God with all your heart so that the thought of sinning against that love breaks your heart. You don't have a lust problem. You have a love problem. If you will change your pursuit to a life of love, everything else will change by default. Mighty man, pursue God with the radical abandon that can come only by knowing that there is nothing and will never be anything between you in this relationship.

~Mighty Man Training & Application~

1. Make it a habit to take time after every and any sin to run to God.

2. Ask God to show you His love for you every day.

3. Think about the verses we read in this chapter from John 15:9 and 17:23. Say out loud, "God loves_____ (your name)." There is something powerful about declaring God's love for you aloud. Now try the even more powerful statement, "God loves _____ AS MUCH as He loves Jesus." Do that until the love of God starts to penetrate your heart.

4. Repent for agreeing with the devil who tricks us into thinking that we need to be better before we're acceptable to ourselves, others and God. Try a prayer like the one below:

Father, forgive me for seeing myself as dirty when you have made me clean. Forgive me for trusting in my actions more than I've trusted in Your love. Thank you that You love me as much as you love Jesus. Thank you that you accept me just as I am. I renounce all agreement with every performance-based idol and receive the free gift of grace in Jesus Christ. I choose to forgive and love myself today, in Jesus name. Amen.

CHAPTER 6

Understanding the Nature
of Sexual Addictions

Sex is designed to be an activity that stimulates us on every level of our being: body, soul and spirit. Consequently, breaking addictions will involve understanding the different nature of temptations and how they affect us on multiple levels and multiple dimensions of our being. It is this multi-faceted nature of sexual temptation that makes it so very ensnaring and so difficult to navigate into freedom. We can be tempted to sin in our mind, in our soul, in our flesh and by demonic forces in the spirit. We can also be tripped up in unhealthy understandings and misunderstandings of sex and sexuality. I believe the fact that we can be tempted time and again on so many fronts is one reason many men are plagued by this for years; and why the enemy can so easily exploit this particular area of weakness. Just when we think we have something that works in one area, we get blindsided by temptations on a whole other level. The devil is an expert at reading us and knowing which area is weakest at any moment.

Understanding the nature of your temptation will help you know how to fight it. This chapter gives a basic overview of the nature of the temptations as well as what makes addictions form. Chapters that follow will serve to equip you with more specific strategies to overcome in different situations.

BEAUTY AND FASCINATION

Even before we begin to delve into temptations on the various levels of our being, I believe that there is one important aspect of this temptation to address that doesn't fall into the category of a temptation but rather becomes a stumbling block due to misunderstanding and bad teaching. I believe that many men do not know how to appropriately respond to the issue of beauty and being drawn to it. This learned and inappropriate response to a natural tendency results in or augments different temptations and contributes to the problem. This then, is more of a dysfunctional behavior pattern and is not a "temptation" in and of itself.

I remember taking psychology classes in college and one of the clinical studies we observed related to the idea of beauty. The study would take infants and show them pictures of different people and gauge responses such as interest, demeanor, pupil dilation, etc. Without exception and across every race, gender and culture, the babies gave more attention, smiled at, and were captivated for a longer duration by the pictures of beautiful people.

They did other studies with adults and photos of people as well. Adult men and women would look at varying photos of men and women and try to determine character traits and rate how well they thought they would get along with the subject. Again, people of all races, ages and genders, on average, ascribed more favorable character traits to more attractive people and also gauged that they would want to spend the most time with beautiful looking individuals.

In the secular realm, I recently heard a bit by a comedian who was making fun of his looks. He made the comment that life is hard as an unattractive man because if you make eye contact with people or smile at them, they think, "Who is that creep and why is he smiling at me?" "But if you are attractive," he jokes, "people want you to look at them. They smile back. They think, 'Oh, what a nice guy.'" There is a lot of truth to his bit.

Simply put, people are fascinated and drawn to beauty. It happens in infants from before they know to judge or form prejudice. Our human fascination and fixation with this isn't limited to human beauty. We love beautiful natural surroundings, beautiful paintings, skillful craftsmanship, majestic creatures... Simply put, things of beauty fascinate us. And do you know what? Our partiality to beauty and fascination with it isn't sin. You can no more repent of seeing a beautiful woman and thinking, "wow," than seeing a beautiful view from a mountaintop and saying, "wow." Now I don't want to confuse what happens in us when we see something beautiful with what happens in us when we see an image that is designed to incite lust or a woman who is dressing provocatively. These instances are overt attacks and are to be handled differently than the way we should process the impact that happens in our soul when we encounter a thing of beauty.

The "wow" factor that happens when we see a beautiful woman or any thing of beauty isn't sin. The sin comes with how we process that stimulus and what happens next in our souls. We need to learn what to do with the "wow." You see attraction to beauty is not the same thing as lust, nor is it sin. You can see a beautiful woman and say, "wow," without lusting after her, undressing her with your mind, or anything sinful and damaging. God made mankind in His own image. We are beautiful creatures. Lucifer was also a beautiful creature... the most beautiful of all created beings. It is no accident that his beauty made him suited to direct all praise and worship in the universe toward God. However, he eventually wanted creation to marvel at his own beauty rather than allow himself to be a reflection of the magnificence of his Creator. And he is perpetuating this tragic slip-up even to this day. Therefore, Proverbs 5 warns not to lust after beautiful women or let them allure you. Misused beauty does have this power. And part of the problem with pornography and lust is simply that we have an innate NEED to gaze on beauty, get caught up in it, marvel at it, and so on. It is a literal need of the human soul. And we must be careful to learn to recognize when this need is being misdirected and perverted.

In my experience, when we see a beautiful woman, we are prone to misdirect the "wow" in one of two ways. Either we pervert our attraction and allow ourselves to begin to lust and desire the woman, or we repress the emotion, wish it weren't there and beat ourselves up for the fact that it is. Both are dangerous and both responses will kill us. Lusting causes us to elevate the creation to a place of an idol. We allow the woman to hold our attention/worship for an undue amount of time instead of saying, "Wow God, you made that one beautiful on the outside. Show me Your beauty and let me be fascinated with that!"

Conversely, the second option, repression, will only cause us to yearn within until something must come out. We lie to ourselves when we see image after image in every walk of life and pretend that they don't affect us. I am convinced that one source of major temptation is that we don't recognize enough our inherent need to enjoy beauty and by the time we fall, we have so much bottled up inside us that we can't think or function normally whatsoever. We begin to dream, daydream, fantasize and mentally rehearse the emotions we repress until we can't take it anymore. Hence, we get fixated on man's beauty and do not spend enough (or any) time reflecting on the beauty and majesty of the Lord in our daily lives.

It is this inherent fascination with beauty that will cause us to be abandoned worshippers of the Lord in this life and in the next: "Oh, worship the Lord in the beauty of holiness (1 Ch.16:29)!" Job tells us that He arrays Himself with glory and beauty (Jb. 40:10). God is beautiful. David was both a mighty man, and at the same time completely fascinated and captivated by the Lord's beauty. David says he had only one desire in life: to dwell in the house of the Lord all his days and spend them gazing upon the beauty of the Lord (Ps. 27:4). That is a pretty serious beauty fix coming from the man who God called "a man after His own heart."

I am designed to love and respond to beauty. So are you. As I was walking out of this sin, I would sit and ache to look at porn. I didn't understand why, however. I hated it. I came to realize that often, it was just a powerful combination of my sex drive, which was created by God, the wounds in my soul crying for relief and my soul's need to meditate on beauty. If you will really lay hold of this truth, it will be one of the most liberating revelations your soul can ever encounter and destroy the devil's ability to take you into a downward spiral of shame. In the following section, we'll discover one of the major heart issues that keeps us from having a normal response to beauty.

THE ROOTS OF SEXUAL SHAME

Sexual shame is a problem for almost 100% of the believers we encounter through our ministry. It is the "glue" that keeps many men stuck in unhealthy behavior patterns and wrong thinking. Sexual shame not only empowers temptation and magnifies the intensity of temptation, but it also puts a wedge between us and God so that in the moment of temptation we are cut off from the divine intimacy and supply of grace that God would give which enables us to overcome in that moment. Shame drives us toward the devil and causes us to identify with our old nature while simultaneously robbing us of the joy of knowing that our sexuality is healthy, good and pleasing to God.

The devil has done an excellent job in perverting sex and sexuality in our culture. Thus we live with this idea, subconscious for the most part, that sex is bad and that our sex drive is bad. But we MUST remember that on the sixth day, God made us male and female – hence, it was God, not the devil, who created our sexuality and said, "It is good." In Genesis 1:28, His first commandment and blessing, the first Holy Sacrament, if you will was, "Be fruitful and multiply" - i.e.: go have sex and make babies. God gave us a sex drive (and make no mistake, it is a driving force). But this sex drive is designed by the Master to accomplish His purpose - and it is good -not bad as the devil would have us believe.

Understand this: when something works according to God's design, that is good. When a dog barks, God is glorified because He designed that dog to bark. When our sex drive operates as God intended, driving us toward sex, that is good - and He is glorified because our sexuality is functioning as He intended.

In that understanding, please don't get ahead of me. I'm not going to condone the gratification of lustful desire in any way - but draw a dividing line that is so critical to understand the dual nature; and necessary dual response to sexual temptations.

I spent most of my life with a dysfunctional, unbiblical view of my sexuality. I'd feel the allure of sexual things and think, "I shouldn't be attracted to that." That sounds like the truth doesn't it? But that was a lie, in reality. For, you see, I have a sex drive that was created by God with Divine purpose. The fact that my sex drive exists is why sexual temptation is tempting in the first place. This is one of the most controversial teachings in this book - and will also be one of the most liberating if you really get it. Again, I have to stress this because many will read this and think that I'm giving a license to sin. I'm not saying and will never say that lust is OK, looking at pornography is OK or that lusting after a woman is OK. ALL SEX outside of the marriage covenant of a husband and wife is sin. Period. Sin is sin - but the sex drive itself is godly.

It is human to be driven toward or attracted to pornography. The simple fact that pornography is tempting doesn't make the temptation sin. The fact that your sexual engine "revs" when you see a beautiful woman doesn't mean that you've sinned. For it to be any other way, one would have to eliminate their sex drive, thus causing us to stop operating by God's design to not be attracted to sexual things. So the *temptation* itself or the drive isn't the sin. Did you catch the difference? Being tempted simply confirms that we have a sex drive - giving into temptation is sin.

Remember, the Bible teaches that the Lord was tempted in ALL ways as we were, yet was without sin (Heb. 4:15). That means that if, while the Lord lived, someone showed Jesus a picture of pornography, it isn't that He would not have been tempted or felt its allure. But He would not have sinned. If we create a theology that thinks that sex wasn't temptING to Jesus, then the Bible couldn't say that he was temptED when faced with temptation. I dislike cooked carrots. It is impossible for someone to "tempt" me to eat them because there is nothing appealing about them to me. In order for Jesus to be tempted in ALL ways as we are, the things that we find tempting also must have been tempting for Him. We also understand that He was sinless. Therefore, we conclude that liking sex and being driven toward sex and sexual things is a function of our sex drive and isn't sin in and of itself; rather, what we do when tempted is either sinful or godly in response to that temptation.

The fact that we, as humans, like sex isn't sinful. God designed us to like sex and made it pleasurable for that reason. We must learn to reclaim the part of our sex drive that is healthy for the purpose of developing a healthy self-image as well as to use this as a tactic in defeating sin and shame.

I remember my first exposure to pornography as a boy. I remember being drawn into its allure - and I also clearly remember the shame of knowing that I wasn't supposed to look at it... and consequently that I wasn't supposed to LIKE it. Without realizing it, there were *agreements* being made subconsciously that were destroying my foundation to respond to the temptation in a godly way.

When a person sees temptations and thinks, "Don't look. Don't be attracted. That has power over you. That is bad." What happens in this scenario is that the person is driven away from God because in their heart, as they try to convince themselves that they shouldn't like the bad thing but realize that on some level that they do, they are forming a shame-based agreement that says, "I'm attracted to a bad thing - therefore I'm bad - my sexuality is bad." Do you remember that Adam and Eve hid from God when they realized they had sinned and were naked? Shame will always drive us AWAY from God in our time of need.

I grew up with this thinking that my sexuality was somehow "broken." Understand something about shame: conviction is healthy - it is the Holy Spirit's work to show you when things you've done aren't right. Shame is the demonic belief that you, yourself aren't right. This is why it is so critical to destroy the foundation of shame so that a proper foundation of love can take root in our hearts. If this is in your heart, you can't come into right relation with God. I spent countless years, then, with this rift between me and God - feeling that I could never be fully acceptable to Him until I was no longer attracted to sexual things - my "curse" of sexuality and urges, then, a constant reminder of how "unholy" I was.

I can't tell you the number of times I prayed prayers like, "God, help me not to be attracted to that. Deliver me from my lustful ways." What I didn't realize was that subconsciously I was saying, "My sex drive is bad. Take away the sex drive that You gave me and is supposed to be there. The devil is running my sex drive." Did you catch that last thought? Is it any wonder the devil had power over me to lead me into lust and sexual addiction? If you feel like your sex drive is out of control and bad, you have given the reins of it to the devil. Let me say that again: if you believe your sex drive is bad, you have already given control of it to the devil - you can't possibly ever be free in this state.

Conversely, when we recognize that God put the drive in us and glorify Him, it empowers God and is tantamount to saying, "I have a powerful sex drive. God gave it to me. He owns it. I can use it for His purposes." This is shocking because it runs so counter to our "Christian" teachings on sex and sexuality: you SHOULD be driven toward sexual things because you have a sex drive. YOU aren't bad for this attraction. Knowing this puts you back in the driver seat of your sex drive. HOWEVER, you must THEN take authority over the lust and perversion so that you don't fall into sin. I submit that this later step is only fully possible when operating in this revelation of your godly sexuality.

When I'm sexually tempted now, I glorify God and often even say humorously, "Thank you God that my sex drive is still working properly. It is good and I am good. I now reject any lust or perversion that the devil would sow through that temptation." If there is a person involved, operating in lust or seduction, I may add, "Forgive that person for exploiting the beauty that You gave them." Wow! Do you see the difference? By acknowledging that my sex drive is good, it drives me toward God. If you feel like your sex drive is bad, it drives you toward the devil. **When a man realizes in his heart that his sex drive isn't going to go away, and feels like it is something that God can't accept, there is no reconciliation for this wound in the soul. But when a man can find himself in the throes of temptation and realize that God isn't discouraged, ashamed or repulsed by his sex drive, the man becomes whole again before his Maker and able to make choices that make the Father proud.** You will always gravitate toward the direction of your core identity beliefs. As we properly lay the foundation of God's love for us, it is so encouraging to know that God loves ALL of us - sexuality included.

If my view of my sexual identity is that it is bad, I will always identify more with the sin nature than with who I am in Christ. If I correctly understand that my sexuality is good and godly, I am forming an identity foundation that leaves no space for the devil to corrupt. When I now see a lustful picture, the temptation doesn't go away. The only way to ever have that temptation go away is to destroy your sex drive - and I promise that you don't want that to happen. But when you see that picture and say, "Wow, God. I'm attracted to that," and instead of feeling bad that the attraction is there and rather feel GLAD that the attraction is there, you will draw closer to God. James 4:6-8 tells us that in temptation God gives a dual grace to resist the devil as well as to draw near to God. Both are critical to walk in victory. You can ONLY draw closer to God when tempted if you understand that you are good, pleasing to Him and that everything is working according to the Maker's design.

When you don't respond to temptation in this way, but repress or feel like you shouldn't even feel this temptation, in your mind you have already sinned before you actually sin in God's eyes - you've empowered the devil and kicked the Spirit of God out of your sexuality. It is only a matter of time before that manifests in some slip-up because you've already empowered the devil and agreed with a lie that is more fundamental than the temptation itself.

Understanding this will give you the freedom to also simply be "normal" when exposed to beauty in a non-lustful setting. I've seen some of the most prominent and pervasive "Christian" resources that tell you to avert your eyes, corral your wild heart, quote scripture and change your mind when you see a beautiful woman so that you don't fall into lust. What a bunch of pseudo-Christian garbage. It is no wonder that this sin is escalating in the church when we have a completely wrong foundation loosely based on scriptures in Job to combat it. Whereas in the book of Job, he makes a covenant with his eyes not to look upon a woman, the context and the other teaching of scripture (and even many translations of this verse) make it clear that this "not looking" is in reference to lusting. To simply not ever look at a woman would require a life of abject reclusivity.

The consequent damage that has been done to men's souls by this prevalent "Christian" way of reaction to beauty has perverted the natural response and made it seem as though we have no power over lust or the devil. I believe in a victorious Christianity and in real freedom that doesn't require our sexuality to be non-existent in order for freedom to become a reality. You can never, will never and AREN'T SUPPOSED TO repress the normal godly response to beauty. And if you call, bad, something that God designed as good, you've just completely changed the nature of things - the word for that is perversion. Furthermore, you've empowered the devil by saying in your heart, "that thing has power over me."

I was recently in a seminar with a fellow men's purity leader. His teaching for men to avoid lust was a montage of powerless circumstantial controls: pick the checkout line with the ugliest cashier (I kid you not, that was actually one of his pieces of advice), don't sit near the beautiful woman in church, etc. What if all the cashiers are beautiful? What if the only open seat is near the beautiful woman? At the end he closed with this impassioned, tearful plea for the men to pray for him because "as a purity leader, he's a 'target' for the enemy… Why, just today while he was driving, a beautiful woman jogged right in front of his car <sob>." I'm sorry, but beautiful women jogging are NOT an attack from the devil. Even if they are, we are called to be mighty men of God. I will not live my life in fear of temptation or under the thumb of the power of the devil and what he can do to me. Rather, I am called to make the devil afraid of what I can do to *him* in Christ! I will not disempower the power of Christ for weak, wishy-washy, pseudo-Christian theology. I will not cower in fear when a beautiful woman walks in the room.

What if you *have* to interact with a beautiful person at work or at school or at church? Will you drop out of society in fear of your urges? Most of the time in our normal life as we interact with people, they won't be overtly trying to be seductive. They aren't empowered by the devil to be beautiful. He doesn't make anything lovely. So much of what we "struggle" with and call temptation isn't actually temptation at all but a **dysfunctional** way of processing beauty and an unhealthy understanding of our God-given sexuality. This simple understanding will allow you to be in control of your sex drive rather than feel that it is out of control and a ticking time bomb just waiting for a spark of temptation to set it off. This revelation is such a blessing. Not only will it bless you as you face the typical day-to-day temptations that we all face, but it will help you simply to react and interact normally with the people around you in life.

When I was a single man, I didn't struggle with attraction the way I did as a married man. One day I realized why. As a single man it was OK in my soul to admit that I was attracted to members of the opposite sex (I'm not talking about lust or entertaining sexual thoughts). I wasn't ever one to pursue relationships per se, but in the back of my mind, as I'd get to know various girls who were attractive to me, there was always the thought and possibility that this one could be "the one." Then when I got married, I suddenly got weird around women. The truth was that attraction didn't go away just because I said vows. So my soul was struggling with guilt and a desire to not be attracted to women any longer. I felt like they had power over me suddenly. My soul had to learn that attraction is part of being human. Just because I realize that a woman is attractive doesn't mean that I'm going to lust after her or jump in bed and have an affair. As a married man and a man of God, I had to give my soul permission to be allowed to be attracted to people. This didn't cause me to lust MORE – it caused me to lust LESS. It took the power and perversion out of simple, human attraction.

When you see a beautiful woman and your heart says, "Wow!", agree with God that she is beautiful (He creates people with a gift of beauty for His purposes). Bless her beauty. Direct your heart into communion with God and take notice of what happens in your soul. A good benchmark of whether you are having a "normal" response to beauty or not is to discern whether the temptation drives you toward God or away from God. If you see someone beautiful and you immediately begin a dialogue with God about what you see (that isn't shame-based and self-berating) there is a good chance that you are processing the stimulus in a healthy way. This will "clear" the temptation and leave nothing to fester in your soul. Thus the stimulus that would have previously been a big temptation becomes a virtual non-event in the course of your day and leaves no space for the devil to corrupt.

However if your thoughts continue to meditate on the person, that's probably unhealthy and creating a lustful response. If you find yourself thinking about the person or temptation later, you definitely didn't process it in a godly manner or may have needed to go a little further with God. (If a woman is overtly trying to exploit her beauty with seduction, simply reject the seduction and the demonic associations - but it is still healthy to allow your soul to admit that she is beautiful.) If you are confronted with a temptation that is overtly sexual in nature, that depicts sexual acts, that is perverted or reminds you of a particular area of weakness, this is the proper time to quickly avert your eyes (but still recognize that the attraction to the sexual nature of things is OK but perversion is not). We see that sexual temptations can be complex - especially in pornography which almost always has an element of perversion - but with this understanding we affirm that we are godly sons of

God and the lust or perversion is bad. It is important to draw this dividing line of understanding.

The devil has blurred this line. We need to understand that our sex drive is godly and pleasing to the Lord, beauty is from the Lord; but lust, seduction and perversion is from the devil. This understanding gives you the freedom to love yourself as you are and trust that God loves you as you are. Your sexuality isn't broken because you are drawn to sexual things or beautiful people. The fact that you are drawn to sexual things only proves that you are working as God intended. Confess something to God even now. Tell Him something that He already knows, "My sex drive is very good, very active and very pleasing to God. He isn't waiting for me to no longer have a sex drive before He loves and accepts me. He loves me today." Now do something just as liberating: forgive yourself. "I forgive myself for being attracted to sexual things. I repent for giving the devil control of my sex drive. I now take it back from the enemy and commit it to God for His intended purposes."

SOUL TIES & ADDICTION

Now that we understand more about how to respond to stimuli that confront us daily, we must also lay a foundation for victory in our thought-life. These unseen temptations may not be as obvious as when we can simply see the thing that is causing us to have a sexual urge. The first area that requires understanding is in regard to soul ties. An interesting (and potentially scary) thing happens during heightened stimulation and orgasm: a combination of chemical and hormonal release and the immense ecstasy taking place in our body and senses opens receptors in our brain that are only open at that moment of extreme pleasure. When those receptors are open, studies show that we get "imprinted" with whatever object or person we are meditating on at the moment of orgasm.

God created this part of the brain to be used in conjunction with marriage. When a man and a woman consummate their marriage, what takes place in the brain should serve to create the soul ties with them. The Bible has a lot to say about how the act of sex "joins" a man and a woman and even talks about this taking place with prostitutes and outside of marriage. (Other chapters have more information and scriptures about soul ties and how to deal with them - this chapter is more of an overview.)

As we give in to the desire to lust upon things like pornography, the pleasurable experience forms soul ties or bonds with the things that we are seeing – it can be individuals, specific scenes or even body parts (giving rise to fetishes, fixations, perversions and such). Once the bond is formed, these images come back into our mind over and over. And the more porn we see, the more we become desensitized to various types of images and also the more fixated and imprinted we get with various things we've seen.

Many people mistakenly assume that these recurring and sometimes obsessive thoughts are demonic in nature. And while I agree that there are aspects to our temptation that are highly spiritual, often the temptation is taking place in the realm of the soul due to these soul ties rather than being a spiritual temptation. Christians who have been raised with a deliverance ministry mindset may grow discouraged, wondering why they keep "binding the devil" with no success. It is very possible that they are trying to bind a soul tie, calling it a devil.

Soul ties within the context of marriage are wonderful. They can also cause intense pain in the event of the death of a loved one. When a person dies, the joy and pleasure and fond memories associated with them have no resolve in the soul any longer. When they die, a part of us dies too... the part that was attached to them. The reality with pornography is that we've formed a bond in our heart with the things we've seen. Those bonds must be broken and addressed before God. And a part of us has to die in order for this to happen. For this reason, a large number of the lessons of this book deal with the emotional pain that comes from severing these soulish desires. Giving up pornography and our fixations is every bit as painful as breaking up with a lover or saying goodbye to a dying loved one.

Soul ties are often compounded by the physical aspects of sexual addiction. There are many books that deal more thoroughly with the chemical science of sexuality and related addiction. The chemistry isn't as important as the fact that at a fundamental physical level, regular and repeated sexual stimulus can be as habit forming and addictive as hardcore drug use due to the chemical release that takes place in the body - but will abate over time.

I went to many counselors who tried to "deliver" me of demonic and spiritual temptations to no avail. The reality of my condition was that a large component of the temptation I faced - especially in the early stages of trying to quit was happening on the soul and physical/chemical level of my being due to doors I had opened. I may or may not have had spiritual temptations going along with it. Why is this so important to note at this stage of the book?

Simply put, there is a lot of opposition to your freedom in the early stages of breaking the cycle of addiction and you have to fight this type of battle differently than spiritual battles and access a different aspect of God's grace for help.

When it comes to the soul ties, the first thing that I'll usually do is obvious: repent. I'll ask God for His forgiveness and covering for the sins I've committed. I'll also usually renounce my association with that woman, image or scene. I'll also renounce my association with any demonic forces that may have been associated with that. I ask God to break those ties, clean my mind and separate me from that torment. I'll also usually pray for the person that may be the focus of that fixation (more on this in later chapters). Finally, I usually ask God for the grace not to run back to old idols and make them stronger. I want to steal the devil's strength, not the other way around.

Don't be surprised, however, if there are still ongoing and strong lustful desires. Just like a junkie will go through withdrawal, you also will have to come to terms with the fact that there will be a withdrawal period that will vary in its severity from person to person. The deeper the addiction, the stronger the soul ties. You will want to get honest with God as to what you need to do to get over and through this time of physical and soulish temptation. These initial stages of withdrawal are most aptly combated by time rather than a swift deliverance. The Mighty Man Manual's workbook provides a great 8-week path for those who may want a little more structure to navigating this time as well as take the cornerstone teachings of this book to the next level.

PERVERSION AND SPIRITUAL TEMPTATIONS

I don't want to overemphasize the physical or soul-realm temptations to the detriment of addressing the spiritual component of this struggle. At the end of the day, I see this as mostly a spiritual issue due to the fact that things that usually get us into this mess in the first place, and can trip up someone who has been avoiding sin for a while, are the spiritual aspects of this struggle and their points of origin in the heart. The devil knows how to exploit our wounds and needs. Thus we must be cognizant of this fact and ready to wage the spiritual warfare that will take us through to a true and lasting freedom.

One good way to begin to identify areas of spiritual temptation is to identify when perversions are present in our thought life and in temptations. Perversions are not natural tendencies. They run contrary to the designs of God. However, they can become an issue, especially as people get deeper into pornography. Perversion is a dangerous thing that should let us know that something is happening spiritually that we can't see. God made sex to exist in marriage between one man and one woman and to build each other up in our masculinity and femininity.

The devil hates everything that God ordained as good. Every time we look at pornography, in additional to escalations of soul ties, we are also making an agreement with the devil and whatever particular perversion we are watching. We are agreeing that his temptation is good and we choose it over the truth of God's ways. As we form these agreements, we open ourselves up to demonic thinking. You will begin to think like the spirit you follow. This is a Biblical principle.

In Galatians, Paul prays that Christ would be formed in the believers' hearts (4:19). In Ephesians, he prays that the Spirit would strengthen the heart, or the inner man so that Christ could dwell in us (3:16). Now we know that when we are born again, the Spirit of God resides in our *spirit*. So we see that despite having ALL of God in our spirit, we must have God's character FORMED in our heart or soul. In our heart/soul or the "inner man" as it is sometimes called, we must CHOOSE what spirit to yield to. If we yield to the Holy Spirit, Christ is formed in our hearts and we are being sanctified. That means we will become more Christ-like. If we listen to other spirits, we will become like those spirits... perverted.

Perversions, then, are areas where we have seared our own conscience and taken on a demonic mindset because of habitual areas of agreement with evil spirits. Many of the books and seminars that address the issues surrounding lust and pornography do very little to tackle the area of temptation that take place in the spiritual realms - so this will be a new concept to many believers - yet it is as essential for our freedom as it is to understand how to deal with fleshly temptations.

Part of the Great Commission that Jesus gives to us is not just to preach the Gospel, but also to cast out devils and demons - early church fathers considered this understanding to be fundamental in basic Christianity. One out of five dealings that Jesus had with people involved the removal of an unclean spirit in order for them to be free. So I would venture to say that it is logical to assume that when we are tempted, there may often be demonic or spiritual forces contributing to the problem. Therefore many chapters will teach us components of spiritual warfare.

Many Christian circles reject notions of deliverance because they don't understand the dynamic between the spirit of a man and the soul. The idea of spiritual warfare for a believer is not that their spirit is inhabited by a demon because we understand that God places His Spirit within us. Rather, we are tempted and agree with the spirits causing the temptation and give them power over our minds - a part of the soul that will conform to the spirit it listens to as we read in Galatians and Ephesians. These areas where we've given the devil permission and space must be reclaimed and the strongholds torn down or the devil will take more and more space until we are destroyed.

We hear about this all too often, a pastor is caught in an affair or sex scandal. Very recently a pastor of a large church made the news. He was caught with a trans-gender prostitute. That level of perversion doesn't happen overnight. Perversions will continue to fester and infect your mind because they are permissions given to the enemy in the spiritual realm. He will corrupt your mind until you think and act like he does. The devil hates God's children. All violent acts of sex and every filthy perversion are human manifestations of a devil's mind and attitude.

Therefore, we can conclude that if a perversion is present, most likely there is an evil spirit present who has been given permission to influence your thoughts and warp your conscience by your agreement with its lies. These agreements must be recognized and broken when they arise. Whenever you recognize that a thought is a perverse thought – one that goes in contrast to the way God presents sexuality and His heart of love toward His created children – you must recognize that it is a devil who has trained you to think that way and that is not you! You do not think that way if the Spirit of God dwells in you, because the Spirit thinks God's thoughts. Start agreeing with the thoughts of God's Spirit in you and you will start to reverse the perversions that are corrupting your mind. This is important. Just as you have made conscious choices to agree with temptations and lies, you must consciously (and I even recommend verbally) make declarations of agreement with God's Word that contradict these temptations.

When you repent of your sin and break your soul ties, you must also repent for agreements you've made with the enemy that have given him permission to follow you around and corrupt you. Ask God to forgive you for choosing the devil's lies over God's truth. Ask Jesus to root out strongholds and footholds in the spirit from doors you may have opened. Ask Him to ransom you back from the devil, purify your mind and deliver you from the presence of your tormentors.

As you begin to do this, God will begin to minister to the need or wound that gave the devil this invitation in the first place. Perversions should cause us to revolt against them. When they don't, there is a lie behind the lie that the devil has used to give you the inclination or proclivity toward that fetish, fixation or perverse urge. We'll deal more with heart wounds and needs later; but these are the open doors through which the enemy enters and whispers lies that we'll believe.

FLESHLY TEMPTATIONS

Temptations that take place in the body can be learned or habitual or they can be literal, understandable fleshly desires. The reality is that the desire for the physical (and emotional) release that comes through orgasm and ejaculation is a real fleshly desire. Sometimes the most difficult times to stay pure are when we find ourselves physically aroused and have no godly outlet for that, or when we have a habitual trigger such as frustration and we have formed an association with orgasmic release as the answer for this. However, outside of God's provision, gratifying this desire is sin and the Bible makes no excuses for it. Nowhere in the Bible do we read a quid pro quo that says, "Men, if thou art horny, God shall look the other way." Rather, it says, "Walk in the Spirit, and you shall not fulfill the lust of the flesh (Ga. 5:16)."

I was talking with a single friend I met on a missions trip. Somehow the topic came up about masturbation. And I was impressed to find out that it had been over three years since he had gratified any fleshly desire with masturbation. We hear much about "men's needs" but he had learned to overcome the lie that orgasm is a need. That freed him to serve God with his body, soul and spirit – and God was definitely using him.

The reality is that orgasms are nice, but they aren't a need. Really, if you never had another orgasm, you would not die. By elevating a pleasure to the level of "need" we create a scenario where we disregard the truths of the Bible and reject the notion that God can actually supply ALL our needs. I think most men either consciously or subconsciously feel justified by their "needs" in their rebellion against God. They think things like, "God, if you'd only give me a spouse, I'd quit." Or "God, if you'd only bless my marriage sex life and make my wife a sex-crazed nympho, then I'll never…" But these thoughts are completely twisted. God can't bless something that you aren't willing to give to him. Masturbation, lust, pornography, etc. are evidences that you have not given your sexuality over to God; you are still trying to control it and be master of your own gratification. We must settle the fact that God is not obligated to bless you. Rather, His sacrifice for us obligates us to honor and reverence Him even if we never were to get one thing in return. But the wonder of His goodness is that He also rewards those who diligently seek Him (Heb 11:6).

Conversely, the devil will use those fleshy desires and cause you to stumble so that he can steal your future, steal your blessings, steal your peace, steal your joy and shipwreck your calling. And we must learn to change our mind when we are being tempted by our flesh. We don't have to listen to the "voice" of our flesh calling to us. There is another voice within us calling: the voice of the Spirit. You have the power to choose which voice to listen to. *"For the flesh lusts against the Spirit, and the Spirit against the flesh; and these are contrary to one another, so that you do not do the things that you wish… For those who live according to the flesh set their minds on the things of the flesh, but those who live according to the Spirit, the things of the Spirit. For to be carnally minded is death, but to be spiritually minded is life and peace. (Ga. 5:17, Ro. 8:5,6)."*

It is time to give God a chance and go after Him with your whole heart. Gratifying the flesh is a learned response to stimulus. The stimulus can be frustration, loneliness, low self-worth or any of a number of emotions. We must simply break the bad habit of gratifying these emotional needs with fleshly sin and learn to set our mind on the things of the Spirit. God has the answers for all of your needs. Fleshly solutions only mask the problem and make us forget about the real need. It is a drug that keeps us stuck in the long term. Many of the sections of this book help deal with matters of the heart and the fleshly response.

So we see that we can be tempted in the spirit, in the heart and soul or in the flesh. We must have God's help and grace to recognize these temptations and to have the strength to overcome them. But, knowing the enemy and understanding what you are being tempted with can make fighting your battles so much easier.

~Mighty Man Training & Application~

Understanding the nature of your temptations is very important as you begin your journey to freedom. As you face temptations try to start to ask yourself key questions and identify the nature of the temptation.

1. Is this temptation simply the result of being a normal human with a sex drive? Has shame about your struggle and urges made you feel distant from God or as though you can't approach Him for fear of rejection?

    a. Remind yourself daily that you are good. Even if you blow it, run right back to the fact that you are pleasing to God and a new creation. Don't throw this truth out when tempted. Draw near to God and resist the demonic nature of the temptation without believing that YOU have a demonic nature. The Bible is clear that we are a new creation in Christ.

    b. When you are out in public or watching a TV show or movie and see a beautiful woman, try to practice godly solutions to deal with beauty in such a way that you don't repress normal emotions or take it too far into the realm of idolatry or lust.

    c. When tempted in this way, pray prayers like: *God, you made my sex derive and it is good. You also made that person beautiful on the outside. I can't wait to see You, the One from whom all beauty flows. I reject any lust or perversion and rejoice that I'm fully pleasing to you.*

    d. Repent if you allowed any lustful thoughts to enter. Remember that this sin didn't take God by surprise and get back on track right away.

2. Recognize thoughts and temptations in the realm of your soul. Is this a repetitive obsession or indicator that you may be experiencing withdrawal symptoms of a physical addiction or soul tie? Does it feel like an emotional longing to see a familiar girl or scene? This may be a soul tie that needs to be broken. In addition to resting in the fact that these strong urges will diminish over time, you may experience some relief by breaking soul ties in prayer.

    a. Try a prayer like this: *Father, forgive me for joining myself to this thing. Right now I renounce my partnership with So-and-so and for finding my comfort in this instead of You. Please break these soul ties, deliver me from temptation and please also forgive and work to save the people I'm thinking about right now. Now I address the object of my desire: So-and-so, I'm leaving you behind. I can never see you again. Goodbye forever. Now Father, please set me free from them and from every devil and demon associated with them and those acts in Jesus name. Grant me the grace and wisdom to know if there is anything else I should do to get through this time of trial. Amen.*

3. Deal with temptations in the spiritual realm. Are the tempting thoughts perverse or indicate that there is spiritual warfare taking place?

   a. Try a prayer like this : *Father, forgive me for the doors I've opened in this area. Forgive me for agreeing with the enemy and giving him space in my heart. I now reject these perverse thoughts in Jesus precious name. These thoughts are not mine, for I have the mind of Christ. I reject, now and forever, every devil and unclean spirit associated with these thoughts and tell you to get out of my life in Jesus name. Now Father I ask that you would restore my mind and heart. Show me the areas of my heart that have allowed this temptation to take shape and heal me. Make me more like You and help me to love the things You love. Speak to me even now and give me wisdom. Amen*

4. Deal with Fleshly Temptations. Are you feeling an actual physical stirring or have you convinced yourself that sex is a need rather than a desire? Do you actually feel something in your body causing you to be tempted or aroused? You need to change your mind and get your mind off that fleshly desire. It will pass soon. Try the following:

   a. Get up and go do something else. Leave where you are and what you are doing.

   b. Start to meditate on godly thoughts. Ask yourself what God is teaching you and doing in your life right now. Dream with God: ask Him to speak to you about your calling and His plans for your life. Ask Him to speak to you about the things He loves about you. Let Him fill you up. Think about the things that you'd like God to do in your life – and that you'd like to do for God. Know that the sin will only put you one step farther from those things.

CHAPTER 7

Destroying the
Foundations of Shame

We have touched on ways that sexual shame drives us from God and perpetuates the cycle of sinful acts. Now, God willing, we will destroy the foundations of shame once and for all.

I love the Song of Solomon. Many people don't realize that this book is not so much a story about Solomon and a woman, but a picture of our relationship with God and His radical love for us. In the first verses of the first chapter, the Shulamite bride is enraptured with the love of the king... until verse four. Here the king brings her into his chambers and she realizes that she must stand naked before him. In verse six she laments, "*Do not look upon me, because I am dark, Because the sun has tanned me. My mother's sons were angry with me; They made me the keeper of the vineyards, But my own vineyard I have not kept.*" The rapture she feels, knowing that she was chosen by the king becomes overshadowed by the realization of her own shortcomings and imperfections.

We, like the bride, are often swept up with Jesus when first saved, but as we continue to sin, shame surfaces in our hearts and we don't feel worthy to stand "naked" before Him because we realize all of our shortcomings. We assume that He wants these things to be out of our lives as badly as we do. We assume that we are less lovely to Him than people who are "more perfect" than we are. We assume that our sin has disqualified us from our calling and ministry. And we, like the Shulamite, downgrade our love level to one that is more acceptable with the level of acceptance we assume that we have - the degree to which we accept ourselves.

Shame drives a wedge between us and God and we live continuously, like Adam and Eve after the fall, feeling as though there is something not right, not acceptable and lacking in us; with part of us hiding from God, settling to have relationship with Him from the bushes rather than walking in full exposure. This feeling is exacerbated after we've fallen; and rather than coming boldly to the throne of grace as the Bible teaches, we avoid God and prayer, go into a cycle of shame and self-berating and live below our heavenly station until we again work up the courage to relate to God as we know we ought. We may theologically know the facts of our position in Christ, but the beliefs of our heart, not our head, dictate our realities.

I mentioned earlier that I always felt as if my sexuality was "broken" and unacceptable to God. Really, I had such an issue with shame that I continuously lived with this heart of shame in other areas also, an overall apprehension that I was missing something - that I was fundamentally unacceptable and disappointing to God. When I would pray, it was always with a feeling that I needed to get something from God that I didn't already have. I was always fighting FOR acceptance rather than FROM acceptance - fighting TO GET my inheritance in Christ rather than fighting WITH my inheritance. Thus there was always a gap between how I saw myself and who I was in Christ; an inability to access the things that I already had in Christ; and a settling for a cheap counterfeit that was more in line with my sinful, lack-based self-perception.

Shame is one of the devil's favorite tools to make us identify with our old nature rather than our new one; and thus, keep us from running to God, keep us from receiving the things God has already given, steal our blessing and calling and much more. Shame drives us toward the devil, isolates us from other people and causes us to settle for cheap, sinful counterfeits to salve the wounds of the soul.

In this shame-based cycle of sinful coping, it is nearly impossible to stop unhealthy patterns until the foundation of shame is first destroyed. Humans need a foundation, an emotional and spiritual springboard or reserve for all things in life. To face the challenges of each day, you need to know that God is with you. Shame is present at some level in most people but is especially pronounced in addicts. Addicts know that they are making unhealthy choices, but this foundation of shame so rapes the soul that this emotional and spiritual reserve is nonexistent and they cope with the pain of their perpetual inadequacy with unhealthy habits that only, in turn, reinforce more shame.

As I began to see the effects of lustful addiction spread to other areas of my life, you would think that would have been a wakeup call to make me stop. But in my heart, I didn't feel as though I had an inheritance with God - so my heart reasoned, why fight for something that I don't have? I didn't *feel* like I had His love and approval and fellowship - so what did I have to lose? When the devil would come with his worthless temptation and dangle it in front of me, I'd go down without a fight because even though his offering was a cheap substitute for the real love that my heart needed, *something,* even if it was cheap, was better than the nothing he had already convinced me that I had. Then after I would fall, it would only serve as confirmation of how worthless I must be to God - and I would beat myself up about having fallen again.

Remember the theme of the last few chapters, "if YOU are disappointed in YOU when YOU fall it is YOUR strength you are counting on." All of these foundational elements are linked and show evidence that we still have work to do on the basic foundation for our souls. The inability to relate and access the graces of God is linked to shame. The inability to receive the love of God is linked to shame. The distortion of our self-perception and godly identity is linked to shame. Shame is a killer and grows with each defeat.

THE SHAMELESS MIGHTY MAN

There is one mighty man in scripture who so remarkably reflected the heart of the One True Mighty Man, the Lord Jesus, that he receives special honor. This, of course, is David, who the Bible identifies as the man after God's own heart.

Let's learn a little about him. David had an adulterous affair and then murdered the woman's husband to cover up his affair. He rebelled against the word of God through His prophet and moved into Philistine lands wherein he had to continuously lie to the king to live at peace with God's enemies. He disobeyed the commandment of the Lord, numbered the people and brought a horrible judgment of God on the nation that cost 75,000 innocent lives. He told blatant lies that resulted in the slaughter of an entire city of God's priests.... and God said, THIS is the man after my own heart. THIS is the man through whom the Messiah will come. My perfect Son will be called the son of

THIS man and will sit on his throne for all eternity. It wasn't David's actions that caused him to have such great favor with God - and this serves as a testimony to every sinful mighty man whose heart cries out for favor and intimacy with God.

What was it in David's heart that made him so special? I believe it was the way in which he so radically embraced God's love and approval for him - even after doing some things that would send most any other "normal" person into a downward spiral for decades. David's attitude after these events would almost be seen as arrogant and shocking - but from it, we can learn a pattern of how to bounce back from defeat, stand shamelessly before God and walk in the fullness of His plans and anointing.

Coming from this shame-based background, the attitudes of David after he "sinned big" were shocking. First Samuel 21 tells of David's escape from Saul's house when Saul first set out to kill him. He goes to Nob, the city of priests and lies blatantly to the High Priest to get him to give him weapons and food (the showbread which wasn't lawful for him to eat according to God's word). When Saul arrives and questions the priest and finds that he helped David, Saul orders the death of the priest and every man, woman, child and beast in the entire city of priests. One young priest escapes to tell the story and David laments to him saying, "I have caused the death of all the persons of your father's house (1 Sam. 22:22)."

When I think of how many families even one pastor touches, I can't imagine the extent of loss that an entire city of priests must have had on the country. The young priest actually stayed with David and his men (and eventually turned on David at the end); and I can imagine that he would be a constant reminder to David of what he had done. But this chapter of David's story doesn't end with shame. God gives him the 52 Psalm to write after this event and we see a picture of David's outrageous repentance. He compares himself to the man who actually killed the priests. In contrast to this man, David trusts in the Lord and concludes that he is like a green olive tree in the house of God - he has a fresh start. David trusts in the mercy of God and can stand unashamed in the presence of God's saints. David realizes that this act didn't affect how God sees him. This didn't disqualify him or steal the anointing from his life.

David is like a rubber ball that always bounces back. He was an adulterer, a murderer, a liar and committed sins of rebellion against God's word that cost tens of thousands of innocent lives. Yet each time, he would bounce back with an undaunted confidence that God loved him, accepted him, had a plan and great calling for his life, that he had an anointing. This level of confidence in the fact that God's goodness is better than his badness is shocking. Yet, over and over we see David take this radical approach of confidence in God and His mercy after the most egregious of sins. This was the thing that made him the man after God's own heart - he knew the heart of God never waivers in love toward us.

Paul is another saint who did horrible things against God, but in the end probably made more of an impact in Christianity than any other person in history. He, like David, had a similar understanding of God's unfailing grace and inexhaustible mercy. He writes that God will never repent of or remove the gifts and calling that He has given to each individual (Rom. 11:29). He understood that he was the "chief of sinners" (1 Tim. 1:15), but still completely qualified for everything that God had called him to do based on God's work, God's calling and God's grace. He opens nearly every New Testament book with a reminder that he is called according to grace and prays for an impartation of grace to the readers.

THE PRIDE OF SHAME

How can these men who were chief of sinners rise so high in God? How did they "bounce back" from sin so indomitably? At times, theologians have accused them both of pride, but in reality, shame is the ultimate expression of pride. That seems counter-intuitive doesn't it?

If you were to tell someone that you were the most humble person on the face of the earth, they'd laugh at you and call you proud. But did you know that God actually moved upon Moses to write that he was the most humble person on the face of the earth in Numbers 12:3? If God told most any person that they were the most humble, they'd probably play it off and say, "No... I'm not really all *that* humble, Lord." But that would actually be pride speaking - exalting our opinion over God's. It takes real humility to agree with the things that God says because so often they are so outrageously good. Moses actually had to be incredibly humble to agree with God and write that he was the most humble man on earth. Shame, on the other hand, exalts our opinion and the devil's opinion over God's, all the while masquerading as humility.

What do we really believe when we agree with the voice of shame? What is our heart saying? Shame will tell you that your sin is SO BIG that it is the one that is bigger than God's love. *Your* sin is the one that He can't cover. Each time you sin, shame says, "Surely that was the one sin that will steal my gifts and calling... Now God will really reject me." But what does the Bible say? God's Word says that He will NEVER leave us or forsake us. He has made us acceptable. We ARE righteous. We HAVE every spiritual blessing. Every lie of shame contradicts the clear Word of God that is to dictate our reality.

Shame ultimately is a way of seeing that taints every area of your faith because your faith is not rooted in Christ if shame is in your heart. Shame exists because we are looking at ourselves rather than Christ... and we will come up short every time. When we look at Jesus as our sufficiency, our righteousness and our means, all things are possible. When we relate to God through Christ and see ourselves in Him, we have an accurate view of how God sees us. But when operating in shame, you feel as though you don't have anointing or calling or capacity for victory because, you know what... you don't! Apart from Christ we are about as spiritually capable as a stone.

This is why John admonishes us that if we abide in Him, we will not be ashamed before Him (1 Jn. 2:28). But when YOU are looking at YOU, you cannot help but be ashamed when standing in the presence of a perfect God. Only when our focus is on Jesus does everything in the Christian life fall into place. The more your eyes are on you, the more shame you will feel in your soul. The person most steeped in shame is proud to the core. But a humble person accepts what God says about them even if it is outrageously good. They don't exalt their opinion of themselves over God's - even if it means trusting in His grace and goodness to such an extreme that you, like David, bounce back immediately after even the most heinous of sins.

Paul so trusted in the grace of God that he wrote that where sin abounds, the grace of God abounds all the more. Remember that grace isn't just the vehicle through which forgiveness comes. It is the vehicle through which every promise of salvation and our calling comes. You and your sin are not greater than God's grace. Your calling isn't about you. Your righteousness isn't about your works. God's opinion and works are the ones that matter.

This is so hard to grasp because we are raised in a world that uses shame and condemnation and guilt as punishment tools. But 1 Corinthians 4:9 says that God puts us on display before men and angels. What a picture. When we stand naked before God and all the heavenly hosts, we expect Him to have disapproval like the world. But instead, His love gushes forth and all of heaven marvels as the righteousness of Christ shines through us. It doesn't matter how dirty you get, you can't diminish the light of the Spirit that dwells in you. No amount of fleshly imperfection diminishes the perfection of the Spirit in you.

People like David and Paul understood something about walking with God. They understood that they could sin but walk away from it knowing not one guilty knowledge against themselves (1 Cor. 4:4). David was so good at fully coming clean on his sin and its consequences while trusting in the outrageous covering of God.

This is the power that we can enjoy as we break free from shame. We bring all of our sin and all of its consequences into the light and rather than hear disapproval from God, we discover that His love, mercy, grace, calling, and Spirit are *greater* than our sin. His ability to redeem a life is greater than our ability to destroy it. We can then walk away knowing that we are rich and with confidence of knowing that His gifts and calling and nature will shine through us. I can say, "I'm perfect" - not because of what I've done but because of who I am in Christ. If He has imputed perfection to me, then it is mine. Who am I to argue with God?

KEEPING A HEALTHY BALANCE

The voice of the devil and the world will want to say, "That is arrogance." Even Bible teachers who can theologically expound on the spiritual realities of our perfection in Christ would balk at the idea that a person should actually be so bold as to apply that truth as a reality in their lives... what about consequences to sin and responsibility? The real issue is that this, like many other Christian truths must be held in balance between the extremes. There are segments in Christianity who preach an "easy believism" or "greasy grace" wherein essentially grace is a license to sin without consequence. Make no mistake, there are consequences to sin and we'll discuss them later. There are other branches of Christianity who preach a gospel wherein salvation is difficult and losing your salvation is easy - leading to a rigid, works-based walk of faith in which shame breeds easily. I believe in balanced theology and that we will find truth and freedom for our souls keeping both aspects of the truth in check.

There are consequences to sin - both in our lives and souls as well as for the people who have been hurt by our sin. Part of being delivered of shame is taking an honest evaluation of these consequences and bringing them before

God. Taking honest stock and store of our situation will help us to get brutally realistic with what we have to do to get out of the mess our sin has created. But getting delivered from a heart of shame won't make us LESS responsible, it will actually give us that emotional reserve to be MORE responsible.

Shame makes us want to hide from full exposure before God and people because we don't have the capacity to really deal with the consequences. We are already operating from a core belief of defeat when shame is ruling our heart. Thus we don't want to really stand eye-to-eye with the realities of our sin and its consequences because that will require something of us that we don't feel we have to give. We don't want to get brutally honest with where our lives will go if we don't course-correct and start to make godly choices - so we hide from responsibility, from God and from reality in our unhealthy coping habits that give us a false sense of security even if the world is crumbling around us.

Many of us need to fully come to terms with our sins but shame wants to keep these things in the dark. We fear that if we really look at all this sin has cost us, the grief would overtake us. Some reading this have lost jobs, money, marriage, self-respect and so much more at the hand of this sin. All of us have lost precious time. But I think of the story of Joseph when he was sold as a slave. Before he was even taken into the house of Potiphar, God called him a prosperous man (Ge. 39:2). That is interesting because as a slave he didn't have a penny that he could call his own. But God called him rich. Similarly, we have been slaves to sin but are rich because of the riches that God has deposited IN us.

Getting brutally honest with yourself and others is healthy and critical to formulating a plan for wholesale life change. When shame isn't part of our foundation, we can face these difficult truths because we have confidence that one thing is certain: God's love for us never falters no matter how badly and how long we've blown it. He is always waiting for us to come to Him without shame and set us back on our feet with all the resources of Heaven and our inheritance in Christ at the ready to help us. That isn't to say that it will instantly be easy. We must sow to the spirit before we reap a spiritual harvest.

Shame-free living is part of the crucial foundation for life and spiritual growth. When this is gone we know that circumstances will be OK because we have a core belief that WE are OK. When shame is gone, grace isn't a license to sin; rather our understanding of our godly nature serves as a driving force to stay pure.

THE ATTITUDES OF SHAME-FREE LIVING

When we are looking at life through the "lens" of shame, its self-view and worldview likely extends into many areas of your life. Jesus said it this way in Matthew 6, "The lamp of the body is the eye. If therefore your eye is good, your whole body will be full of light. But if your eye is bad, your whole body will be full of darkness. If therefore the light that is in you is darkness, how great is that darkness!"

When shame is tainting the way we see ourselves and God, we look in the mirror and feel that we are not enough. We look at our bank statement and feel as though we are not enough. We look at our anointing and feel as if we are not enough. You name it. We disqualify ourselves from virtually every good thing eventually as this cancer spreads. It may start small and just seem like "normal dissatisfaction," but any self-perception that is based in lack is a root of shame that can grow. The voice of shame says, "I don't have..." When you are delivered from this, your heart can say, "I HAVE... I am enough."

The Bible is clear that Jesus already HAS given us ALL things that pertain to life, Godliness and our calling. He HAS already blessed us with every spiritual blessing (2 Pe. 1:3, Eph. 1:3). He HAS made us acceptable. He HAS put His Spirit in us. Every spiritual blessing that I can think of is listed as a past-tense reality for us. **One of the reasons that we don't access them by grace is because we are still trying to get them** rather than trying to receive grace for the faith for what we already have. Grace is the conduit through which every heavenly reality manifests on earth. Shame blocks that conduit by stealing our faith.

Christianity, as a general rule, has faith upside-down. What happens when we are sick or when we need something? We plead and petition God to give us healing or give us what we need. When that doesn't work, we may try to pray and fast and clean up our act to convince God further. But this is all backward faith. Jesus already paid for healing and defeated all disease. We already have the same Spirit that raised Christ from the dead living in us. We already have ALL things that pertain to life and Godliness. We already have every spiritual blessing. Thus we conclude that the goal isn't to get God to give us the things we need because we already have them. So when we relate to God out of our feeling of lack rather than from an understanding of His fullness, this is nothing more than faithlessness. Faith is the EVIDENCE of things not seen, the title deed if you will (Heb. 11:1). God has given us the title deed to

ALL things unseen. But without faith it is impossible to please God (Heb. 11:6). When you go to God without faith, asking Him to give the things He has already given, is it any wonder when you don't receive?

Acts 3:5 tells a story of Peter healing a lame beggar at the temple. He says to the man, "Silver and gold I do not have, but what I do have I give you: In the name of Jesus Christ of Nazareth, rise up and walk." This verse always intrigued me because Peter recognized that HE HAD something that was tangible enough to give away. We also possess an inheritance that is tangible enough for us to spend if we will only receive the grace to walk in it. It is important, when we approach this struggle to know that God has already defeated the devil, changed our nature and that our victory is certain.

Conversely, shame creates a hole in the heart that can never be filled. The blessings of God are directly linked to the prosperity that we perceive in our soul (3 Jn. 1:2). As we walk free from shame, walking in our calling will come naturally. However, if shame is in our life, it hinders our calling and blessing because we are putting things into a hole that can never be filled. The bottomless pit of shame also steals glory from God because all the glory that should go to him goes right to our needy soul. Having people's respect, approval or a flourishing ministry at church are blessings that God wants to give - but when shame is part of the picture, we NEED these things to fill the void of these things in our hearts. We crave "God's validation" on the things we do because we don't feel His validation of who we are.

There are many people who God would love to prosper financially but can't, because if they had wealth it would make them feel better about themselves or superior in a destructive way. God would like to pour out the anointing on more people, but His "stamp of approval" on our ministry would cause us to devour the admiration of others rather than give all glory to God. When you compare our reality to the realities of heaven found in the Bible and see that there is a discrepancy, it is usually because there is a hole in the heart that is stealing the blessing that God wants to and has already given. Being healed of shame is part of the foundation - not only of walking free from sin but for launching into your life's calling and purpose because God can add things to you without feeding your demons.

I always found it interesting that God put His stamp of approval on Jesus' ministry BEFORE it started. As Jesus came out of the water, having been baptized by John the Baptist, the Holy Spirit descended upon Him and the voice of God spoke saying, "This is my beloved son, in whom I am well pleased (Mt. 3:17)." Jesus had the Father's approval before He ever did anything to earn it. **We, as sons of God, enjoy that same blessing and unconditional approval.** It is so amazing to stop and consider that God not only loves us, not only accepts us but actually is pleased with us. God enjoys you. You bring Him pleasure. He loves the way He made you.

If you have to remind yourself 100 times a day that you are pleasing to God and that you have a calling, do it. Ask God to show you the great things about being you. Then use this knowledge to defeat self-condemning thoughts when they arise. Something amazing happens when you realize that you are pleasing to God: you want to please Him more. Something amazing happens when you realize that you have access through grace to every spiritual blessing: you start to access them.

What if you really believed that when you pray you would receive from God? Would you pray more and be excited to pray? What if you really believed that when you leave your home, God is going with you and that His favor is upon you? Wouldn't you have an expectation of great things coming your way? What if you really believed you have a calling and an anointing from God? Wouldn't you step out in faith more? What if you really believed that you have something worth fighting for? Would you be so quick to sacrifice that for a cheap counterfeit in sin? Do you see that the attitude of living shame free creates a platform for growth in every area of life? This is the key that makes faith begin to work.

The moment after you sin, you should be able to look yourself in the mirror and say, "Man! I'm something special in Christ. He has gifted me. He has forgiven me. He has called me. He has crowned me with righteousness and tender mercies. He loves me. I bring Him pleasure. He has a future and a hope for me... etc." If you do this, you won't go into a downward spiral that makes sin come naturally... because sin isn't natural for you any longer. It is time for our identity to become the one that God says we have.

Is it any wonder that the loving kindness of God is what leads us to true repentance rather than fear or condemnation? There are so many ministries that use shame and condemnation to achieve a "godly" result. But if there is no condemnation in Christ as the Bible teaches (Ro. 5:16, 8:1), then we understand that God is understanding - that there is a higher law than "try harder." God's ways truly are the good news. And this foundation of love is the very thing that you have needed to soar with God.

What is stopping you from casting off shame forever now? There is no sin so great or heinous that it took God by surprise or that God can't and hasn't already forgiven. You may feel unqualified or too weak for the mountains in your life. Good. You never were qualified or mighty - your qualification and might are through Christ. Your sexuality, as we previously learned, isn't something of which God is ashamed. You have a mighty calling on your life. The worst that you have done serves only to give glory to the depths of God's mercy and redemptive power. Stand "naked" and unashamed before Him now, fully accepted as a full son and as a full heir in the inheritance of Christ. Know that you have gifts, a future and a calling. It is only a matter of time before they start to manifest because God is a rewarder of faith.

~Mighty Man Training & Application~

1. It is time for us to live shame-free before God. Go to Him in prayer now. Imagine yourself standing in His presence before His throne. How do you feel? Do you feel as though the things you've done make Him love you less? Repent.

   Lord, I don't know how Your love can be so big, but You say You love me as much as You love Jesus, even after all my sin. You have given me Your Holy Spirit and gauge my acceptability by the perfect work of Jesus. I haven't related to You as though these things are true, however, I repent. I thank You that I am fully righteous. I thank You that I have gifts and a calling that I can still walk in. I thank You that You are never surprised by my sin, knew my ways and still desired to save me. I am good enough. I am smart enough. I am spiritually acceptable. I am attractive enough. I am prosperous. I am loved. I am accepted. I am new. I can go on with my life as though I had never sinned.

2. Change how you see yourself for good. Don't think that because you have a great time with the Lord right now as He reveals this in your heart that shame will be gone forever. Patterns of thought that have dominated for years will want to come back. This is true of most of the lessons in this

book. We must daily rehearse and practice walking, thinking and acting in the truth because we have habitually walked in lies for so long that they often feel more natural and real than the truth. Every morning you should "put on" shame-free relationship with God just as the Bible tells us to daily put on the whole armor of God in Ephesians 6. In fact, the belt of truth is very much what we are putting on when we agree with the truth of God's word.

3. Daily Affirmations: as you go through your day, remind and affirm the truth of God's opinion by saying aloud:
    a. I am God's beloved son in whom He is well pleased. I bring pleasure to God.
    b. I am fully righteous. Even after sinning I can never be more righteous than I am now.
    c. I have a spiritual inheritance and access to every heavenly blessing.
    d. My sexuality is good and pleasing to God.
    e. I have unique gifts and a calling in the Lord.
    f. God loves me.

~ Part III ~
Fighting Battles & Winning the War

The lessons you have learned: love, grace, your identity, etc. will serve you for the rest of your life – but they don't make sexual temptation go away. Rather they give you the foundation necessary to relate to God properly and access everything you need to walk in victory. They make the tactics work where they failed before.

It would be nice if we could just go to bed and wake up free the next morning. There is no magic pill for instant and total freedom that I know of. But I've realized that heart change takes time and the enemy won't take a holiday from tempting you just because you are pressing in for victory. Temptations will come in various forms at various times. This part of the book will help you identify and overcome various temptations as you journey toward real heart change. I trust that God has already begun to do an amazing work in your heart to reveal His powerful love for you and deliver you from shame. But we must prepare for the struggle mentally, emotionally and physically so that we aren't taken by surprise when we find that we still have sexual thoughts and temptations.

This part of the book can be tough at times. It is intended to tear down false beliefs, strongholds and show us ways of thinking and tactics that will contribute to our success one fight at a time.

CHAPTER 8

Getting Ready to Face Your Demons

MENTAL PREPARATION FOR THE BATTLES TO COME

The horse is prepared for the day of battle, But deliverance is of the Lord.
– Proverbs 21:31

I used to watch G.I. Joe as a kid. At the end of every show, they'd have some constructive message about what to do in a certain situation. They'd tell you what you needed to do and end with, "Now you know… and knowing is half the battle." I don't know about taking strict dogma from G.I. Joe, but knowing and being mentally prepared for a situation has proven time and again to improve the chances of victory when the time comes.

Studies have shown that when a person visualizes doing something, it actually activates and "trains" the same part of the brain that is stimulated in the actual doing of the task visualized. Coaches and scientists have used this information to help train Olympic and high-level athletes, astronauts, and even help people improve written exam results. The old cliché holds some truth: if you fail to plan, you plan to fail.

Have you ever heard someone say, "Put on your game face."? That is another way of saying, "We're about to go up against a challenge. Get mentally prepared." As we prepare to talk about fighting our battles, the first battle will be to be adequately prepared mentally and emotionally for what is coming. If you have a sexual or pornography addiction as I did, you are in for the most emotionally challenging fight of your life. It will take you to the end of yourself and exhaust every ounce of strength within you.

I think of the movie Beowulf. Part way through the tale, the main character falls prey to lust and weakness. His partner is a demon and their offspring becomes a deadly dragon who terrorizes Beowulf's peaceful kingdom. In the final climactic scene, the dragon is about to kill the woman he loves and in order to kill his devil which threatens everything he holds dear, he must, while dangling from a chain, sever his own arm in order to gain the final few inches to pierce the heart of the dragon. The wound and the subsequent fall to the rocks below with the dragon result in his own death. This is a poetic picture of how we all must fight our own dragons.

Jesus said it this way, *"And if your eye causes you to sin, pluck it out and cast it from you. It is better for you to enter into life with one eye, rather than having two eyes, to be cast into hell fire* (Mt. 18:9)." Cutting sin out of your life requires extreme sacrifice and determination. Whereas there is a part of us that eagerly desires freedom, there is another part locked deep within that is still habitually and emotionally dependant on this crutch. I believe what follows is how we must prepare to defeat it.

THE EASY PART AND THE HARD PART

I've been in this spot so often: broken, repentant, sorrowful over my sin, wanting so badly to be free, hoping that the last time will truly be the last time, trying to come to closure over it… even finding resolve and peace to believe that I'll never go back to it ever again. This is the easy part. It is easy to think to yourself while you are at church or with friends, or in a small group or reading parts of this book that inspire you that you'll never go back to your old ways. The decision is easy: "I'll never do it again." It rolls convincingly off the tongue. I've been fully convinced of my own fleshly repentance and professions 1000 times. In those moments, I had indomitable resolve, unwavering clarity of thought and mind, and a surety that I'm making the change once and for all that I'll never go back to my sin. "I've turned a corner this time. Next time it will be different."

The hard part comes in "the next time." When the temptation arises the next time, suddenly all the former commitments go out the window…

then clarity isn't so clear. The struggle didn't seem like a struggle until you find yourself struggling… and that is the problem that we all face. All the things you are fighting for and the reasons you are fighting seem murky, far away and the furthest thing from your mind when all you can think about is lust and porn.

The moments of repentance are indeed sincere; but they don't prepare us for what comes next: the moments of testing. All there is in those moments, it seems, is you and an overwhelming pull toward your sin that doesn't make sense logically. It is at these times we wish we could muster even a fraction of the resolve we had in the safe place of the sanctuary where we made our commitment to "never do that again."

WHAT IS THE ANSWER (AT LEAST MY ANSWER)?

We hear a lot of buzz words like stamina, endurance, perseverance. At the end of the day, all these thoughts only amount to "try harder." For me, "try harder" wasn't the answer, per se. I want to talk about a familiar concept that we don't often associate with conflicted emotions and struggle: sowing and reaping.

All things follow a cycle in the universe God created. There are big cycles such as the four seasons that govern our year. Major changes take place in major cycles. There are smaller cycles such as the months. We have even smaller cycles such as weeks and days. There are infinitely smaller and even infinitely larger cycles that are currently taking place throughout the cosmos; and these cycles mentioned are just smaller instruments in the grand symphony that God has ordained in His universe.

Our bodies also follow cycles of all sorts. Agriculture follows cycles. Light moves in cycles. You get the picture. There is a rhythm that weaves its way into everything and everyone… our will and emotions also follow cycles and we must be aware of this as we make our choices. And then we must be aware of the ramifications of the cycle.

No human can understand God's reasoning why so many things operate in such a long cycle of growth. But I think one lesson can be learned from the law of sowing and reaping. The cycle of sowing and reaping gives space for grace. If you miss a day or two of watering, the seed you planted can still grow.

The cycle actually serves us. Aren't you glad that there isn't usually an instant consequence when you do something wrong? You have the space to come right and make good choices before the bad ones overtake you. It takes time for bad decisions to take root and bear bad fruit. It also takes time for good ones to bear fruit. This time delay allows room for grace to cover us and overtake us with blessing. But in a system of sowing and reaping, we must understand how to apply it and live by its rules.

PLANTING TIME

During those times of decision, we find it easy to make a choice for God that we hope and believe will last forever. Even these truths we've learned can lead us into an place where we are tempted to think, "I've arrived and I'll never sin again." As we've already pointed out, and I'm sure you already know heartbreakingly well, those decisions will be met with a time of testing. The reason we fail when we are in the time of temptation is because we are not cycle-minded. We did not take measures to protect that decision, knowing that the time of testing would surely come around.

We have to understand something about the cycle of the soul. Decision time is like the planting of spring for decisions of the soul. We make a decision in the easy times because we are receiving the water of the Word usually at those times. God is moving on our hearts and speaking life into us. Our hearts are fertile soil and respond easily to God's prompts. However, because we don't have a cycle mentality, we aren't mentally prepared for the next season of our seed's growth which will test the decision we planted.

In our time of decision we must respond to God with humility, not like Peter, thinking that we will continue in the strength we FEEL at the moment. But in humility we plant our seed of decision saying, "God, with all my heart I want to serve You and love You, never giving space to the devil. But I know that I will be tempted again. When that time comes, I choose to remember the grace that brought me to this time of planting. Give me the grace in the day of temptation to love You with all my heart, soul, mind and strength."

GROWTH

As surely as the summer follows the spring, there will be seasons of the soul which test the godly desires of the heart. Summer is a difficult time for plants; yet it is the time of maturation. The heat and the sun can scorch plants. The lack of water can make them dry up.

Watering must be deliberate and come from a water reserve. These are the rules of summer. Every farmer who plants knows in the spring that summer is coming. He knows what he must do in order for the plants to survive and grow until harvest time. I think we fail when our "seed" of decision reaches its testing time because we don't have the mind of the farmer. We don't have a sober preparedness ingrained in our minds for what is to come. Jesus said, "For which of you, intending to build a tower, does not sit down first and count the cost, whether he has enough to finish it (Lu. 14:28)." Every decision we make must be sober and not based on feelings. We must know that a costly time of testing is coming to shake our decision… and knowing is half the battle.

Work, stress, busyness, the hum-drum and all the things of life are elements that wage war against our sensitivity to the Spirit. The devil knows and waits until an opportune time arises to test us. And in that time, we are usually not "soft" to the word. Testing comes when we are far from the broken vessels that told God we were never going back to our sin. The soil of our hearts is dry and scorched by life at these times. We must know our reasons and own our resolve so that in these times we have reservoirs to water our seed and overcome. We must have anticipated the next battle and the one after that and the one after that and have a plan how we will not give in to the temptation. Where will your "water" come from the next time one of your familiar triggers causes you to want to turn to lust?

I have recently gotten into jogging. I came to realize that pacing yourself is crucial to finishing a race. If I just go out and start to run with no plan and no benchmarks, I seldom can finish the distance I set out to go. However, when I remember to pace myself, anticipate the fatigue that comes toward the middle and end of the run and picture myself finishing, I almost always run at my peak and break previous personal records.

The mental preparedness gives us 50% of the victory before we even have to face the battle. You must decide TODAY how you will respond to the pain and difficulty of tomorrow's temptation. It WILL come. What are the times and temptations that trigger you to fall? Get real about them and do whatever it takes to make sure that you don't have the ability to fall prey to those times of testing. If you have ones that you can't safeguard against, mentally rehearse what you will say and how you will respond until you are certain that when faced with that temptation, you will act just as you have trained.

The times of testing WILL be worse than you are imagining right now, so don't let them take you by surprise. Know in advance how you will react. It will still feel a bit like chopping off a part of ourselves at the time, but by the grace of God we overcome and gain the victory. The prize is growth. I promise you this. Every battle will make you stronger in the spirit and soul than you were before. Every victory puts us farther from the bondage and closer to freedom than we were before. Just as the plant grows and matures in the summer, this process will grow and mature you. It is worth the fight. The juice is worth the squeeze. Ask God for the grace to set these forces in motion even now.

HARVEST

The farmer knows that the work of the summer will bear a blessed harvest. Nobody loves difficult work. Bringing in the harvest takes work. We must sacrifice. If you are at all like me, the struggle reveals what is really in your heart. This will set us up for later key victories where God delivers us from the heart issues that keep us bound to the sin. I've had to come to grips with the fact that there is a part of me (that is my carnal mind and flesh) that really likes the sin, pleasure, escape and feelings that porn brings. I wish that weren't the case, but it is the reality of what I saw in my heart. I had to kiss those idols goodbye in order for God to heal those areas of my heart; and it was like Beowulf cutting off his arm to kill his demon. It does get easier - but I'd be setting you up for failure if I didn't go out of my way to impress this upon you.

We look forward to the harvest. This is the only consolation for a person who has a sowing and reaping mindset. We sacrifice immediate pleasure, because we know that a far more valuable weight of glory is being sown which will reap a harvest. Likewise, a sowing and reaping mindset is needed to overcome, because we must get it through our heads that each act of sin steals the good seed we've planted and sows evil seed which will cost dearly to pull out when it starts to grow.

The farmer knows the labor will be great, but he has a sowing and reaping mindset that brings him consolation. In our culture where everything comes fast, faster or fastest, we have a hard time relating to this mode; and it kills us when it comes time to water our seed. We can't win this battle unless we know that it will cost - and we can't find a willingness to pay the cost unless we believe in the harvest.

Did you get that? It is so important. The decision that I liken to spring is usually emotionally based. It is during the time of testing that I liken to the scorching dryness of summer that the emotion is gone and if you don't have a harvest mindset, you will never, never, never, never, never make it!

God is a rewarder of those who diligently seek Him. The thing that keeps this reward/harvest mindset from working is usually shame and a feeling like the reward is unattainable. Thankfully this is not the case. We have the favor of God on us and He won't be mocked. We will reap what we sow in the Spirit.

But then what happens when we bring in our harvest – when we are at a place when we can feel like we are walking in victory over this sin? It will be tempting in that place to feel proud, as though YOU are the one who has made this happen, when the reality is that you've simply learned how to apply the grace in your seasons.

In harvest time, you have abundance. What will you spend your harvest on? You will find that you have more spare time and a deeper intimacy with God. Who is the man that will emerge in your time of harvest? What will fill the space that was once filled with pornography? Dream with God and plan for your harvest.

Preparedness for the next season is what gives us the ability to make it through the one we are in. This is the life-cycle of growth and freedom. When there is no vision the people perish or cast off restraint (Pr 29:18). When you don't have the mental preparedness that a sowing and reaping mindset gives, you will cast off your restraint when the time comes. But when the harvest comes and you start to see joy, you will know it was worth it in the end.

WINTER

We can't forget about winter. The winter of the soul is the long season when there is no new growth or visible activity. It is easy to think that you've beaten your sin when you start to enter that harvest time. I went through a period of great victory. I even started talking to people about how I beat my habit. I started seeing myself as a great victor. And then my winter came, and I wasn't prepared.

The farmer knows that even in the joy of the harvest, he must store up for the winter. There is never a time when the farmer is not sober-minded about the realities of the world. He knows what he has to do for his seed to take root. He knows what he must do to tend his crop to bring it to harvest. And he knows that harvest must be divided into food for eating, food for winter and additional seed for sowing again in the spring.

The joys of seeing a harvest in my life where the struggle seemed over gave me a false sense of security and a fair measure of pride. I thought that the fight was over and I had won. End of the story. But the reality was that I had brought in the harvest and was eating all my fruit and not storing up any to last me through the winter of the soul. I let my guard down and got sloppy, worldly, carnal... and fell. I wasn't prepared to sustain my harvest through a lifetime - to continue walking in lock-step with God and trusting that it was by His grace only that I had achieved any measure of victory. After a while, I started to guard my heart less and then a wake-up call came in the form of a fall.

I wasn't struggling daily any longer. It had been months since I really experienced any measurable temptation. This is a wonderful place to be and it is easy in this place to think that God has done all the work He'll need to in your soul. It is easy to feel like you have risen above. But sooner or later the thrill of not feeling like an addict is gone and you realize that now this is life... When I stopped seeing growth, when life became status-quo, it required a kind of spiritual endurance I wasn't prepared for. The choices we make are for life. Then you have to sustain your choice. This is the "winter time" for our souls.

When we start to see victories and when we aren't struggling on a daily basis, we can't afford to think we're out of the battle. When Jesus was in the wilderness and had resisted all the temptations the devil left... until an opportune time. The battle will always be there; but it will get easier. We need stamina in order to finish the race. This is the cycle of growth. Real freedom is available for every one of us. We're made in God's image and He is forming Christ in us. The victory is certain, but will come at a price. And we must be sober not to think that we're above temptation at any time. God will lead us to higher and higher levels of freedom, but pride will lead to a fall. We also will learn many lessons as we go through this book. We can't afford to get sloppy and go back to old things that lead to temptation once we are enjoying the freedom of harvest time.

Brothers, be sober. Know the seasons so that you can prepare for them. If you prepare your heart in this way, the lessons of this manual will bless you greatly.

~Mighty Man Training & Application~

1. If you have made the decision to never look at porn again, ask God to bless that seed and help you water it through the difficult times of testing.

2. You WILL be tempted again. It will be horribly difficult. Stop and remember what it feels like to be in that situation. Now think what you will do when the time comes. Grit your teeth and make your decision today.

3. Remember the reasons you want to be free. List them. They are your harvest. As you think about the pain of enduring temptation, think about the greater reward of finally bringing in your harvest of freedom.

4. Plan for the long haul. I promise you this: temptations will get easier, but won't go away. As you think about fighting your temptations the next time, settle the fact that you will have to fight them the time after that, and the time after that, etc. There may be some lifestyle changes you have to make in order for freedom to be a lifestyle that you can sustain forever. But know that it will be worth it and you will be glad.

CHAPTER 9

Sowing and Reaping in the Fear of the Lord

The Fear of the Lord. I think this is a really misunderstood concept in Christianity. Both the Old and New Testament teach us to learn the Fear of the Lord... but it just doesn't sound like fun... it certainly isn't on any pastor's list of "feel good" sermons. I also think many tend to avoid this topic because it has the potential to really be taken to extremes - either brushed aside as meaningless in our age or distorted to the point that God's character comes into question.

Let me say this about the nature of God: He's wonderful. I really do fall more and more in love with Him every day. The more I get to know His ways, the more I love them too. I think the less we know of God, the more we tend to shy away from learning about things like "holy fear." Maybe some deep part of us doesn't really want to find out what it means - perhaps we get nervous that maybe God is carrying a big stick and waiting to smite us after all.

Nothing, however, could be farther from the truth. When you read how God describes Himself in the Bible, never once does He say things like, "I am an angry God who delights in misery." God can BECOME angry... but it isn't how He defines Himself. He IS love. And so even if God were to get angry, it would never undermine His character and nature. Everything He does flows from this nature of love – even chastisement. And we can count on this through all times. So we can learn about scary sounding concepts like "fear of the Lord" knowing that nothing that God does can be bad. It is His loving kindness that will ultimately lead us to repentance, not fear (Rm. 2:4).

UNDERSTANDING THE FEAR OF THE LORD

While teaching Sunday morning groups at my church, between series, I often liked to open the floor for open question and answer classes. People could ask any question that related to God, the Bible, Christianity, etc. One morning, someone asked if I could explain the "fear of the Lord." I wanted to know what the general knowledge was on the subject, so I opened the question to the group first for input. I found several of the answers interesting. One woman made the comment that the Fear of the Lord was an Old Testament teaching and didn't really apply to Christians today. Another person made a similar comment that because of Jesus, we don't need to fear God the way they did under the law.

It is true that the Law has been cancelled by Jesus – praise God! But there is still an element of holy fear that is as much a New Testament teaching as it is Old Testament. I asked the group to turn to 2 Corinthians 7:1, *"Therefore, having these promises, beloved, let us cleanse ourselves from all filthiness of the flesh and spirit, perfecting holiness **in the fear of God**."* Then we turned to Acts 9:31, *"Then the churches throughout all Judea, Galilee, and Samaria had peace and were edified. And walking in the fear of the Lord and in the comfort of the Holy Spirit, they were multiplied."* A quick concordance search also revealed that the concept of the Fear of the Lord and Holy Fear comes in many other instances throughout the New Testament. In fact, walking in Holy Fear seemed to be a common denominator for breakthrough in the early church.

Clearly the Fear of the Lord is not an "Old Testament" concept despite public opinion and misconception. So what does it mean for us today? I'd say this: its definition hasn't changed without warning from one Testament to the next. Ultimately, as we'll see, it all comes down to this: *"Do not be deceived, God is not mocked; for whatever a man sows, that he will also reap"* (Ga. 6:7). This is not an Old Testament verse. In fact, Galatians is perhaps the most bold, clear teaching in the New Testament to the fact that believers are not under the law any longer! So we must understand that sowing and reaping in the fear of the Lord are concepts that we must embrace as New Testament believers. You can't play with sin and not be burned. You will reap what you sow sooner or later.

OK, we'll reap what we sow. So what? What does the Fear of the Lord actually and practically mean? How do we apply the fear of the Lord in the New Covenant? The entire first chapter of Proverbs is some of the Bible's clearest teaching about the Fear of the Lord. Most of us have heard one of the familiar passages from this chapter, "The fear of the Lord is the beginning of knowledge, But fools despise wisdom and instruction" (v.7). This concept of refusing to learn from your mistakes and their consequences continues throughout the rest of the chapter:

> *Turn at my rebuke; Surely I will pour out my spirit on you; I will make my words known to you. Because I have called and you refused, I have stretched out my hand and no one regarded, Because you disdained all my counsel... When distress and anguish come upon you. "Then they will call on me, but I will not answer; They will seek me diligently, but they will not find me. Because they hated knowledge **And did not choose the fear of the Lord,** They would have none of my counsel And despised my every rebuke. Therefore they shall eat the fruit of their own way, And be filled to the full with their own fancies (vv. 23-31).*

This is a pretty shocking passage. We don't like to think that God would actually sit back and let us reap what we've sown. We definitely don't like the idea of eating "the fruit of our own ways." All that seems so... Old Testament... after all, don't we have mercy now? We much prefer sermons and books about God's blessings. Can't we skip to a happier chapter... one that doesn't talk about the fact that there may actually be consequences to our sin?

Does all this mean that God is an angry god or waiting for us to mess up in order to smite us... or could it be that God may allow us at times to see the "wages of sin" so that we can learn to trust that His ways are the best plan for our lives? However, if that is the case, what about the cross and grace and Jesus?

GRACE AND THE FEAR OF THE LORD

I have heard a wonderful definition of grace that has a lot of truth to it: grace is the space and ability to come right. I'd add to this definition that it is God's ability to us and through us that gives us the space and power to overcome sin and obstacles. Grace is NOT a license to sin. Grace is not a happy pill that allows us to say, "God understands and forgives me if I keep on sinning." God does understand and He does forgive. But He still hates sin; and we abuse grace when we think that we can just keep on sinning "in grace."

People glibly and conversationally use verses like we read earlier, "God is not mocked, a man reaps what he sows." However, many Christians don't live their lives as though they actually believe that their sins will affect their life and calling. Somewhere in Christian circles, despite the vast weight of scripture's teaching against this, an idea has come about that because of grace we can sin and get away with it without bearing any subsequent consequences of our sin.

This attitude that grace is a license to sin is pure rebellion, not Christianity. A person with a hard heart toward God, who has no intention of forsaking sin and who is using "grace" as a blanket cover-all excuse is most likely not even truly saved; for how could they have been saved if they have never repented of their sins? This attitude is very different from that of an earnest believer who truly hates their sin, wants to come right and is seeking the Lord to do so. This latter type of believer is immature but under grace. In fact, Paul teaches such a radical understanding of grace, that for the immature believer, they can literally never out-sin the grace of God (Ro. 5:20). This understanding of grace then helps us see that it indeed gives us the space to come right with all glorious freedom and confidence before God but doesn't by any means enable us to continue sinning. This fact of our position before God, however, does not mean that sin does not carry natural consequences, emotional consequences and even chastisement from the Lord.

WISDOM OR CURSES

Consequences are not the same thing as curses. Curses are spiritual injunctions or judgments that give the devil "legal" space to afflict us because of sin. We need to understand that there is a difference between consequences and curses for the sake of the Gospel as well as developing trust in God's character and love. Many Christians live in fear of God allowing them to be cursed for their sin. I used to be one of them.

Fear of the Lord throughout scripture does not teach that God is going to curse us, but rather is inseparably linked to growing in wisdom, gaining understanding and knowledge, BLESSINGS that a good father gives to instruct his child. God may allow us to eat the fruit of our own way so that we grow. What He isn't doing is slapping a curse on us in anger. All God's wrath was poured out on Christ; and all His spiritual judgments through the law have been paid in full by Christ.

The Bible says clearly that when God fulfilled the law in Christ, He *"wiped out the handwriting of requirements that was against us, which was contrary to us. And He has taken it out of the way, having nailed it to the cross. Having disarmed principalities and powers, He made a public spectacle of them, triumphing over them in it* (Col 2:14, 15)." So we conclude that the law, being abolished, can no longer give the devil "legal" space to afflict us because of sin. Furthermore, "Christ has redeemed us from the curse of the law, having become a curse for us" (Ga. 3:13).

Despite the fact that God has paid for ALL curses and will not, Himself, curse ANY believer for any reason (**for there is NO condemnation in Christ** (Ro. 8:1), and there now is NO Law with which to pronounce judgment), there are still, however, millions of Christians with curses operating in their lives - but NOT because of sin. I have to say that again because of all the wrong teaching out there on curses: SIN cannot, does not, will not EVER again be an open door for curses in the life of ANY believer. Here's why (and this is the MOST important thing that you can ever learn about how curses operate under the New Covenant): when the devil, **unable** to go to God now for condemnation, **unable** to use the cancelled law to curse you through sin, seeks to curse us, he then goes to the ONLY thing left that can pronounce a curse, the ONLY thing that has power and authority in the spiritual realm to empower the dead law. He goes to YOU, the one created in God's image who now has the spiritual authority in Christ to reenact the law and its curses through our **agreement** with the devil.

Curses are real. They do affect believers. But it is OUR agreement and authority that empowers these spiritual contracts. If the devil parades all the Old Testament curses of adultery in front of you, telling you that you'll be cursed with poverty and shame and all the rest because of this sin, the only way that gains power is if YOU believe it and add your faith to that lie. Faith works whether it is in good things or bad. That is the power you have as a believer.

However, if you spend all your time looking at pornography and not living up to your full potential, you may still be in poverty as a consequence of sin rather than as a curse. If this sin has stripped your soul of confidence and your internal realities are now dictating your external circumstances, this is a consequence that may have brought cursing into your life by its attitudes and agreements. But in grace and through the fear of the Lord, you can change all of that today! You don't have to clean up your act to have fellowship with God. You don't have to pay the wages of the Law to work your way out of a curse and work your way into blessing. Praise God the Law has been cancelled and fulfilled!

It is the wrong mingling of Law-based theology into this glorious Gospel of grace that has perverted our spiritual understanding. Christianity has curses horribly, horribly confused. Ministries either don't teach about them at all or teach that sin brings curses and that we must break them one-by-one along with the fear of generational curses for sins that we didn't even commit. You are a son of Abraham, a full heir of all the blessings of God and the law has been fulfilled on your behalf. These blessings trump any curse.

For the purpose of this brief teaching, we must understand that because the Law has been cancelled and Christ has become a curse for us, because there is and never will be condemnation for us in Christ, we can live without fear of curses. But there are still consequences of sin and wisdom that will serve us if we learn about them and understand the fear of the Lord. (If you would like to learn more about curses, how they operate and how to break them, please write to our ministry.)

GOD'S CHARACTER

There is a widely popular mode of thought in Christianity that, for lack of a theologically better definition, thinks that God is out to get you. I can't count the number of times I've heard people say things like, "Oh, be careful if you ask God for patience, 'snicker,' He'll give it to you the hard way." "Ask God for wisdom and He'll put a hard choice in front of you... and you better make the right one or you'll be sorry." The list goes on and on of stupid, damaging things that people attribute to God's character. Somewhere we've gotten the idea that God is just waiting for us to ask a loaded question so that He can do what He's been gleefully waiting to do and say, "Aha! Now I've got them!" and slam us with calamity. In what universe's bible are people reading that this is the nature or character of the God who is love and who can neither tempt nor be tempted (Jas. 1:13)?

Is it God or the devil who comes ONLY to steal, kill and destroy? Isn't God the One who gives only good and perfect gifts? If the devil is allowed space in your life, it is because you were playing in his yard or because God has set you up to crush his stinking head.

We have this idea that if we ask God to teach us the fear of the Lord that we are in for it – that we just asked the question that will allow God to open up hell-on-earth in our lives until we have learned the fear of the Lord through every horrible trial imaginable. God can't give you what He doesn't have. He won't release hell into your life because all He has is heaven to give. The Bible teaches that the fear of the Lord operates through wisdom and understanding. These are the gifts that God gives so that we don't have to go through hell on earth.

The "law" of sowing and reaping, the fear of the Lord, and the chastisement of the Lord are New Testament concepts that directly relate to our RELATIONSHIP with God, as we are now in a relational covenant through grace. This is important to understand. The old covenant was designed to lead us by the hand. In the New Covenant, God wants to lead us by the heart and cause us to understand His love and ways. Therefore, the chastisement of the Lord is always done out of love, designed to bring us into deeper intimacy, directed at tearing down every obstacle of love and serving to protect us and others from the more dangerous and dire consequences of our sin. The Bible is clear that the Word of God is God's preferred method to "wash" us and cleanse us of sin (Eph. 5:26, 2 Tim. 3:16). However, we need to walk with the sobriety of knowing that God loves us too much to let us continue to walk in self-destructive ways.

So let's take a moment to clear God's character. The fact that God chastises us in no way contradicts His love. Quite the opposite. *"For whom the Lord loves He chastens, And scourges every son whom He receives. If you endure chastening, God deals with you as with sons; for what son is there whom a father does not chasten? But if you are without chastening, of which all have become partakers, then you are illegitimate and not sons. Furthermore, we have had human fathers who corrected us, and we paid them respect. Shall we not much more readily be in subjection to the Father of spirits and live? For they indeed for a few days chastened us as seemed best to them, but He for our profit, that we may be partakers of His holiness. Now no chastening seems to be joyful for the present, but painful; nevertheless, afterward it yields the peaceable fruit of righteousness to those who have been trained by it. Therefore strengthen the hands which hang down, and the feeble knees, and make straight paths for your feet, so that what is lame may not be dislocated, but rather be healed. Pursue peace with all people, and holiness, without which no one will see the Lord* (Heb. 12:6-14)."

This is the heart of the Lord in chastening: that we be healed, that we become strong, that we yield fruit, that we have greater fellowship with Him. I love verse 6. Many translations say that He chastens the son in whom He "delights." This translation says "receives" – but understand the picture either way: even in the midst of chastisement, God is still delighting in us and receiving us. As an earthly father I understand how damaging it can be to chastise my children out of anger. We are told to correct, train and instruct our children. This is God's way.

If you are disciplined, that has a different connotation in our minds than if we become disciples. But the word "disciple" means "a disciplined one" or one undergoing discipline. God corrects, chastens, instructs – all these things are the process of being a disciple. Let me tell you something: living a disciplined life is much better than living an unfulfilled one.

Jesus loved His disciples. God doesn't discipline us in wrath or anger. All His wrath has been poured out on Christ. While sin does anger God, His anger is never directed at us, the sons in whom He delights even in the midst of chastisement. However, we *feel* the opposite don't we? We feel as though God is rejecting us when going through times of correction. His chastisement is always directed at removing the sin that will harm us more than that by which we are being chastised. Nevertheless, let us not sin in hopes of discipline. Sowing and reaping are a wake-up call that should tell us that something is wrong because we aren't experiencing the blessing that should be coming to us as God's children. Fear of the Lord is the instruction that helps us avoid chastisement altogether.

We cannot take lightly the consequences of sin. *Every* New Testament writer talks about reaping from bad choices (as we'll read later in this chapter), Jesus Himself warns us about the consequences of unrepentant sin in His letters to the Churches in Revelation? *"And I gave her time to repent of her sexual immorality, and she did not repent. (therefore) Indeed I will cast her into a sickbed, and those who commit adultery with her into great tribulation, unless they repent of their deeds"* (vv. 2:21-22). Those are strong words that should give every believer pause if they want to play with sin and not repent.

Look at the wording in the passage from Revelation. God gave TIME to repent, THEREFORE... I believe we have a time of grace upon us as believers to get certain sins out of our lives before it escalates and does worse damage to ourselves and others than could be repaired. Grace gives us this space to come right. However, if we don't listen to the conviction in our hearts and do what we ought, there comes a time when our sins will catch up with us and we will start to see consequences play out - not because God wants to smite us, but because He wants to show us that the wages of sin are death and that He has better things in store for us. This is a function of His love.

I think back to a time when God allowed the grace for a sin of speeding to wear off in my life. As a young Christian and newly saved, I was a speed-freak behind the wheel of a car. I loved to drive fast. I had been pulled over many times for speeding and for a long while, I had a grace or favor on me to the point where I never got tickets. I don't think it was until the sixteenth or seventeenth time I was pulled over that I even got my first ticket. One time, I was even pulled over for doing TRIPLE the speed limit and didn't get a ticket.

However, God began to work on my heart after I was saved and reminded me that His word teaches us to respect authority and obey all the ordinances and laws of man for the sake of our testimony and a peaceful life. Speeding is sin. One day my "luck" changed. I was speeding, got pulled over and actually got a ticket! Then the very next day, I was pulled over again and got another ticket. I had been pulled over roughly twenty times before this and only ever got 3 tickets - now I got two tickets in two days? The following day I was going to be pulled over a third time... but I turned onto back roads and ditched the cop (more sin). Without fail, EVERY SINGLE time I allowed myself to speed, there was a cop sitting there waiting for me. Every stop sign I blew, there was an officer waiting for me. I once got 3 tickets in 2 days! It was like I was *cursed*, or something. All my GRACE for that sin was gone. I was now reaping the consequences of my actions. Did my salvation change? No. Did God or His character change? No. Did I deserve what I was reaping? Yes. Suddenly I was very sober about my sin. I thought, "Maybe I should start to watch my speed." God wasn't cursing me or waiting to smite me... my own sin was reaping its consequences and God simply had to remove the grace, take a step back and let me begin to eat the fruit of my own ways.

As I counsel men who have lived with a sexual addiction for some time, the list of damage that this sin sows into lives is devastating. Lives ruined, loved ones crushed or lost, financial destruction, reputation and authority destroyed, incarceration. The list of consequences are endless. Let us not be slow to learn that we can't play with fire and not be burned.

There are seasons of grace on Christians at different stages of their walk. Many Christians may still have a grace so that the devil isn't allowed access to "sift them like wheat" as the devil asked to do to Peter. I believe other Christians have been in this sin so long and are reaping the consequences of their sin, but never made the connection in their minds that it could be the law of sowing and reaping in full maturity of harvest time.

This will be a wake-up call for most Christians: whereas God's love IS unconditional, all of His blessings are not. Even though our gifts and calling are irrevocable, the degree to which we bear fruit is not set in stone. The anointing on us can lift. The Bible even warns that we can experience "shipwreck" of our calling and get into heaven with all of our works and rewards burned up. The Bible is full of "if-then" promises. We can lose earthy and heavenly reward, destroy our calling and "eat the fruit of our own way" because of agreement with sin. These are not Old Testament concepts, they are found over and over again even through the New Testament.

Your destiny isn't set in stone. Sin will steal your future and your calling in Christ if you don't ever get over it. Your promises from God are not concrete. Allowing a lifestyle of lust will eventually destroy the blessings that God has planned for you and like Esau weeping over his lost birthright, there is no guarantee that you can get them back. We can't play with sin. I quote this verse many times, but it is worth repeating: *"by means of a harlot A man is reduced to a crust of bread; And an adulteress will prey upon his precious life. Can a man take fire to his bosom, And his clothes not be burned? Can one walk on hot coals, And his feet not be seared?" (Pr. 6:26-28).* It is only a matter of time before serving Hell brings Hell in your life.

FEAR OF THE LORD AS A BEGINNING

"The fear of the Lord is the beginning of knowledge, But fools despise wisdom and instruction... The fear of the Lord is to hate evil; Pride and arrogance and the evil way And the perverse mouth I hate."
– Proverbs 1:7. 8:13

It is important to understand that the fear of the Lord is not an ending point but a beginning point. The purpose of the fear of the Lord is not to teach you conformity through fear for the rest of your life but to teach you wisdom and understanding and the heart of God. Of the 27 passages in the Bible that talk about the fear of the Lord, the concept is ALWAYS coupled with this higher truth. In about half of these passages it is linked to knowledge, wisdom and understanding. In about a quarter of the others, its purpose is to help you learn the heart of God – what He loves and what He hates. The purpose of the fear of the Lord isn't to keep you in fear but to cause you to walk in wisdom and begin to think like God thinks.

You see, sin does harm us, harm others and pains the heart of the God who IS love. He loves us too much to see us destroy our lives without a few wakeup calls along the way. He loves us too much to see us squander our inheritance as sons on worthless things. He loves us too much to see us live a vain life adrift and devoid of purpose and fulfillment. He loves others too much to allow us to go on hurting them through our actions without some reminders of how He feels about this also.

However, chastisement is not His first choice or the end result. The first chapter of Proverbs shows the progression of warnings that God will go through. It says if you hate knowledge, won't hear the counsel of God, despise His rebukes, refused His call, and don't notice when He stretches out his hand… THEN He says, you will eat the fruit of your own way. THEN He will take a step back and allow your consequences to catch up with you. This is a long list of warnings before God allows your sin to bear fruit.

Do you see how gracious God is? He could allow you to suffer consequences from the FIRST instance of your sin, but He shelters you in grace and gives you so many chances to come right. So you see, as plainly illustrated in this passage of Proverbs, that the fear of the Lord and its chastisements are not a direct consequence of sin. If they were, God would have to allow the consequences instantly. Rather He uses it with patience and discretion with those whose hearts are hardened to His preferred methods.

What are God's preferred methods? That you LISTEN to Him. "But whoever listens to me will dwell safely, And will be secure, without fear of evil (Pr. 1:33)." God washes us by the water of the word to cleanse us of sin (Eph. 5:26). The word of God is His tool for reproof, correction and instruction (2 Tim. 3:16).

Fear of the Lord is a beginning of instruction in wisdom for those who won't hear God – NOT a beginning of judgments of sin. Its results are not an end, but a beginning. Its purpose is to give you wisdom into how God feels and lead you into love. **While fear of the Lord may keep you from sin, it will NEVER free you from being a sinner, which is God's highest ideal, that you learn to walk in the new man and become sanctified in heart, not in actions alone.**

If I, as a grown man, see a person in need of help and want to pass by but suddenly think, "If I don't help them, my dad will give me a spanking," there is something horribly wrong and stunted in my emotional development. If, as a mature man, my motivation is still fear of discipline and I have not taken personal ownership of my parents' ideals, they have failed miserably in training me in the way I should go. The same is true of our Heavenly Father. Fear of the Lord is for the immature, to cause us to understand the heart of God and know how the person of God feels about sin. Fear of the Lord is for the believer ABUSING grace, not USING grace.

The Bible says that if you perfectly keep God's word, the LOVE of God, not the fear of God has been perfected in you (1 Jn. 2:5). **There comes a time in your Christian walk where the greatest fear that you can muster is that you should hurt the heart of the God that loves you and whom you so love.**

SIN AND YOUR CALLING

God put you on this planet and equipped you with gifts and talents that enable you to serve Him and make an impact in the world around you. Walking out your ministry and calling, however, is not set in stone. I have heard some people quote Romans 11:29 *(The gifts and calling of God are without repentance)* in the context that you can sin all you want and still have a fruitful calling or ministry. But this is wishful thinking and imbalanced theology. There is a difference between *having* a calling and *walking* in your calling. You can have a calling your whole life and never fulfill it.

Jesus tells a parable about three servants who are given talents and told to use them while the master is gone. Two use their talents and multiply them. One buries his gift in the ground and does not multiply it. That servant who does not is also cast out and his talent given to the one who was the best steward (Mt. 25, Lu. 19). The moral: there is no reward for those who squander what God has given them.

While sin doesn't steal the fact that God equips us with gifts such as teaching or serving, and those gifts carry the promise of a calling, how we steward those gifts affects whether we use them for God's purposes or not. Jesus tells a parable in Matthew 22 where homeless and derelict people are invited to a great banquet. They are all given robes to wear, but one man does not. He is taken and cast into outer darkness. The moral at the end of the story: many are called, but few are chosen (v. 22:14).

Paul warns us in 1 Corinthians about Christians who get to heaven and discover that they have no heavenly reward. They are saved… but barely. In the very next verse he then warns us not to defile your body in which the Spirit of God dwells (vv. 3:15-17). Do you see a pattern emerging? You can destroy all your calling and all your Heavenly reward by living like Hell.

Paul again warns us in 1 Thessalonians 4 that sexual immorality will interfere with the will of God for your life and stymie the sanctification that God wants to do in you. The truth is that you and I should be further along in our sanctification process than we are now. We should know how to "possess our vessel in sanctification and honor." We should not so casually pass over the warnings that God has put throughout scripture that serve to steer our life and calling from ruin.

Peter warns us to be diligent to make our calling and election certain (2 Pet. 1:10). That is to say, if you are not careful, you may forfeit the call on your life through laziness and sin. He teaches that just being a Christian doesn't guarantee your calling. He urges us to escape lust and add virtue, diligence, self-control, perseverance, godliness and other qualities to our lives or else we will surely miss our purpose on this earth.

Jude also speaks of people who began in the truth but got sidetracked by earthly pleasures and lusts. He warns that the end for them is worse than if they had never come to the truth in the first place.

James warns us that faith without works is dead and powerless to save. Let us wake up and respond with holy fear. Every single author of the New Testament without exception warns us about the consequences of sin in our lives, calling and blessing. Every single author!

Christian men, CATCH ON! We aren't called to get saved and live however we want while we wait to "cash in" on our free ticket to heaven. If all you want from God is a free ticket to Heaven, you are living so far below your potential and destiny – and I question if a real believer can truly live that way. We have been made sons of God. His Spirit burns in us for greater things. I have to believe that there is a heart in you that beats for more: more of God's fellowship, more purpose in your life, to see the Kingdom come to you and through you.

In heaven God will wipe away every tear. I believe those tears are shed when we realize all that we could have done, all that we could have been, the lives that we could have saved. You are in for a very rude awakening in heaven

if you don't get sin out of your life now by walking in the new man:
Nevertheless the solid foundation of God stands, having this seal: "The Lord knows those who are His," and, "Let everyone who names the name of Christ depart from iniquity." But in a great house there are not only vessels of gold and silver, but also of wood and clay, some for honor and some for dishonor. Therefore if anyone cleanses himself from the latter, he will be a vessel for honor, sanctified and useful for the Master, prepared for every good work. (2 Tim. 2:19-21)." I don't know about you, but I don't want to get to Heaven and discover than I was a vessel marked for dishonor because I refused to get the iniquity out of my life. You will one day stand before God and have to answer the question of what you did with your calling and gifts.

If you continue in this, the reality is that you are stealing the blessings that God wants to give you in this age and in the age to come. Every time we walk in sin there are spiritual consequences that interfere with our sanctification and calling. Furthermore, there is only so long you can play with this sin before you start to see natural consequences. Each time you dabble, you gamble that it won't be this time. But even if we don't see them, there are consequences every time. At the very least, every time you open doors to lust and pornography you have lost the time spent, seared your conscience a little and generated memories and soul ties that will make freedom more difficult to attain. Let us pray that God, in His mercy doesn't allow greater reaping than this... but how long will you play with that fire? How many divine appointments have you missed while sitting in front of your computer? How many blessings were you not positioned for while you gratified your flesh with a passing pleasure?

I had to come personally to the realization in my life and ministry that I could not live with one foot in God's Kingdom and the other in the world. I could not live by day as a son of God and by night like a lost man. I had to make a choice to be a Christian or nothing; to love God with ALL my heart or not at all (just as Paul warns in 1 Th. 4:8 that if we reject purity we reject God, Himself). I could not live one more day dreaming of the things I'd like to do with God and see my reality fall short. I knew this sin was stealing from me in various ways. I had to draw a line in the sand and trust God for what I felt I was "giving up" to forsake it completely.

Let us start to be sober about this now. Let us not respond in shame and look at what we don't have or what we have squandered. Let us rather be sober about the time we have left and be grateful that we have a calling and a grace upon our lives to reach people in a way that only we are uniquely equipped to do. God has a plan and calling for you. He doesn't want any of us to have further loss in our lives. He begs, *"Turn at my rebuke; Surely I will pour out my spirit on you; I will make my words known to you. (Pr. 1:23).*

GOOD NEWS

Many of you reading this may indeed see the fruits of your sin at play in your life. The good news is that God never ceases to love you even when He allows you to walk in your sin's consequences. If God allows chastening into your life, He is simply showing you a plain truth: sin has no good end. And this fact helps us understand why the Bible teaches us that the Fear of the Lord is the beginning of wisdom. To understand that sin has consequences will cause you to act wisely and not sin. For the person truly trying to come right, grace is there to pick us up when we fall.

There have been many times that I chose not to sin because I knew that the act would have consequences in the natural as well as spiritual realm that I was simply not willing to bear. The Fear of the Lord is God's way of leading us by the hand while He teaches us understanding of His ways so that we can be eventually led by the heart.

I personally believe that the most pure motive to not sin is actually the love of God and not the fear of sin's consequences. The ultimate goal of this book is to take us to the point where we are motivated to righteousness by love. But as a very practical truth, the fear of the Lord should not be overlooked.

~Mighty Man Training & Application~

If you have been playing with sin and thinking that it was OK, simply repent. *Father, forgive me for lightly esteeming Your Word. Forgive me for thinking that I could have my cake and eat it too. Forgive me that I thought I could mock You and not reap what I sow. I ask You now to turn the tables. I choose to sow to the Spirit. Please lead me in paths of blessing and restore the gifts and calling to my life. Grant me the grace to be a good steward of my time and walk worthy of my calling. Bring my soul to full and real repentance. I want sin out of my life forever. I resolve to never again look at pornography or lust. I ask these things through grace, in Jesus name, Amen.*

Ask the Lord to show you the ways that this sin has stolen from you. Ask Him to show you what will be stolen if you continue in it. Then be sober and make a decision to depart from such ways so that the blessings of God begin to overtake you.

CHAPTER 10

Where there is no Vision...

WHAT ARE YOU FIGHTING FOR?

It isn't enough to have what you want. You have to want what you have.
- Anonymous

God has given each of us a calling. What is more, He has deposited a facet of His own uniqueness in each one of us as the guarantee of this call. The unfortunate thing is that we spend more of our time and lives fantasizing about other people's calling and uniqueness rather than contemplating and cultivating our own. It is easy to envy another person's abilities, physique, checkbook or perfect family. Meanwhile they are busy envying someone else's too.

Genesis 25 depicts a story between two brothers. The elder brother Esau came back from a long hunting trip and was extremely famished. He tells his brother Jacob to get him some food because he's so hungry. Jacob does something a little back-handed and tells him he'll give him his food in exchange for Esau's birthright. Esau was the older son and in those days, the larger portion of the inheritance and blessing was given to the firstborn. Despite the audacity of his brother's proposition, Esau sells his birthright to his brother for a pot of stew. He sacrificed future honor and blessing for the sake of what his carnal nature was calling for in the moment. It says that later he sought to get it back and wept with exceeding bitterness, but it was too late. You can't change the past.

In reality, both brothers despised their destinies in different ways. The younger brother wasn't happy with what he considered to be a smaller portion. The other brother didn't think that what he had was worth enough to fight for. I fear that I and many Christian men around the world are daily selling their birthright - their gift, calling and blessings in Christ for momentary gratification and the promise to live vicariously in a fantasy reality.

TV, movies, society - these all try to sell you someone else's birthright. They give us glimpses of people "living the dream." Glorified lives, glorified bodies, clever situational plot lines with witty scripting and heroic endings... All this lets us vicariously experience all the emotion of living their lives within a short window of time and whatever happy ending we want. Porn also gives us the ability to indulge in any or every sexual fantasy with our dream partner du jour. The blessed sex life God intends for us to have and the satisfaction with our wives gets sold for a fantasy. We have enough fantasy outlets bombarding and entertaining us in our fast-paced culture that we can easily drown out the fact that our lives are supposed to have purpose and meaning.

Do you know how you spell destiny? T-I-M-E. What you spend your time on will shape the course of your future. I always said to God, "Lord help me get free from pornography and then help me set other men free also." This calling required action in order for it to go from thought to reality. *"A dream comes by much activity, but a fool's voice is known by many words"* (Ecc. 5:3). It isn't enough to dream big. You can die with a head full of big dreams and no fruit unless you take the time to act on your dreams. You can't wait until tomorrow to begin to do what is in your heart today. The lessons you read in this book represent **hundreds** of hours of prayer and travail. The actual writing of the book you are reading, adds countless hours on top of that.

Think of all the time you have spent looking at pornography over the years. How could your life be different if that time had been spent pursuing something beyond passing fancy? Time dictates how high and how far you go in life and in your call. We all have the same 24 hour timeframe to do our work, take care of our families and pursue God and His plan for our life. Once a day passes, you can no more redeem its time than Esau could redeem his birthright by crying about his loss. It is gone.

We have to shake ourselves of the mindset that living in sin doesn't cost us anything. We need to start to dream with God, set the vision for our lives before us and learn that there are things to come that are worth fighting for. How much more of your life are you willing to give away to things that only cause heartache in the end?

I hate to think of the number of hours I have spent doing awful things online; taking my precious time and life that God gave me and squandering it on things that won't last. How much further would I have taken my dreams if I had put those hours into them? How much deeper would I know the Lord if I had sown that time with Him? How much clearer could my vision be than it is now? It isn't enough to dream big. Addictions will keep you living small and keep you from ever achieving the things that bring true satisfaction and success.

"Do you not know that those who run in a race all run, but only one receives the prize? Run in such a way that you may obtain it. And everyone who competes for the prize is temperate in all things. Now they do it to obtain a perishable crown, but we for an imperishable crown. Therefore I run thus: not with uncertainty. Thus I fight: not as one who beats the air. But I discipline my body and bring it into subjection, lest, when I have preached to others, I myself should become disqualified" (1 Cor 9:24-27).

SET YOUR VISION BEFORE YOU

For years I knew I wanted to be free from porn, but I don't think I really knew why other than "because God said so." Because of this shortsightedness, when I was being tempted, I didn't have anything worth fighting for or to fight with. Knowing what you're fighting for is absolutely imperative. Throughout history, some of the most stunning military victories were not won by people who had the most equipment or advantage, but by those who had the most to fight for.

If we are to really win our battles, we must know what we are fighting for. We need to live with vision and purpose and allow that to be the prize we set before us. What will your prize of victory be? Even Christ had to live with this mindset. Hebrews tells us to look at Jesus, *"the author and finisher of our faith, who for the joy that was set before Him endured the cross, despising the shame, and has sat down at the right hand of the throne of God."* The cross was His greatest trial. Even Jesus needed to have a vision and set it before Him. The promise of salvation - knowing that you could have eternal life with Him and the Father motivated Him to make it through the pain of His trial and emerge victorious. We also have great promises that will take us through the pain to the other side of this struggle. The Christian walk doesn't end when we get saved. In fact, salvation is just the beginning in this life and the next.

The Bible tells us that there is a high and "upward call" for each of us in Christ. We don't get saved and then sit around waiting to get into heaven. There is a destiny for us; gifts that must be searched out and developed. There are talents for which God will require an accounting to see what we did with the treasure He deposited in us. There are increasingly deep realms of fellowship with God and deeper ways to hear His voice. All of these things are dependent upon how we respond to His Spirit.

Most Christians, however, live like they got in the door and they're just waiting to get to heaven to cash in. They either don't have a greater vision for their life and call; or have settled with unbelief, mediocrity and complacency - thinking that the Christian life we read about it is out of reach for them. But we MUST live with vision. Vision and a high call is one of the much needed fundamental truths essential to overcoming sin and complacency. If you don't have a bigger vision for your life... get one! It won't take much time with God and His Word before you start to think God-sized dreams.

What will it look like when you've "arrived"? What are the things you hope for in God? In your marriage? In your finances? Proverbs 29:18 says, *"Where there is no vision (revelation about the future), the people cast off restraint (and perish)."* If you don't have a reason to fight, you won't. It really is just about that simple. Habakkuk 2:2,3 teaches the same truth: *"Write the vision And make it plain on tablets, That he may run who reads it."* When the vision is plain, you will have something to run after, fight for, live for and protect.

The book of Lamentations is unique. In it we hear God pour out His sorrow and heartache over the ruin of His people. They gave away their valuables and destiny for worthless things. The strength of the mighty men and princes was reduced to nothing. Read these phrases from Lamentations 1: *"the enemy has become their master... because of the multitude of transgressions... the princes flee without strength... in the days of affliction, she (Jerusalem/God's people) fantasizes about pleasant things... and did not consider her destiny, therefore her collapse was awesome... they have given their treasures for food* (like Esau).

These words paint a sad picture of God's people who have allowed sin to creep into their lives and forgot to live with destiny and purpose. They flee without strength – they've lost their fighting edge, because they're more concerned with their fantasies than with the reality that they have a destiny that must be fought for. God's people have always had to fight their way into their Promised Land and stay vigilant to posses it.

Vision gives pain a purpose. And the stakes are too high, my friend, to not live with vision and deliberate purpose. The devil wants us to think that our sins are small and insignificant; that they won't really hurt anything or amount to any real damage. I believed that for years.

HARNESS YOUR PASSIONS

God made you a sexual, passionate being. That fact doesn't have to detract from your life's vision and calling as it has in the past. Rather, it will serve your purpose when properly harnessed.

In interviews I've read of highly successful people, they almost universally consider themselves to be highly passionate, sexual individuals AND use their passions to fuel their drive. In short, they are in the driver's seat of their sex drives. They have harnessed that sexual energy and don't squander passion foolishly. The devil loves little more than to see a person with powerful passions exhaust their energy, time, thoughts and essence on something worthless.

Paul instructs us this way, "For the flesh lusts against the Spirit, and the Spirit against the flesh; and these are contrary to one another, so that you do not do the things that you wish (Ga. 5:17)." Either your fleshly passions will destroy your spiritual passions or the other way around. You only have so much physical and emotional energy to expend in any given day. You are in a war for how you use it.

When you realize that your sex drive doesn't make God blush, rather that He is proud of what He put in you, it makes you free to then do something productive with those energies. If you are a married man, yes, you can direct them into fantasy, love and passion for your wife. But you also have to realize that life isn't all about sex. There will be times when that simply isn't an option – and for good reason. It is very good for a man to learn the drive that properly harnessed sexual energy can give.

So whether married or single, the primary lesson is this: set your vision before you and use your energy as a motivator not a hindrance. When I'm sexually tempted, I'll often say two things. First, "Thank you, God, that everything is working like it is supposed to work." Secondly, and very importantly, "Thank you for this reminder that I am a passionate, powerful man. Stir up my real passions!" When I allow a sexual temptation to stir up my

REAL passions in life, I rob the devil, using the very thing he would have used to rob me. I love that.

Sexual temptation used to remind me a hundred times a day of how "unholy" I thought I was. Not it serves to remind me of how called I am. What a blessing this sexuality can be!

HIGH STAKES GAMBLING

Life without greater vision and purpose gambles away important blessings that are available to us now in this life.

We are gambling our relationship with God:

The reality is that each sin is more significant than we know. You lie to yourself if you think that each sin doesn't harden your heart little by little, grieve and quench the Holy Spirit in your life, and ruin your fellowship with God.

God tells us to abide in Him and show our love for Him by obeying His commands. This familiar passage in John tells us plainly that His intent isn't to make us mindless obedient servants, but to help us understand that we break fellowship with Him if we don't obey His commands. Sin separates us from God, and the more we walk in it, the less we are ready to hear and respond to the subtle leadership of the Spirit. We bounce from one fix to the next and wonder why we can't discern the voice of God or hear what He's telling us in our lives.

We are gambling away our marriage intimacy:

Another high stake gamble we make is with our spouses. You are deceived if you think that your marriage and sex life isn't affected by this sin. Lust destroys healthy marriages. It breeds dissatisfaction with your wife's beauty and trains your mind, soul and flesh to think that lust is the same thing as desire. Many men wrongly believe that their wives don't "do it for them" because they've trained themselves by lust to think that its sensation is synonymous with arousal and desire. Nothing could be further from the truth! Lust is a devil. God can't give you the sensations for your wife that you feel when you are looking at porn (or when you were dating for that matter) because He doesn't have it to give! God can't give you lust for your wife.

The sexual union is designed by God to be much deeper than lust. We must learn to make love in marriage, not revel in lust. Love is uniquely designed by God to make men feel like men and women feel like women. Lust does neither of these – in fact it tears down healthy sexuality. Love builds up. Lust destroys. One creates union, the other is selfish robbery.

Love should make a woman feel like the most gorgeous, desirable thing in the world – the apple of your eye. And when a woman loves her man, he should be built up and affirmed in his masculinity and manly power. Lust seems like this at first, but actually cheapens the woman and leaves a man feeling like less of a man in the long run. When you learn to really make love to your wife, and she to you, it is amazing, pleasurable and fills up a man's need for physical love in a way that no lust ever can.

We are gambling our finances and blessing:

When we play with lust, we gamble with our finances for a number of reasons. In many places, the Bible speaks of curses associated with immorality, harlotry and adultery. They are almost too numerous to speak of. They include curses of poverty, diseases, broken fellowship with God and more.

Aside from these spiritual injunctions which inhibit blessing, pornography steals our precious time. If your time and energy is spent meditating on these things, how will you find time to learn new things and improve what you do know? Pornography is a practical and spiritual problem.

You have too much at stake to continue to walk in your sin. By expanding our vision, looking past immediate desires to see more important virtues to be attained, we become sober and realize all the things that are worth fighting for. So how do we begin to set the vision before us and live lives of purpose?

THE BELT OF TRUTH

Let's boil down the concept of "vision" to a more foundational element: truth. Vision is nothing more than knowing what you want and why you want it. These are the "reasons" we should fight. These are the truths we are fighting for.

If the devil can steal your truth, he can beat you without a fight. And that's the truth. There are lots of "good reasons" to stop looking at pornography. But the funny thing about them is that they are often the last thing on our minds when we are being tempted. We tend to know what we *should* do, but the lie of the devil has more weight in the dark moments of temptation than the reality of God's promises about our lives and calling. So for lack of vision - a lack of clear truth - we cast off restraint and exchange the truth of God's blessing for the consequences of our sins.

We can't win this battle for our soul if we don't have a strong foundation of truth - for why we want to win and get free. "Because the Bible says so" will only take you so far. You must "take ownership" of your truths. Paul calls this "putting on the Belt of Truth..."

Ephesians 6 talks about the armor of God. *"Put on the whole armor of God, that you may be able to stand against the wiles (attacks) of the devil (v. 11)."* The first piece of armor we are told to apply is the belt of truth. The belt, when speaking of armor, is more like a large belt that you'd use for weight lifting. It was both to support the back as you wear additional large, heavy armor around and it provided a final layer of protection against an attack that found its way through the outer armor to the organs of the midsection.

One step God taught me to take toward winning my battles was to "write the vision" - write all the "truths" I could think of for why I wanted to be free. Before I did this I knew all the 'truth' of the Bible, but it wasn't ingrained in me - so it was easy for the devil to steal it away at the time of temptation.

But something happened when I began to wrestle with the truth and rehearse it: it was there as a wall between me and my temptation. The temptations would still come and come hard. But then I'd be confronted by my wall of truth and I'd wrestle for a while. Sometimes the wrestling match would go on for hours and even days. And it seemed instead of simply being gripped by temptation and lust, I was now caught in the middle of a battle royal between truth and lies.

If you also will take the time to write your vision (the truths that you believe are worth fighting for), and rehearse these truths so that they are fully equipped in your mind, you will have a powerful new defense that will help you overcome many battles.

~Mighty Man Training & Application~

Do this now. Take time to write your list of truths. Ask God for help doing this. Here are a few of mine to get you started.

1. If I don't overcome the temptation this time and every time, I'll never be free. "I'll win next time" is a lie.
2. As long as I allow myself the option to sin, I'll always be a slave of sin. I must close the door permanently and pray that I come to the place where I truly resolve to never go back again.
3. Lust and pornography aren't harmless. Just the opposite.
4. Lusting after other women will always affect my sex life and satisfaction with my wife.
5. Lust and pornography is adultery of the heart. And that makes me an adulterer.
6. I won't feel better after looking at porn, I'll feel worse about myself and that will perpetuate the cycle.
7. I can't have the fellowship I desire with God as long as I keep walking in sin. Sin breaks fellowship and grieves the   Holy Spirit.
8. I have a future, hope and calling in God – a Holy purpose for my life. And the Bible makes it clear that we must walk worthy of that calling or it can be lost. I am not willing that this sin steal my birthright, calling and blessing in this life.
9. Right is right. Wrong is wrong. Even if there were no benefits or consequences to walking in purity, in my innermost man I want to be a good, godly man. I want to do what is right simply for the sake of right and wrong.
10. God is worthy of my obedience. He loved me enough to die for me and for this sin. He redeemed me and the thought of trampling on that love breaks my heart and fills me with remorse for my sins. I want to honor Him with my body because He broke His for me.
11. These girls (and guys) are people… God's children. He loves them desperately and wants their freedom too. When I lust after them, I am thinking like a devil and agreeing with the devil and putting on demonic mindsets that will corrupt and pervert the way I see all of God's children eventually. Not just the ones on the screen.
12. The devil hates me and wants to destroy me.

13. There is a real spiritual war going on around me. It is easy to think that this act of sin isn't significant; but there are literal devils that despise me waiting to feed off me and destroy the works of God in my life.

14. Every act of disobedience steals an act of obedience. How many people have suffered that I don't know about because I have walked in disobedience over and over. How many thousands of hours for the Kingdom have I squandered thinking about only my fleshly gratification. If you added them all
up, what great good is now missing in my life and in my fruit?

15. I can't pretend that these actions won't escalate. Every fall will desensitize me and create greater perversions.

16. There is nothing new that I haven't seen 100 times before. I'm not ever going to "miss" anything by doing what is right.

17. Each fall opens doors for my soul to be joined to more and more of these scenes and thoughts. I can still remember my first Playboys... what has that exposure done to my soul over time as thousands of women have become objects of lust and seared into my mind?

18. There are most likely spiritual consequences that I don't even know and can't even imagine associated with this sin. I am not willing to take that risk and dabble in things too great for me to understand.

19. I am righteous. Christ made me that way. I'm not going to tarnish what he has made shine. I'm not going to dirty what has been made pure.

20. I love my wife. She deserves my fidelity.

21. The Bible speaks of sins passing down through the generations. I must win so my children can be free.

22. I have promises from God. They will be fulfilled. But some promises are dependent upon obedience.

I'm sure there are more truths for each one of you. Write and rehearse your truths until they become a part of you.

CHAPTER 11

The Stronghold of Sensuality

How is a mighty man made? I can share with you the secret of the mighty man. Try this: stretch your arm out in front of you as far as it will go. Do that now. Now that it is stretched out, stretch it just a little bit farther. Did you discover that when you really tried, you still had just a little bit of stretch left in you?

Coaches tell their players to give it 110%. I think this is what they mean. When a runner is running their fastest, if they have to, they can dig down deep and find a little bit more. When you are lifting weights, there is always that little extra push. We can do more than we think, it just costs us. When an athlete gets used to giving it 110%, they find that they can hit "the zone" more easily. And after a while operating at the zone, they find that they can stretch themselves even farther.

I think this is what Paul was thinking about when he wrote, *"We are hard pressed on every side, yet not crushed; we are perplexed, but not in despair"* (2 Cor. 4:8). When the chips are down and we feel like giving up, deep within us, the Spirit of God is waiting until we are at the end of our strength - then God's strength gives us what we lack. I'll be honest, even though God says we won't be tempted beyond what we can bear, there will be times when you will most likely be pushed to the end of yourself as I was. At those times we will need to use the mighty man principle and dig deep for that last push. This mindset will serve you well through the trials to come. But watch out, there is another mindset that will oppose this.

The notion of pushing – of fighting for something – it seems like…
WORK. You see, objects and people tend to follow the path of least
resistance. Water runs downhill not uphill. Wheels roll over smooth ground
better than rough terrain. Electricity passes through more conductive materials
before it will arc to other avenues. The list goes on and on… and you're on the
list.

It is easier to watch TV than it is to pray. It is easier to play a video
game than watch a sermon on TV or read your Bible. It is easier to do nothing
than it is to volunteer at church or with a ministry. It is easier to snack than to
fast. It is easier to sleep in than to get up in time to enjoy quality time with
God. Easier to gratify the lust of the flesh than to struggle and overcome. You
get my point.

THE GOD OF AMERICA

What do you want to eat right now? You can go get it. You don't
even have to wait for it. I heard a funny statistic. Orange sales have been
declining over the last five years. When the panel results came in from focus
testing as to why people aren't buying oranges, do you know what the number
one reason someone will pick another fruit or snack over an orange? Too much
work. That's right. People aren't buying oranges because it takes too much
effort to peel them. You can pop open a bag of chips and a soda in less than a
second… but an orange takes upwards of half a minute before you can eat it.
Unhealthy choices are easy. Healthier choices take a little more effort.

We have a big problem in our country. We have too much. Billy
Graham made a speech in one of his crusades, "If I wanted to destroy a godly
nation, I'd give it too much of everything." Now, having things is wonderful.
I've got a lot of stuff. It isn't necessarily a problem to have stuff… the problem
is if stuff has us. We have stuff for every whim and craving you can imagine.
And the more quick solutions we have, the harder it gets to make a choice that
doesn't follow the path of least resistance. When we are bored, we have 20
different types of instant amusement. When we are sick, we have every type of
pill and quick fix. When our emotions aren't what we want, we can chemically
induce a blissful emotional state with all kinds of prescription and non-
prescription solutions. When we are hungry, we have every imaginable food at
our disposal. When we want a pick-up, we have church. When we are horny,

we've got porn. We have a quick fix to every need and emotion you could possibly have. We truly want for nothing – so the thought of placing ourselves into a situation that creates lack or suffering is almost unthinkable.

Lack is not a word our generation understands. However, have you ever heard an older person use phrases like, "Do without... it will build character." That is what people were taught a few generations ago. They didn't have instant everything. They often had to do without what they wanted. That's just the way it was. They didn't see not having something as a bad thing. It is only within the last few generations that we have lost the ability to conceive of life without every convenience.

As Christians and as a nation we are prone to be fat, lazy, complacent, and comfortable. We are the definition of the Laodicean Church in Revelation: we think we've got faith... just as long as our faith doesn't cost us anything or make us uncomfortable. It is a way of life in our country if not THE way of life. It is America's "Do what feels good mantra." Its name is sensuality. And it is the god of our country.

As we prepare to walk out of our sins and sexual addictions, this mentality must be broken.

UNDERSTANDING SENSUALITY

Most people associate the term sensuality with other terms like lust and sexuality. Sensuality, however, is not the same thing as lust. At its root, sensuality simply has to do with the senses: what you can see, touch, taste, smell, etc. Sensuality, then, is a lifestyle that glorifies gratifying the senses. Lust is just one aspect of sensuality that has to do with the libido. When our flesh is crying out for attention and gratification, a sensual person will give in to that craving instead of doing without.

I believe that for most Americans, there is no higher ideal than getting to the place of total comfort where we don't lack for anything and where we don't need God... except to make us feel better about ourselves and give us a quick-fix solution for eternal security. We treat God like everything else... a convenience. Obedience is a word that has a pretty negative connotation in our society because our real god is sensuality. Obedience means that we can't do whatever we want whenever we want. What a drag.

While we are in church, it is easy to think, "I'll never look at porn again." Why? We feel like doing what is right at church. That is what our emotions (and the Spirit) are feeling at the moment. But that only lasts until the feelings wear off. And then we don't think twice about acting however we want to act because our actions are following the feeling of the moment. So our god isn't God, but our feelings. We don't do what God tells us to do... we do what our senses tell us. Philippians 3:18-19 speaks about this phenomenon: *For many walk, of whom I have told you often, and now tell you even weeping, that they are the enemies of the cross of Christ: whose end is destruction, whose god is their belly, and whose glory is in their shame-who set their mind on earthly things.*

You can't flip on the television without finding some preacher giving a feel-good version of the gospel. Pastors are also conditioned by their congregations to tell them the "Christian highlight reel." Feel-good messages build big churches. And so many of us get the travel brochure version of Christianity that tells us all the good things we can experience in life while we wait to arrive at our luxurious final destination. We aren't being fed a healthy dose of reality in our culture. Not even in church. It seems every aspect of society is giving us a feel-good message... and then we wonder why it is so difficult to actually stand up and fight when we are tempted by lust and to make other choices that take a little willpower. And so, like Israel, we make bad choice after bad choice and find ourselves in worse and worse bondage.

When you think about sin on a cosmic scale, it is really the ultimate stupidity. The uncreated author of the universe has told us not to do something, but in our pride, we do it and think, "He won't notice. He won't care. He won't be hurt. He won't be offended. He will forgive us. He won't punish us for it." Why do we think this way? Could it be because we really are giving lip service to God but serving a more convenient god: our sensual desires?

Contemplate something for a minute. Have you ever been pulled over for speeding or a traffic violation? What is the first thing we usually do? We "repent" and pray that God would get us out of trouble. Why did we not have the conviction before we got caught? Have you ever been caught in a lie? Lying came so easily and we didn't think twice about the "little white lies" before we got caught. People lie every day right? "I'm working on that right now... I'm five minutes away... I didn't say that." Most people tell white lies all day long. A little lie is still a lie. Do we steal? Do we download songs and videos that have a copyright? For the most part, Christians lie, cheat, steal, break the law and sin every single day and we don't feel bad about it until we get caught. Then it seems convenient to repent and hope that God bails us out. Sensual, carnal Christians. We just want a big genie in the sky to help us and give us what we want.

This has to change if we want out of our lust addiction. Lust is just one aspect of a much larger stronghold of sensuality and carnal living. You can work and work to get lust out of your life, but if you tolerate other forms of sensuality, you still have lust's big brother in the back alley ready to open the door for a "do it if it feels good" relapse.

You will go through some horrible withdrawal as you come out of this. And if we walk according to the god of this nation and are unwilling to suffer a little, you just won't have what it takes to get through what's ahead.

SUFFERING

Suffering. The word just sounds so wrong. When we are suffering, what is the first thing we do? We try to make the suffering stop. The Bible, however, teaches a different perspective: *"In this you greatly rejoice, though now for a little while, if need be, you have been grieved by various temptations, that the genuineness of your faith, being much more precious than gold that perishes, though it is tested by fire, may be found to praise, honor, and glory at the revelation of Jesus Christ (1 Pet. 1:7)"* James also tells us to consider temptations pure joy because of their work in us (Jas. 1:2).

God doesn't view suffering in the same negative light that we do. In fact, when sin entered the world, God promised us that we would have to work and toil. Actually, He even says He cursed the ground "for our sakes." Work, toil and a little suffering are the tools that help us grow. If you want to grow, you have to accept a little suffering.

"In the day of prosperity be joyful, But in the day of adversity consider: Surely God has appointed the one as well as the other" (Ecc. 7:14). Suffering isn't ungodly or outside God's will. God appoints suffering for us to go through because He loves us and will use it to bring us closer to Him.

God suffers more than any being in the universe. Does that statement shock you? We don't think of God as suffering... after all, He's God. Shouldn't He be living the American dream and get to do what feels good all the time? God made us to be His friends and have fellowship with Him. He wanted a people that He could love and walk with in the cool of the day. But when we made the choice to rebel against Him, we broke His heart. We chose to do what felt good over fellowship with Him. He still so loves us that He was willing to sacrifice divine fellowship with His Son and allow Jesus, the Suffering Servant, as Isaiah called Him, to come to earth, suffer and die for our sins. Jesus' sacrifice enabled us to have fellowship with God again, but we still choose our sins over fellowship. The Bible says, love suffers long. It believes all things. It bears all things. It endures all things. If you want to know the heart of God, find a concordance and look up "longsuffering." Over and over God tells us that He is longsuffering – waiting for us to run to Him. Waiting for us to choose Him over things that won't last.

His heart breaks every time we shut Him out. But He thinks we're worth the wait. So He'll suffer a little longer. We must take on the character of Christ and be willing to suffer - to deprive our souls of their cravings so we can walk in victory. We must be willing to choose God over our comfort just as He chose us over His.

~Mighty Man Training & Application~

1. Break your mind free of the mentality that suffering is bad. Equip your mind and emotions with the character of a mighty man - a willingness to stretch yourself a little farther to see growth take place. *Father, you chose to suffer for my salvation and fellowship. I accept that fellowship and freedom has a price tag. I'm willing to suffer a little just as You suffered for me.*

2. Examine yourself to see if sensuality is prevalent in your life.
    - Do you have a hard time making right eating decisions?
    - Do you have a hard time disciplining yourself for quiet time with God?
    - Are other important time commitments easy to sacrifice for the sake of easy distractions?
    - Is much of your free time spent with TV or entertainment?
    - Do you find it easy to commit "little sins"?

Father, forgive me for letting my decisions be made by what feels good. I confess that I have lived in a carnal and sensual way. I renounce a sensual lifestyle and ask you to help me have balance in my life. I want to make good choices in every area of my life. Please help me grow in strength and character.

CHAPTER 12

Giving or Getting Strength

LEARN HOW TO TURN WEAKNESS INTO STRENGTH

He who rules his spirit {is stronger} than he who conquers {an entire} city… Whoever has no rule over his spirit is like a city broken down without walls…
- Proverbs 16:32, 25:28

I'd often read the passage above and think, "If only I could be one of those strong men who can rule over his own soul. But I felt more like the man in the second verse. Defenseless. Helpless. Weak. I knew I was weak in this area. It didn't take much more than a passing thought to make me fall into temptation and lust. The slightest provocative woman would cause me to start to go off the deep end.

I can't tell you how many times I would cry out to God and ask Him to take this temptation from me. "Change my heart!" "Deliver me from this temptation!" "At least give me strength to overcome the temptation." But those prayers year after year were never answered and it left me feeling somewhat abandoned by God. I knew He wanted me free, but I couldn't understand why He would never deliver me so that I could be. "I know God wants me to be free… why doesn't He do something?"

I don't know why it is this way, but some things you sail over easily in God, other things you go through with travail. The things that you go through make you stronger. God could have made it so that lust is easy to combat. But He didn't. I wish He had, but I'm not God, so there's nothing to it but to learn

His ways and discover the hidden blessing in this fact. This isn't one of those things that you sail over, so you may as well embrace that this battle is a tool in your life to make you stronger.

This is a hard truth to stomach however. For most of my life, I just wished that the struggle would go away without a fight. I always thought that the temptation wasn't supposed to be there or that there was something wrong with me because I was so easily tempted. I wanted the temptation to get lesser rather than have my soul get stronger. I had it backward. God's plan was to make me a mighty man after the One True Mighty Man, Jesus. "… he who rules his spirit is mightier than he who takes a city" (Pr. 16:32). It is this process of learning to conquer the desires of the soul through the victory of the Mighty Man that builds strength and character to make you a mighty man in Him.

YOUR STRUGGLE MAKES YOU STRONG! You aren't born strong. No untrained person competes in the Olympics. That strength is cultivated over time, begins with a single decision to train, is tested through endurance and is rewarded with victory. Likewise, no person automatically has all the character that will be required to walk in the fullness of their calling without the strengthening that comes through resisting temptation. Neither should we wait until we feel like a "spiritual Olympian" to start training. Every gain of strength starts with the next single decision.

If God removed the temptation from you so that you don't have to grow, He'd be taking away the very tool that is needed to train you to lean on Him, make you a mighty man and qualify you for your calling. If God were to just take away the sin and the struggle, sure, you wouldn't keep messing up… but you'd be a weakling who doesn't have the character to stand up to the next temptation that would come along.

Most of us like the idea of being a mighty man of God. But if we are honest, we hate the process that brings forth might. When I got saved I told God that I loved Him and would do anything for Him. How I've wanted to take back that last part in the intense trials of life at times! But afterward, I'm glad for the testimony and character that is borne of travail.

Resisting temptation, depriving your soul's gratification, and learning that a little suffering isn't a bad thing are all lessons that build endurance, inner strength, character, resolve, confidence, emotional stability, and cause us to fall on Christ as we come to the end of our own strength time and again. By coming face-to-face with our weakness, we learn to tap into God's strength and our "inner man" begins to be conformed to the character of Christ and imbued with divine strength.

This process has other profound benefits. If God were to suddenly give you incredible resolve and willpower, you would never come to realize your utter dependence on Him. Furthermore, as you fall to temptations and then call on God to say, "What went wrong?" you come to realize the areas of your heart that need that sin as a crutch. You see, your sin is linked to wounds in the heart that we'll address later. Our weaknesses give illumination to the areas that God wants to heal.

Trust me, you don't want to just have this sin whisked away and out of your life. This is an area that you want to overcome and look back at the man it makes you. The temptation is the proving ground for your call. The stronger the temptation, the stronger the man you'll be at the end and the more God will be able to entrust to you. A man struggling with temptation and sin, is a king in the making. The devil's plan for your sin is to steal that call... God's plan is to use it to ensure the call on your life.

The Bible warns us, *"Do not give your strength to women, Nor your ways to that which destroys kings"* (Pr. 31:3). Solomon speaks of this in Proverbs 30:19, saying there are forces in the universe that make him marvel: the way a man gets when he's with his virgin was one of those marvels. Women can affect us and cause us to lose sight of what it really means to be a man. Mighty men and kings can be destroyed by this area of weakness. We see it over and over again in the Bible. Samson was one of the mightiest men of all, but was reduced to a lying, helpless coward around Delilah (Jud. 14). Solomon, the wisest man and a great king was warned by God about women but he nevertheless allowed his heart to chase after women and it was his greatest downfall.

A NEW REASON TO FIGHT

As I came to understand the dynamic that was happening in the spirit realm, I suddenly had new wind in my sails - a new determination to use the devils' own attacks to make me stronger. The thought that each battle was actually a tool in God's hands to make me a powerful man meant that there was purpose for the pain.

The devil was using one of the oldest tricks in the book to steal my strength and calling. He'd dangle some alluring thing in front of me, sit back and let her do her thing. It would distract me from how weak I felt, and for a moment, I "felt like a man." But afterward, I'd only feel weaker than ever, miserable and worthless. God however, had a plan to take what the enemy had used to defeat me time and again and, through the struggle, shape me into a man who could, in turn, defeat the enemy. God is not without a sense of irony. If this sin isn't one of those things in life that you simply get delivered out of easily, use these battles to shape you into the man you are called to be. Thus we must stir ourselves up and declare to the devil, "If you think this is making me weak, think again! The very attacks you have been using will become your own undoing when God is finished with me!"

My entire attitude changed. Instead of fearing temptation and failure, I'd say, "God in your grace let me not be tempted beyond what I can bear, but may I endure enough to grow in following Your Spirit." When the temptations would come, I didn't shrink back and wonder why God didn't deliver me. I came to understand the dynamic that was going on. The devil was trying to steal my strength. But I was now determined to "steal his." Every temptation was an opportunity to realize my own weakness in the flesh but to allow the strength of God to fill my spirit and turn me into the mighty man I had hoped to be. I believe that the greater the temptation a man is allowed to endure, the higher the call on his life and the more strength of character he will need to walk in that call.

In all your strengthening, do not get puffed up in pride, thinking that it is your own strength that has allowed you to overcome. Even the most mighty man can get in over their head (it is still all about grace, remember?). Dwell in grace that God should not give you more than you can bear. But you will never learn how to defeat the devil if you never have to face one. So may God also not allow shelter you to the point that you never be strengthened and shaped into the mighty man who can destroy the works of the devil and be led by the Spirit and not by his loins.

David passed a great kingdom to his son Solomon. But Solomon let women turn his heart from God and there was never another king like David. The glory went out from the kingdom. How would history have been different if Solomon had heeded the warning and kept his heart pure? Could he have passed an even greater kingdom to his sons? How will we write our history and what will we pass to our sons?

Christianity needs the mighty men again - men who are not afraid to look life and struggle in the face because their hearts have been made strong in Christ through their struggles. The simple prayer, so easily regarded as mere words, "Thy Kingdom come" requires that we look an earthly obstacle dead in the eye and say, "Kingdom come HERE, NOW!" with steely resolve that doesn't faint or quit until heaven invades earth. Our families need mighty men. The world needs mighty men. The size of your struggle is directly in proportion to the size threat the devil fears you will be.

~Mighty Man Training & Application~

1. Do something crazy: get grateful that God hasn't taken away your struggle. For the first time in your life, look at your temptations as an opportunity. Think of it. The next time you struggle, God's Spirit can make you stronger. Won't that be a nice change?

2. Think about how tempered steel is formed. It goes into the fire and is then pounded repeatedly. If you were the steel, the tempering process wouldn't be fun, but at the end, tempered steel is incredibly strong.

3. Take a deep breath. Accept the fact that you are like steel to be tempered. You will go through the fire, but at the end you will know the strength for which your heart yearns.

CHAPTER 13

Change Your Mind

TEAR DOWN STRONGHOLDS THAT WAR AGAINST YOUR THOUGHT LIFE

As a man thinketh in his heart so is he.
-Proverbs 23:7

     If you plan to change the way you act, you have to change the way you think *and* what you think about. You can't stop sinning by trying to stop sinning. Your thoughts and identity must change. In most cases, the battle of lust and pornography is lost long before you ever touch your computer (or yourself). Addicts like to say, "I can't control myself." However, if your pastor were to walk into the room, I'm sure you'd miraculously have plenty of self-control to turn off the computer. So we realize that the battle isn't really against fleshly cravings too strong to control. Rather, the battle is fought in the mind. Flesh will be flesh - it will always have carnal cravings and desires. But how we process those desires and what we decide to meditate upon will dictate how we *act* despite any temptations in your body or in the spiritual realms.

     You are fighting a war you can't see! The Bible tells us that we do not wrestle against flesh and blood, but against various powers and spiritual forces in heavenly places (Eph 6:12). Again we find more insight about this concept in 2 Corinthians 10: *For though we walk in the flesh, we do not war according to the flesh. For the weapons of our warfare are not carnal but mighty in God for pulling down strongholds, casting down arguments and every high thing that exalts itself against the knowledge of God, bringing every thought into captivity to the obedience of Christ"* (vv. 3,4,5).

It would actually be nice if we did war against flesh and blood or things we could see - at least we'd be aware of the fight. Can you imagine if you had to actually wrestle a physical devil in order to be tempted? We wouldn't be so quick to think that sin is harmless then. But the reality of our battle is that we are constantly under attacks from the enemy, the media, our past experiences and memories and much more that send silent messages to our mind. On the other hand, there is the voice of the Spirit of God quietly and steadfastly calling you to intimacy and rest. You have the choice what to listen to. You have the power to shape your destiny according to what you allow your mind to dwell upon.

THE CARNAL MIND VS. THE SPIRITUAL MIND

Do you know that you can have the entire Spirit of God living within your Spirit, and still be totally carnal in your mind and thoughts? Paul prayed for the churches over and over that they would GROW into maturity. Maturity doesn't mean that you have more of God's Spirit in you – you've already got all of His Spirit living in your spirit that you will ever have. But you must yield to the Spirit so that you can be filled "with all the fullness of God" as he prays in Ephesians 3. Again in Galatians 4:19, he prays that "Christ is formed in you." How can Christ be formed in you if you already have the Spirit in you? He is talking about your soul, your heart, your inner man. These terms are fancy ways to say your mind, your thought life and your emotions. This is the part of you that you MUST learn to change if you are to have victory.

Paul again says it this way, *"For those who live according to the flesh set their minds on the things of the flesh, but those who live according to the Spirit, the things of the Spirit. Because the carnal mind is enmity against God; for it is not subject to the law of God, nor indeed can be"*... *"Therefore, brethren, we are debtors-not to the flesh, to live according to the flesh. For if you live according to the flesh you will die; but if by the Spirit you put to death the deeds of the body, you will live. For as many as are led by the Spirit of God, these are sons of God"* (Rom 8:6-7,13-15).

You will become like and act out the things that you think about – the agreements that you make in your mind – the identity from which

you choose to live. The Bible over and over warns about corrupting your mind and searing your conscience. We find one such passage in Titus: *To the pure all things are pure, but to those who are defiled and unbelieving nothing is pure; but even their mind and conscience are defiled. They profess to know God, but in works they deny Him, being abominable, disobedient, and disqualified for every good work"* (vv. 1:15,16). As we defile our mind and conscience, we grow weaker and weaker to temptations and open ourselves up to other temptations that would not have been there if we were pure in heart. Therefore we must guard our hearts so that we do not continue to erode our conscience.

God has given us free will. He will never force you to think good things. He calls us to be disciples, a term that means "one who disciplines themselves." It is not God's job to sovereignly change our minds. He has already done His full work to help our thoughts by placing His Spirit in us if we have been born again. Through His Spirit, He does change our desires and thoughts, but we must yield to His work. We must spend the time in His word and in His presence that brings about this change. The presence of the Spirit in us gives us OPTIONS of what to think about as well as the desire to do what is right and conviction when we do what is wrong.

So when a thought or memory surfaces that is lustful or wrong, we must learn to quickly change our mind, stop thinking that thought and start thinking about something else. **The more time you give a thought, the more power it gains.** I've gone through days where I've had to put down tempting thoughts every 30 seconds or more. Over and over the temptations would come, but I've come out of those days victorious. The real difficulty arises when you give even a little space to keep thinking a wrong thought. "Space" is agreement. When we think these thoughts, we are agreeing that they are good and rejecting the truth of God. This only fuels the enemy and gives him more strength and tenacity.

We must learn ways to start to take these thoughts captive and change our mind if we are to walk in freedom.

AGREE WITH THE SPIRITUAL MIND

From the moment God places His Spirit in you, you have a Spiritual mind. The Bible tells us time and again that this new mind will be at war and will never agree with your carnal mind. It is a wonderful thing to have the

Spirit in you even though you now feel the conflict warring in you to sin or to be holy. Since you have the ability to agree with carnal thoughts or Spiritual thoughts, what do these new godly thoughts look like?

We are tempted in the things we think about, who we think about and how we think about ourselves. Usually we know that a lustful thought isn't a godly thought. But it is easy to start thinking ungodly things about ourselves - or even to become unbelieving that God is working good things into our lives - no matter how undeserving we may feel. God is good to all His creation. And every thought that is godly will build up, cherish and empower ourselves or others.

Godly thoughts always agree with God's Word, speak the truth and fly in the face of the devil's lies and how they make you feel. I remember a pastor bragging about one of the young ladies in his church. She was a waitress at a restaurant in their town and worked with a young man who was homosexual. She knew enough to know that God does not make anyone gay or desire that for their lives. So she asked him one day, "Why do you act the way you do?" He responded that he was homosexual - however, she promptly told him, "No. You're not." This infuriated the young man, but she persisted to speak the truth of God's Word about him despite his angry protests. After about a month of this and many heated and angry conversations, he came to work one day and said, "You're right. I'm not gay." God's Word was able to change this man's perceptions about himself and overcome a mountain of lies and perversion!

This story illustrates a powerful point: the truth of the Spirit trumps the lies of the flesh. We must start to see ourselves and speak out over our lives the truth of how God sees us. For many of us reading this book, you have agreed with so many lies and perversions for so long that you may believe the lies over God's word. Reality check: if God's Spirit is in you, if you've given your life to Jesus Christ and asked Him to forgive and save you, if you've truly been born of the Spirit, you have a NEW nature and heart and you ARE NOT who you've been or how you've acted in the past.

Let me say that again. You are not who you've been or how you've acted or what carnal devils you've agreed with. You are not a pornography addict. You are not a pervert. You are not any of the things you fear you are becoming. You are a new creation in Christ Jesus. All things have passed away. All things are new (2 Cor. 5:17)! When a lustful or perverted thought enters your mind, that is not your thought any longer. Perversion is not your nature. It is a devil or at the very least your dead carnal flesh or a wound in your heart trying to resurrect some old habitual pleasures, bad habits and coping mechanisms. Count yourself dead to your old nature.

To change our mind, we must know God's thoughts and think God's thoughts. Agree with the truth that you find in God's Word about you. That means you must increase your exposure to God's Word.

GETTING FULL OF THE WORD

In order to know what thoughts we should be thinking, we have to get familiar with God's thoughts. If you want to overcome this area of sin and temptation, you have to start to feed the Spiritual mind. Get full of the Word! Go to church as much as you can. Read the Bible as much as you can. Pray as much as you can. Go to activities such as Bible studies or small groups as much as you can. Listen to sermons online, on TV or on the radio.

David said, *"How can a young man cleanse his way? By taking heed according to Your word… Your word I have hidden in my heart, That I might not sin against You!"* (Ps 119: 9,11). Something magical happens the more we are exposed to the Word, it begins to affect and change us. We get the very real sense of God speaking right through the pages or from the sermon we may be hearing. He speaks about what He's working OUT of us. He speaks about what He is working IN us. He speaks to us about WHO we really are. He speaks about our gifts. He speaks about His promises. He speaks about our calling. He speaks about our situations and circumstances. The Word of God is WONDERFUL! It gives life to us and a vision greater than ourselves.

Being full of the Word will cause you to discover the life of God in a fresh way. It will build greater desire and determination to overcome the sin of lust and pornography. Show me any Christian who IS and who STAYS "on fire" for God and I guarantee they are getting plenty of exposure to God's Word through various sources.

Many Christians think back to times when they were "on fire" and either wish they could get back to that or wonder why the fire dissipated. I've asked them what was happening in their lives at that time or any events that got them fired up and they will often relate a time when they were away at a Bible camp or crusade, or they were a new believer and going to this Bible study and this campus group and excited about the Word, etc. Almost without fail, when I've asked them how much time they spend in the Word now compared to those times, it is far less (or not at all). This is the problem. Most Christians spend less than five minutes a day praying and reading the Word... yet we can easily spend hours looking at pornography or even "innocent" worldly influences such as TV or video games. You will think like and think on the things that you fill your mind with. How can you grow your love for God if you are feeding your lusts more than nurturing the Spirit?

There are two truths that your soul needs to know. First, no matter how dry and dead spiritually you may feel, no matter how long it has been since you cultivated your relationship with God, the journey back is quick because your soul is designed to come alive in God's presence. The second thing you need to know is that even if your quiet times aren't always magical, they ARE bearing fruit. You may not feel it. You may not see it at first. But before you know it, you will be changed. Every time you spend time with God there is seed being planted, watered and nourished. When you plant a seed, you don't see what is happening below the surface, but sooner or later it grows and bears fruit. This is the way of the Kingdom.

The more you spend time with God, the more you'll love Him and the more you'll start to think the way He thinks. Time in the Word may seem like a chore at first, but it will start to affect the way you think and you will know what God has to say about who you really are on a much greater level. You will become more and more like whatever spirit you feed on (good or bad). So get full of the things that fuel your mind with thoughts of the Holy Spirit.

CUT BACK ON WORLDLY INFLUENCES

What goes in will come out. The more time you spend meditating on the things of this world, the more you'll think like the world. Think about what happens after you have watched a movie. The next few days, you are thinking about lines and scenes from that movie. The same thing is true with porn, music, TV or any other influence. After you have watched or listened to it, it still continues to influence you.

Begin to cut back on worldly influences and remove anything altogether that is sexual or that glorifies sex and carnal sexuality. As you get full of the Word of God and less full of the carnality of the world, your desires will change along with your thoughts. You will have more desire and thoughts about the things of God and less for the things of the world.

I can honestly say that at this point in my life, my every idle thought is about God and His ways. When I wake up in the morning, He is the first thought in my head. When I go to sleep, He is the last thought. Sure I have times at work or when something is dominating my thoughts that I'm not specifically thinking about God; but as soon as I have a free moment, He's right there again. When I'm tempted, I start thinking about God and the things that He's doing. That serves as my fuel and my passion instead of the passions of the flesh.

KNOW YOUR WEAKNESSES

This is a point I will touch on over and over. Learn the things that you simply can't expose yourself to without it affecting your thought life. Get rid of them. Also learn the times you are the most weak. For me, it was always in the morning. I would wake up with an erection and carnal thoughts would almost certainly follow. I had to simply settle the fact that I needed to get up (without touching myself) and start doing something else to get my mind off my physical arousal. Otherwise, it was all too easy to start fantasizing and then down the slippery slope I would go.

Another time that was difficult for me was late at night. Often I'd have a hard time going to bed. I felt like something was missing from my day. I've come to realize that feeling was a deep yearning to connect with God in a meaningful way. But often this desire for intimacy would drive me to seek comfort in the familiar stimulation of porn. You also must know when you are vulnerable and know what you have to do to change your mind at those times. Take the time needed to really identify your triggers and weak times. Then make a plan for how you can avoid them altogether or make a plan for exactly what you will do when triggered if it is unavoidable.

Know when you have to walk away from conversations or situations. Know what stirs up frustration that leads to carnal cravings. Put down thoughts right away. Don't entertain old fantasies. You may as well invite the devil in for a cup of tea. Don't watch things that stir up lust, etc. Get to know what you can and can't do safely. Know that whatever you have to "give up" will be more than worth it in the end.

KNOW WHAT TO MEDITATE ON

Paul instructs us in the epistle to the Philippians, *"Whatever things are true, whatever things are noble, whatever things are just, whatever things are pure, whatever things are lovely, whatever things are of good report, if there is any virtue and if there is anything praiseworthy-meditate on these things"* (v.4:8).

You can't turn FROM something without turning TO another. In a lot of ways, even reading this book can initially stir up temptation because thinking about NOT thinking about porn, in a roundabout way, is still thinking about pornography. If you sit and chant, "Don't think about porn. Don't think about porn." What are you thinking about? Porn. You can't stop looking at porn by trying to stop looking at porn. This isn't how the Kingdom works, but unfortunately is how most ministries want to teach people how to overcome.

The Bible teaches that you will unfortunately always have a carnal mind that is at war with the spiritual mind (Rom. 8:7). He won't even take away a lustful thought for you. Asking God to take away fleshly desires or take away bad thoughts is wrong thinking. God never takes. He is a giver. He will give you better thoughts if you learn to live by the Spirit and walk with Him.

As we fall more in love with God, living for self becomes more and more unnatural. We've been taught to think that we'll be "closer to God" when we stop sinning. This isn't how it works. Your relationship with God will be better when you work on bettering your relationship with God. He has already paid for the sin part of this equation. You don't have to double-pay.

This change does not come naturally at first. However, the more we "feed our spirit" the more natural it will become. Even if you are getting plenty of doses of the Word, cutting back on worldly influences and avoiding things that obviously tempt you, you will STILL have temptations. Being full of the Word isn't a magic pill - but it does give you options when your thoughts start to come under attack. Using the Word, you must now learn to change your mind.

When you are being tempted, you must "take that thought captive." I find at the times my thoughts want to wander, I literally have to say, "I will NOT think about that right now! I know exactly where that thought is going to lead." Instead, I start thinking about the things of God that excite me and agree with those truths. You see you have to go FROM thinking something TO thinking something else. If you can't think of anything that distracts you from that tempting thought, you need to simply DO something else that distracts you. Otherwise, the same old thought comes back to fill its empty space.

There is nothing the devil offers us that is worth thinking about anyway - he has nothing of any real value. He is a master at getting us to trade something truly valuable for something utterly worthless. He convinced Adam and Eve to trade the title deed of the world to him for a piece of fruit. He takes bondage, despair, self-hatred and ruin, polishes it up and places it in a box called "Porn and momentary pleasure" and somehow convinces you to trade your fellowship with God and your calling for that. How about if we trade those lies in for the blessings of God's Word!

I am convinced that if we really believed God's Word, we'd never even be remotely tempted to sin. We'd see reality the way Paul did, *"Yet indeed I also count all things loss for the excellence of the knowledge of Christ Jesus my Lord, for whom I have suffered the loss of all things, and count them as rubbish, that I may gain Christ"* (Php. 3:8). When we begin to really start to believe the Bible and that we can have the things it says we can have, the things we used to meditate on will become worthless to us as well. But until that happens, we will have more faith in the devil to meet our needs through porn than for God to meet them.

Again, your carnal mind will always be at war with the Spirit. You must settle, then, that carnal thoughts are not "opportunities." Temptation seems tempting because the devil promotes it as an opportunity for us. This is a lie! You know exactly where sin will lead you. When the lie arises, I find I must tell myself, even if I have to do it 100 times a day until it sinks in, "No! That is not an opportunity. That is not something I REALLY want. It will only breed perversion, discouragement and defeat. The devil ONLY comes to steal, kill and destroy. This 'opportunity' is nothing but death and destruction!"

Do you see why we need a mind change so badly? We can't go on as we have been. We can't listen to our flesh, to the world or to the devil any longer. Those roads all lead to death. Settle it now before the next time you are tempted because all the happy feelings you have now will be gone then. The devil will be dangling his new, bright, shiny temptation in front of you and you'll need to change your mind or you'll make a worthless trade. Every time you yield your mind to the devil, the "next time" will be harder. Don't let there be a next time. Take wicked thoughts captive instantly and start listening to the Spirit. *"I say then: Walk in the Spirit, and you shall not fulfill the lust of the flesh"* (Gal 5:16).

The more you listen to the Spirit, the more you will start to think like God and the more foreign these thoughts will become. You may have corrupted your heart and seared your conscience, but it doesn't have to stay that way! It won't be easy at first, just as it isn't easy to start a 500 pound ball rolling, but it will get easier and easier. There is real freedom for the person who overcomes.

To the pure, all things are pure. This means that things that used to set you off become less tempting. *"He whom the Son sets free is free indeed"* (Joh 8:36). There is coming a day when you will be so free, that the struggle will seem like a distant memory. You won't have to keep the internet under lock and key. You will have conquered your devil and learned to subdue your mind.

~Mighty Man Training & Application~

Don't think you can "fight" a temptation without changing your mind! You must recognize all ungodly thoughts as dangerous, corrupting and as something to quickly get far away from. When you are thinking ungodly thoughts about something, someone or about yourself, they will overtake you and have power over you until you "take them captive" and start to meditate on godly thoughts to combat their lies.

Question: What things have you done and lies do you believe about yourself that you need to stop agreeing with?
- Do you choose to see yourself as pure and forgiven? Or do you still see yourself as tarnished, unforgivable and hopeless?
- How would you feel about yourself and how would you relate to God if you really believed that you were PERFECTLY righteous? This is how we can relate to God in Christ!

Engage your mouth and speak out truths over your life:
- I am a new creation in Christ
- God loves me
- I am forgiven and lovable
- I am not sexually perverted (Break agreement with any particular perversions or fetishes you may have)
- I am not doomed to be a slave to this sin. I am free.

Rehearse the truth that temptations are not "opportunities" when they arise:
- Know where they will lead
- Remember how you will feel after
- Count the cost of a fall

What do you have to change in your life to get more of God's Word and less worldly influence? Can you give up some TV time and exchange it for some God time? Take a minute with this question. Make a decision to add a new or add to an existing godly influence to your life.

When are you vulnerable to sin? Plan ahead. Know how you will act the next time so that it is easier to "change your mind."

CHAPTER 14

Sobriety

IDENTIFYING TEMPTATIONS & FOLLOWING THE SPIRIT

The word "sobriety" usually makes us think about alcohol and alcoholics. Alcohol has an interesting effect according to the scriptures. It dissipates our sensitivity to the Spirit and therefore our ability to make godly choices. Peter warns us later about being sober... but he isn't speaking about alcohol or drugs, but about lust and carnality. You see, you can dissipate the Spirit on more than just wine... and our culture wants us drunk.

We live in a society that continuously "line shifts." We push the lines of morality and acceptability until everyone is comfortable... and then we push the lines a little further. This has been going on for years and it affects us far more than we can imagine.

In an over-stimulated culture, it seems the most effective way that entertainers and advertisers have found to get your attention is to shock you. Sex sells. Having been in the advertising industry for years, I encounter this reality more often than I could comment. The advertising, marketing and communications world knows that subtle and not-so-subtle sex, innuendo and sexual content sells more widgets and gets people's attention quickly and they deliberately exploit that fact.

TV ads either overtly use sexual images or subtly work them into more ads than we realize. Magazine ads overtly sell using sex and also use hidden images to excite without the reader's understanding. Radio will often use suggestive sounds so faintly in the background that we can hardly recognize them on more than a subconscious level. TV shows exploit sex constantly and especially during times they need to boost ratings. We're under attack from all sides!

We must learn that everything around us wants us to drink in and be drunk on sexual stimulation. We must become sober about what we've considered "harmless" in our surroundings and acknowledge many things that appear "normal" but are actually working against the Spirit in our carnal mind to open doors for the devil.

THE TROJAN HORSE

Troy was a city once considered militarily impregnable. Most of us know the story. The Greeks presented a "gift" of a giant horse to the Trojans, but secretly hid away a troop of soldiers inside its belly. Once nightfall came, the soldiers crept from the statue and opened the city gates, allowing the Greek army to lay siege from inside the walls. The fall of Troy was inevitable once the army was past their defenses.

The Bible warns us to be sober. In other words, "Watch out!!" First Thessalonians teaches us, *"Therefore let us not sleep, as others do, but let us watch and be sober."* Titus 2:6,12: *"Exhort the young men to be sober-minded... teaching us that, denying ungodliness and worldly lusts, we should live soberly, righteously, and godly in the present age."*

We are not to be conformed to the image of this world. Why then do just as many, if not more, Christian men have a problem with pornography as unsaved men do? Why are the divorce rates actually higher among evangelical Christians than in the world? Why are just as many Christian singles having sex as lost people? Why do we go to the same movies, listen to the same music, watch the same TV shows and laugh at the same comedians? The devil is trying to slip Trojan Horses past your defenses and destroy you before you ever know what hit you. We must start to learn to be sober about what we watch and learn that it will affect us far more than we know.

I'm not preaching from a soap box here. There was a time when I was completely worldly. I thought like the world. I acted like the world and I accepted the things that the world accepts. Just out of college, if you had asked me, I'd have said that I was "on fire" for God... but I'm not sure what that meant. I had a roommate who had a subscription to a non-pornographic, but sexually charged men's magazine (with monthly pictorials featuring semi-nude women), and I thought nothing of flipping through it... after all, the girls in it aren't *completely* naked. I'd watch movies with suggestive content. Laugh at sexual jokes in movies. Not turn my head away from sex scenes on TV or movies even if they "didn't show anything." My thinking was, "If it isn't pornography, but falls into society's standards of 'OK', then I'm not doing anything wrong or dangerous." Society is constantly pushing back the lines of morality. They CAN'T be your guide of right and wrong. The young generation now doesn't even think pornography is wrong! That doesn't mean that men in that generation have an excuse to look at it. Many things that are "socially acceptable" will open the doors wide for the devil's stronghold of porn addiction to stay in your life.

Just as an alcoholic can't avoid just whiskey but still drink beer, you can't hate porn and love the things of this world that are getting you drunk with sexual images and undertones. Sobriety means you will have to recognize what things aren't in agreement with God's standards, remove many of them altogether and tone down others.

Some people will think this chapter is legalistic, but truthfully, it is just reality. Legalism is an attack-word used by people who want to justify living however they want without consequences. You can't take a recovering alcoholic to a bar. That's reality, not legalism. The point of this chapter, however, isn't to give you a list of rules. That won't work either; but to set up a mindset that allows you to be led by the Spirit into real freedom and victory. That mindset, however, will require breaking fellowship with what the world views as innocent and OK and raising yourself to a higher standard.

You must come to understand that if you want to be free, your freedom comes with a price tag.

CLEANING HOUSE

Most of us know that we can't keep our "stash" of porn. If you haven't gotten rid of every trace of porn in your possession, that is a "no brainer." You absolutely can't have any of that. But that is just the beginning. You need to get brutally honest with everything that presents sexuality in some way and ask if you'd be comfortable looking at that or laughing at that with Jesus by your side. There are no "rules" to this process of cleaning house, but I can give some suggestions. Owning movies with nudity and sexual themes is ungodly. You can't have subscriptions to "innocent" men's magazines - almost all of these have sensual pictures of women in them. You need to "change your mind" as we have talked about elsewhere and break agreements with TV shows when they show people outside of marriage having sex. Recognize these things as ATTACKS on godly truth. Also recognize when advertising is trying to entice you with sensual images. Hint: shampoo commercials showing women having orgasms because they love the shampoo are not OK and should be turned off when they present themselves. You can't play video games with seductive women in them. This is not a comprehensive list - you must come to hate all the things that chip away at your moral foundation and slip their subtle messages past your guard.

Agreement is powerful! It is a Trojan horse. If you live your life by what the world considers innocent, you will always be fighting your battles within the city walls and you will likely stay addicted to porn for the rest of your life. The Trojan horse will already be inside the gates. Agreement with the world sows a seed of death in you. You may not fall that moment, but you have an open door that the devil will exploit at an opportune time. Romans 1:32 says it this way, "[they], *knowing the righteous judgment of God, that those who practice such things are deserving of death, not only do the same but **also approve of those who practice them**.*" Did you get that? Approval is agreement. How can you own, watch and laugh at things without admitting that you approve of them? How then, if doing worldly acts produces death can we desire to watch people and characters who do these things and not be sowing death into our own lives?

A soldier must think like a soldier because his very life is at stake. He can't walk around carelessly in hostile territory with bullets whizzing past his head and then gear himself up only when he's ready to fire his gun. He must always be on his guard and also think clearly enough to evaluate the threats around him.

Likewise, we mustn't think that we can go through our day accepting this sexual thing over here, laughing at that sexual thing over there and then think we'll suddenly have the strength to fight our battles when the time comes. We are fighting our battles 24/7. We must be on guard when we see the magazine covers at the grocery store. We must be on guard when we rent the movies at the rental store. We must be on guard from the girl who flaunts her body because she likes the attention. We must be on guard against the TV shows' indoctrinating situations. We mustn't agree with the "innocent" commercial that is subtly and suggestively selling its product. We must be on guard against every lie the enemy throws at us.

We must train ourselves to see, not as the world sees, but as God sees. The Bible calls this sobriety. Sober-minded thinking extends to all the things that can make us think in ungodly ways. Being sober minded allows us to be led by the Spirit. That's where we're going with all of this. I don't want to give you a list of rules, but to show you a mindset that empowers sober minded thinking. **Having all the rules in the world won't keep you from sinning. The devil can always think of a way to tempt you that you don't have a rule for yet.** Sobriety leads us away from the deceitfulness of the world into a place that is fertile for the Spirit to lead.

SPIRIT LED SOBRIETY AS OPPOSED TO LEGALISM

1 Peter 1:13-15, 5:8-10:

> *"gird up the loins of your mind, be sober, and rest your hope fully upon the grace that is to be brought to you at the revelation of Jesus Christ; as obedient children, not conforming yourselves to the former lusts, as in your ignorance; but as He who called you is holy, you also be holy in all your conduct." "Be sober, be vigilant; because your adversary the devil walks about like a roaring lion, seeking whom he may devour. Resist him, steadfast in the faith, knowing that the same sufferings are experienced by your brotherhood in the world. But may the God of all grace, who called us to His eternal glory by Christ Jesus, after you have suffered a while, perfect, establish, strengthen, and settle you.*

Peter says it best in the passage above. Sober-minded thinking will cause us to suffer for a little while. But soon, you will be strengthened, established and settled. The fact that you can't go and watch any movie may seem restrictive at first. This is what Peter means when he says that you will have to suffer a little. But as you learn what is safe for you to watch and then see it set you free in regard to your struggle with sin, you will begin to love the *greater* freedom you experience. What is more, as you train your mind to think like God's, you'll love letting God pick the movie. You still get to enjoy entertainment... and it won't open doors for other bondage. It is in this place you find real freedom.

The "suffering" that is most common in being sober is really just the emotional pain that comes from having to cut back a part of your fleshly "freedom." The Bible teaches us to "circumcise our hearts." Your heart is your soul, the area of emotion and desire (not to be confused with your spirit). Someone who wants to lose weight must cut back certain foods that their soul craves and restrain their desire. Over the past year or so, I have begun cutting back my portions and making a few other diet changes. At first I wanted to eat as much and snack as often as I was used to. But over time, smaller portions have become a lifestyle change for me and I've lost weight and don't miss the way things were. This is what Peter is talking about. When we begin to sacrifice the things our soul desires, it causes emotional pain. That pain, however, only lasts for a while and then real freedom comes.

We must, therefore learn what absolutes we must set for ourselves with a sober mindset, and also learn that there will be areas of "freedom" that must be surrendered to the Holy Spirit and learn to trust His leadership.

ABSOLUTES

There are some absolutes we must set in our lives if we are going to break the hold of addiction to porn and sexuality off of our lives. We simply cannot watch movies with nudity and sex. This should be a no-brainer for any Christian... even if we don't struggle with porn. Why should any Christian watch any movie that they would be ashamed to watch with Jesus? You may have to stand up to your friends and choose to leave or at least look away if you accidentally find yourself in a movie that has undesirable content.

We need to watch the places we go. Many bars and clubs should automatically be off-limits for us. Some may be OK. You'll have to learn to follow the Holy Spirit as we'll read later. Any place that is "sexually charged" should be a no-fly-zone for a Christian man. Even places like the well known sports bar chain (which shall remain nameless, but whose name is a slang word for breasts) should be on a strict "no-go" list. I've heard many Christian men argue that the outfits the girls wear aren't overly revealing. But let's get sober-minded for a minute. The name of the place and the outfits are all designed to make you think about a woman's breasts. The girls are trained to flirt with you. It is a sexually charged atmosphere and you can't view it as innocent or you will be fighting an enemy that you let through the outer defenses!

129

We must watch where we go! I was on a beach in Italy with my wife. As the beach got more crowded, many women started going topless. I said, "God, how would Jesus have kept His mind pure in this place?" I heard a clear answer in my spirit, "I would not be in a place like this." We needed to leave that beach. There are some places you simply can't go.

For some of you, there may be some TV shows you can't watch. For me, I was always a channel surfer during the commercials. The problem is that you never know what you are going to accidently surf your way into. There is a lot of trash on TV that will whack you out! I am now extremely careful in what I watch. I can NEVER allow myself to channel surf, and I prefer to simply not watch any TV except a select few shows I know to be OK.

You need to be SOBER! Notice the things that are stumbling blocks for yourself in regular life and go on a sober-minded diet. Your soul may suffer a little, but your spirit will grow. Society may think you are weird, but do you want to be free or to be "normal" in society's eyes? Frankly, our culture seems to now consider porn to be a "normal" activity. TV shows, comedians and many media influences have begun introducing porn into their scripts regularly. It is a classic foot-in-the-door technique: if you want to begin to have mainstream acceptance of something, get the mainstream laughing about it and make the topic "lighter". Once people laugh about it long enough, it is no longer taboo. Yes, we are well on our way in this society to having porn become normal and acceptable; and if godly men do not begin to take a stand, perversion will continue to escalate in our culture and every trace of morality will be eradicated.

LEARN TO FOLLOW THE SPIRIT

In addition to knowing the absolutes we must set up in our lives, we must also become sensitive to the Spirit. This takes practice. Get in the habit of simply conversing with God about everything. Ask Him if the movie or TV show is a good idea. Learn to recognize the "check in your spirit" when something may be damaging or the "peace in your spirit" if it is OK.

This has happened to me recently with one of the TV shows I watch from time to time. This show is usually innocent and the commercials on this channel are usually OK. One night, however, I was on my way downstairs to watch, and I really felt a tug on my heart that I wasn't supposed to watch it tonight. I thought about it for a few moments but brushed it aside. I thought, "This show is always fine for me." (I've since learned nothing is ALWAYS OK.) As it turned out, this particular show's plot revolved around a crime taking place at a beauty pageant. After about 20 minutes of bikini contests and scenes taking place in girls' dressing rooms, I was totally whacked out and over-stimulated. The Holy Spirit gives me freedom to enjoy certain things and warns me at other times. This is the blessing of walking with God and not living totally by legalism. We have freedom to do many things we enjoy such as watching certain shows, but must give God the space to warn us when we may walk into danger (and we must listen).

Sometimes I have the freedom to do one thing or see another. Other times I don't. I don't know myself well enough to know when I'm susceptible and vulnerable. I don't know the future and can't tell if I'll encounter something during normally "acceptable" activities that will be too enticing. But if I walk in the Spirit I can be safe and still enjoy freedom. If I turn to legalism, I would have to say, "I can never..." And that isn't the best answer.

We just don't know ourselves as well as God does. Sometimes I can take my laptop downstairs to do work late at night when everyone is in bed. Other times I simply can't. The temptation is too much. Sometimes I just need to go to bed early and get a good night of sleep. We don't know our own hearts and we can't predict the accidental exposure some situations may create. So we must learn to tune into the Spirit's voice. He knows when normally OK TV shows will be a problem or if the commercials are going to be a problem (ads for Girls Gone Wild videos, etc.) or the show that comes on afterward is about "the hottest women in..." And again, the Spirit can protect you from weakness of the flesh and situations that would open doors in your heart.

I've turned fellowship with God into a lifestyle. When I go to rent a movie, I always pray, "Lord, what movie will I enjoy that you can enjoy with me?" When I use the internet, I keep the communication open so I don't accidentally do a search that brings up trash or click a video link that may take me to a site that could have objectionable banner ads. I don't go see movies that I don't have peace about seeing. God is my best friend. I want to do the things that I can do with Him. There is immense freedom in this!

You may feel the sting of self-restraint for a while. You may also have to tell your friends that you can't go see the movies you used to see with them. But these things are often the price of freedom. We must be sober and vigilant.

Sobriety will teach you to walk in such a way that you are not opening doors to sin as you walk through normal life.

There is no such thing as innocent sexuality in the world. If we want real freedom, we must understand that freedom isn't the ability to do whatever we want. Freedom is the ability to make choices that bring freedom. Carnal sensuality enslaves us and all who serve its sinful ways. Being Spirit led may restrict your actions at times, but it always leads you in freedom.

~Mighty Man Training & Application~

Be your own watchman on the walls. Seeing that there is no set formula to what you can watch on TV or movies that are "safe" or set times to let your guard down, you must learn to follow the Spirit and recognize your own Trojan Horses. You are your best watchman on the wall.

What places, activities and things do you have in your life that could be opening doors for sexual stimulation in your heart? Are there any movies, magazines or games that you need to get rid of? Don't keep these open doors. They are areas of agreement with the enemy.

Don't let a single failure or slip up go by without learning from it. Every time I would fall again, I'd stop and say,
- "God, what was the open door or reason I blew it this time?
- What do I have to watch out for next time?
- Is there action I have to take to know that the devil won't get me with the same tactic again?"

Take some time and pray about these things. Ask God if there are any open doors in your life. It doesn't happen instantly, but God will teach you how to close the doors that keep the devil from getting in. We are in the beginning stages of victory. We must apply a stricter standard for ourselves so that we can stand.

CHAPTER 15

Fight Fire with Fire

The devil is a jerk. He doesn't fight fair. I'm sure anyone who has struggled with this sin has experienced some degree of this battle. It's the "movie projector" in your head. You see some scene you've lusted after playing over and over; or some girl you can't seem to shake the memory of.

You put down the thoughts over and over, but they come back over and over again. Often it can be overwhelming. The same thoughts for hours or days until you just can't take it any longer. Sometimes these temptations can be demonic in nature. However, most of the time, these yearnings are what the Bible would call a soul tie, a joining that takes place in the heart - "two becoming one."

UNDERSTANDING SOUL TIES

This is a common theme in the scriptures, especially when it comes to two topics, sex and idolatry. Over and over the Old Testament refers to people or their souls being joined to idols. Hosea combines the two concepts in chapter 4:17,18 stating that "*{he} is **joined** to idols... they commit harlotry* *continually."* 1 Corinthians 6:16 says, *"Or do you not know that he who is joined to a harlot is one body with her? For "the two," He says, "shall become one flesh."*

Soul ties are not always bad. God intends "the two to become one" and for a man's soul to be joined with his wife. The Bible also speaks of Jonathan and David's friendship *"the soul of Jonathan was knit to the soul of David, and Jonathan loved him as his own soul"* (1 Sam 18:1). Soul ties then are simply immensely profound connections with people - good or bad.

In this case of a soul tie that is formed through ungodly sexual activity, we have a doubly profound and doubly negative effect. We get attached on a soulish level to these women for the sake of the sexual connection as well as the fact that pornographic lust is a form of idolatry.

It is important for your recovery to take the time to remember as many girls and scenes and themes as you can and to name them before God individually, ask Him to forgive you for each occurrence, ask Him to break the soul ties that may be keeping you tied to these girls, concepts and memories, ask Him to deliver you from any curses associated with these people and acts, and ask God to make you whole again. This is profoundly helpful and I've seen a noticeable release from doing this.

This act of breaking all demonic soul ties will probably take a long time. Hours. And most likely will not happen in a single sitting. But as you take time and remember different people and scenes, bring each one before God and do this. The point of this chapter, however, isn't to address the concept of breaking soul ties, but to learn how to fight when their yearning causes temptation.

TURN HELL'S ATTACKS AGAINST THE GATES OF HELL

Even after you break soul ties with certain people and mental images, don't be surprised if you still have lingering thoughts about them from time to time. I did.

It began to discourage me. I did everything that I knew how to do to get rid of these thoughts. One day I decided that I was tired of this and it was payback time. I wanted to try to frustrate the devil like I was frustrated. I wanted to fight fire with fire.

For years I've turned weakness into a weapon in other areas of my life. For example, my dad struggled with insomnia most of my life growing up.

Then during high school, it started to affect me and I found myself lying awake night after night. My father was always troubled and frustrated by his insomnia. I decided I would take a different route and use that time to pray... before I knew it, I was falling asleep instantly. I don't know if my insomnia was an attack and the devil backed off or if God just honored His Word that promises to give His righteous ones rest. Either way, I started falling asleep easily when I would just pray.

Similarly, when I'm sick, I praise God and pray constantly. I hardly ever get sick now. I think satan doesn't want me to have that kind of time on my hands.

This tactic worked so well in other areas of my life, I decided to apply this principle of prayer to my struggle and allow temptation and weakness to become a weapon... I started praying for the girls that the devil would try to use to tempt me. What a wonderful concept! The devil puts a thought in my head or reminds me of the scene and I use his own weapon against him by praying for the very girl that is tempting me!

Since then, I've made this a standard response to temptation. I've really had some fun with this and have seen great results. My attitude is, "I'll make the devil regret every single attack." I'd take 2, 3, 5 minutes and just begin to pray for the various girls I was being tempted with. I'd pray and ask God for revelation for her; for His love to see her the way He sees her; for Him to save her; take her out of their lifestyle; to heal her broken heart; for God to take whatever issues and circumstances have brought her into that lifestyle and use these very factors to draw her to Himself.

You know what? It works. In fact, it works so well that this form of attack has become very rare for me now. I believe I was starting to beat the devil at his own game. If he doesn't tempt me, I win. If he does tempt me, I start praying that we would steal another soul from Hell's grasp. He can't win when this is our mindset.

I've even started doing this if a temptation doesn't involve an actual person. If I'm being tempted, I'll often just pick a porn star randomly and start to pray for her. Temptation time became spiritual warfare time – "Father forgive them, for they don't know what they're doing."

SUCCESS IN THE MIDST OF FAILURE

I remember one girl who I was repeatedly tempted by. This happened for months. I prayed many times for her during those months. However, one day came and I blew it. I got online and started looking at porn. I went to one of my usual sites and to my surprise, there was nothing new from this girl in the months I had been clean. So I curiously checked a blog site. Much to my surprise, she had left the industry. Now only God can save a person (and let's not get some crazy notion that we are called to a porn star ministry or anything so preposterous), but I believe my prayers had an effect that just may have contributed to her decision.

We don't realize how powerful prayers are. I remember one occasion when I was talking with a Christian friend at the gym. I asked him if there was anything I could pray about. He asked me to pray for a friend of his who had turned away from the Lord. All I knew about this person was his name, and that he went to Christian high school with my friend. Nevertheless, I prayed for him every day for about a month. I didn't know what to pray - I just asked God to lead me in my prayers for him. One night I went to a different friend's house to watch a movie after a Bible study he led. I started talking with one of the people attending, and he told me his story. He had grown up in Christian school, turned away from God and then God started drawing him back about a month ago. As he told me some of the things God was doing in his life, I realized that they lined up perfectly with my prayers for this unknown individual over the last month. Excitedly, I blurted out, "Is your name Chris and did you go to this high school?!" To my surprise, he was the very person I had been praying for! God allowed me to meet this guy to prove a point, even if we don't know someone we are praying for, our prayers still have great power!

Think about this for a moment: what if every Christian man struggling with porn started praying for someone's salvation? I believe with all my heart we'd start to see revival and salvation sweep through the porn industry. These women and men are God's precious daughters and sons. He hates seeing them used as objects. It is God's will that none of them perish but that they come to Christ and receive salvation, healing and forgiveness. We are just as guilty as they are in this sin. Let's not think this is all about us. We have sinned along with these people. **Perhaps as their sin has dragged us down, our salvation can pull them up!** The devil used them as our stumbling block and an enemy of God. But the Bible tells us to pray for our enemies and to bless those who curse us.

It is a lot harder to lust after someone when you are loving them with God's love. When you see them as a little sister in the faith or as a brother in the faith, temptation loses its zing. I often like to picture these girls in church singing and praising God with all of their hearts or leading a women's Bible study. If you really get a picture for someone in God, you won't want to picture them in sin. I say let's use the devil's own tactics against him, plunder hell and gain sisters and brothers in the faith. I hope someday I get to see one of the girls I've prayed for walk through the doors of my church so I can truly say, "what the devil purposed for evil, God turned to good."

~Mighty Man Training & Application~

Now take action. Think of a person or thought that has tempted you many times. Who are the actors or porn stars in that scene? Take a moment now and pray a prayer for you and a prayer for them as we see below.

Lord, forgive me for my illicit thoughts and lusts and idolatry with this girl. Please break every soul tie and curse associated with her. Have mercy on me and close the doors that I've opened.

Now I also ask that you would have mercy on her and start things in motion to save her soul and save her out of a life of sin. I pray that you would arrange the circumstances, people in her life and emotions she feels to cause her to seek you and find you. I pray that she would be able to leave pornography behind and find a church that will fill all her needs. I pray for strong Christian friends and influences in her life. I hope to see her in heaven one day as a sister in Christ and not as an object of lust. I choose to think of her in this way from now on.

Also take a minute of reflection and ask God if He can lay anything else on your heart to pray for them.

Do you see how powerful this type of warfare can be? Did this prayer change the way you think about this porn star?

CHAPTER 16

Get Violent

EQUIPPING A MIGHTY MAN MENTALITY TO FIGHT THE ENEMY

Think about something for a moment: "What are the qualities that our modern society values in a man?" How should men act in our day and age? It isn't hard to come up with a list. We see them portrayed over and over in TV shows and movies. We are taught that a man should be soft spoken. He's better off if he shuts up and listens to his wife, who knows better. He shouldn't be hot tempered or have outbursts of anger... that would be too "Neanderthal." He's not good for much except fixing things around the house. He's just a sex-crazed pig. The list goes on and on I'm sure, but these are the things we see over and over. And the adage holds true for the most part, "Tell someone something enough times and soon they'll start to believe it."

We may not be consciously aware that we agree with these modern stereotypes, but believe me, they get in. I hear the scornful voice of society in my head every time I want to speak up or have an impulse to react strongly to something, "Calm down. It's not a big deal. Don't be so unsophisticated." And so many of us agree and act, if not consciously, on a subconscious level in agreement with these "virtues" of the modern man.

We are becoming conditioned to think that violence or strong, violent emotion is bad. But you know what? I really don't see that in the scriptures. In order to change our mind... we have to change the way we think. There is a time and a place for everything. That includes strong emotions and reactions.

Now let me make something clear up front. This chapter isn't about PHYSICAL violence. I'm not telling anyone to go out and punch a stripper; nor do I condone violent acts or acts of aggression toward other people and things of that sort. This chapter is about SPIRITUAL warfare in response to the violence of the devil's attacks against you. I hope to shake some godly men from the sleep of passivity that considers temptation harmless and wake them to the need for violent faith and for godly, scriptural response to spiritual attacks.

My goal is to have you retrain your mind! The Bible teaches us ways to respond to sin and the attacks of the devil that are anything but meek, mild or gentle. We will need to kick out the sensitive, passive, metro-man that society has told us we should be and replace him with a passionate warrior who knows what attitudes will cause the devil to flee and who doesn't repress his passions only to see them resurface later in fantasy and pornography.

In society's eyes a passive man may be desirable, but this is not the way God intended us to be. I fear passivity and complacency seriously handicap us in two ways which we'll cover in some detail. Passivity and complacency are the opposite of how we must react to temptations and the devil if we are to overcome. And secondly, we are training ourselves to suppress emotions and reactions that are natural, only to have them resurface later in more destructive ways.

THE ATTITUDE OF FREEDOM

I'm going to tell you something your Sunday School teacher probably never did: hatred is not necessarily wrong. Many of us are taught you shouldn't hate anything. You won't find that teaching in the Bible, however. Now we are not to hate PEOPLE (how can we show people the love of God if we hate them?). But there are many passages which tell us what we should hate. Yes, the Bible tells us that we should feel that strongly about some things! *"You who love the Lord, hate evil (Ps. 97:10)!" "The fear of the Lord is to hate evil; Pride and arrogance and the evil way And the perverse mouth I hate (Pr. 8:13)." "All their wickedness is in Gilgal, For there I hated them. Because of the evil of their deeds I will drive them from My house (Ho. 9:15)." "Hate evil, love good; Establish justice in the gate.*

I'm here to tell you that you need to start **hating** your sin, **hating** the devil, **hating** the attacks of society against your sexuality, **hating** complacency, **hating** bondage, etc., etc., etc. Wanting to be free of your sin but not allowing yourself to feel passionately about it will deprive you of the attitude that is needed to overcome. We must become strong men of the truth, not complacent, passive-aggressive dreamers. Complacency is another way of saying, "I accept my bondage and the lies of society." We may not think things like that, but if you aren't tired enough of being a slave to sin to get riled up about it, you will be stuck in it for a very long time. I promise you that.

The Bible tells us things like, "be vigilant," "fight the good fight," "wage the good warfare," "put on the armor," "tear down the strongholds," "destroy the works of the devil." Similarly, in the book of 2 Kings 13 we read a story of King Joash and Elisha. Elisha tells the king to shoot an arrow that represents his victory over his enemies and then to take the remaining arrows and strike the ground with them. Joash weakly strikes the ground and Elisha reprimands him. Elisha's lesson: he should have beat the arrows to the ground with the same vigor with which he wanted to see God rout his enemies. I wonder if God doesn't violently come through to deliver us in some cases because our attitude is one of apathetic complacency.

We cannot be like King Joash when it comes to this sin. We must get violent. We are tired of the devil kicking us around, but too numb and mild-mannered to get angry about it. We want freedom, but we're too domesticated to go to war for it. We are made to be passionate warriors and destroy sin. However, the devil has convinced us to subdue ourselves instead of him! Joash needed a heart like David toward wickedness and his enemies: *"I beat {my enemies} as fine as the dust of the earth; trod them like dust in the street; spill them out like water"* (2 Sa. 22:43). David, the man after God's own heart, saw everything that rose up against God as an adversary to be destroyed to the uttermost.

Most theologians will agree that God used Israel as a physical, visible example that parallels our modern Christian life. He led them by the hand and He leads us by the heart. What they were called to do in the physical relates to how we are to act in the spiritual. God trained mighty warriors that He used to tear down strongholds. The price of freedom for us today remains the same: raise up men with a warrior mentality that will tear down the strongholds of our heart and society. If you are ready to violently beat the attacks of the devil into powder, you are ready to be free.

YOU ARE UNDER ATTACK!

General William Sherman coined the famous phrase, "War is hell." War may be all hell, but all hell is at war with you. The devil is constantly on the prowl looking to devour God's people (1 Pet. 5:8). The devil wants to kill you, steal from you and utterly destroy you (Jn. 10:10). He wants to kill your marriage. He wants to kill your children. He wants to steal your success. He wants to destroy your calling and anointing. If you don't fight back, you'll give him the whole thing like Esau selling his inheritance for a pot of stew.

Too many brainwashed Christians either live their lives as though the devil doesn't exist or they hide behind false theology that thinks that the devil can't touch you once you are a Christian. Nothing could be farther from the truth. You are attacked every day by the devil. We just don't think in those terms because we can't see the enemy, but he's there. The proper mental response to attack is not passivity or ignorance.

I think the most common thing we do when we are attacked is simply push it down and pretend like it isn't there. Think about this: what do you normally do when you are out with your girlfriend or wife and see a woman who is inappropriately dressed? You look away and pretend she isn't there. What do you do when you see the billboard ad that has women scantily dressed and posing suggestively to sell their product? You look away and pretend it isn't there. We get bombarded by sexual messages on magazines and we are trained to ignore it and say, "That doesn't bother me." We see the billboards and the TV ads using suggestive imagery to pitch their goods and think, "Don't be influenced by that." We get assaulted by the casual sex and scantily clad women in TV shows and movies and are pacified to think, "That's just the way it is. It is harmless."

The devil's attacks are not harmless and they can't just be brushed aside. When we train ourselves to simply look away and pretend this attack isn't affecting us, we are committing spiritual suicide. If someone were shooting at you, "ignore it and look the other way" is not a wise tactic if you want to live. You have to shoot back, put on a bullet-proof vest or run (we'll cover all of these as spiritual warfare tactics). Some Christian books on this very topic even tell men to ignore these things and just look at something that doesn't excite them - I feel bad for the men who read these books and think that tactic will help them.

Think how you would react if you walked in on someone trying to rape your wife or girlfriend. Would you tell her, "Don't worry. That's harmless. It won't affect you."? How enraged would you be if you knew someone was about to molest your child? Why then do we not stir ourselves up in our minds and hearts over the devil's attacks against them and us? You are allowed to get angry. The Bible says we are not to sin when we are angry... but that's about it. Anger is not an ungodly emotion - especially if it is directed against satan. God will one day pour out His wrath on the devil and wickedness. The Bible tells us we can do the same against the attacks coming against us right now.

EVERY attack that you don't rise up and deal with properly will affect you. These messages and images are attacks from hell and the enemy and they are not to be brushed aside as innocent and they are not to be ignored or repressed. I spoke earlier in this book about the proper response to beauty. This is not the same thing at all. Intentional acts to stir up lust require a different response than the normal attraction to beauty inherent to all humans.

The Bible says, *"As a ring of gold in a swine's snout, So is a lovely woman who lacks discretion"* (Pr 11:22). The corruption and misuse of beauty is an attack of the devil against you. Suggestive ads are intended to exploit beauty and incite lust. A woman who is dressed in such a way as to incite lust is walking in partnership with demons and devils – you can't see them, but they're present and they want access to your mind and emotions. Ignoring the devil doesn't make him go away.

I believe there are three appropriate, biblical responses depending on the situation. Defend, fight or flee.

DEFENDING

The Bible tells us to *"resist the devil and he will flee from you. Draw near to God and He will draw near to you"* (Jas 4:7,8). Many times, such as when we see something enticing on the magazine rack or in a movie, the best response is to recognize that as an attack against you and violently oppose it in your mind. You must recognize that a devil wants you to agree with him or at the very least ignore him so that he can stick around and torment you later by bringing up the lustful thoughts that you pushed down.

When you say, "NO!! I reject that temptation in Jesus name!!", you have willfully rejected the devil's overt advance toward you. He will have no means of entry or future chance to torment you. I will usually also pray quickly because James tells us to also draw near to God right after he tells us to resist the devil. So I'll often pray something like, "Lord, keep me in perfect peace and righteousness. I forgive that woman for partnering with the devil. Let the enemy have no rights to me."

FIGHTING

When we know there is overt spiritual warfare going on around us, often the proper response is to engage in warfare of our own. Overt means the temptation is an intentional and willful ploy to entice lust, arousal and excitement. The scriptures teach us to tear down spiritual powers, principalities and strongholds. Jesus said the Kingdom of Heaven suffers violence from violent attacks, but the violent take the Kingdom back by force (Mt. 11:12). We need to train ourselves the right way to pray in order to do damage to the enemy.

How fervent are your prayers? I always wanted God to come and powerfully deliver me... just not enough to get fervent about it myself. We read in James that the fervent, effective prayer of a righteous man is powerful/effective/having great effect. Energeo is the Greek word for 'fervent' in that passage. Obviously, this is where we get the word energy from and it carries the notion in the text of violent, erupting, uncontainable energy. When was the last time you would classify your prayers as uncontainably violent and energetic? Most of the time I think we have problems just staying awake to pray, let alone getting excited enough to consider our prayers fervent. I'm not saying that this is the way that our prayers should always be - but I do want you to rethink the way you think when it comes to spiritual warfare. It really is that: a war. Powerful prayer that puts life in your fight will often be the fight of your life.

Very often, temptations that arise in private or in public may require that we take action as well as pray - or determine some combination of action and prayer. Many times I've been around women who were inappropriately attired. I've asked women to button their blouses, pull up their necklines if they are showing cleavage, fix their skirts, etc. Never once have any of them gotten mad. Most often they are very apologetic. What I've done is given a clear message to their devils, "I don't want seduction." What I didn't do was shame or get haughty with the person who has a love need that isn't being met. We are fighting devils, not people.

I remember one situation that was solved simply with prayer. When I was in Bible school (of all places), there were plenty of young men and women around, but something happened when two girls in particular came in - it seemed as though every eye was on them and every man needed to pick his tongue up off the floor. There was just something about these two. Later my friends and I (we were all single at the time) were commenting about these two girls and how attractive they were, etc. The next day the same thing happened. Later I was praying and I just mentioned it to the Lord, that these two women were alarmingly distracting and I wanted His help to stay focused. The Holy Spirit actually spoke to me and revealed that these women had literal spirits of seduction operating with them. So I prayed and repented for agreeing with these seducing spirits and asked God to give me sobriety and the ability to overcome. The next day when they walked in, I immediately prayed under my breath, "I reject their spirits of seduction in Jesus name." One of the girls was far out of ear shot when I prayed this but turned around quickly and looked right at me. She probably didn't even know why or what just took place. There was a literal breaking of power between us. These two ceased to have any power or influence over my mind or emotions from that point on.

I use similar tactics on a regular basis when the situation calls for it. Many women trust in seduction, especially when they are feeling bad about themselves. There are spiritual forces at work with most women who are dressing inappropriately. You will often need to pray God's protection and deliverance from their devils. I have found that it is helpful to pray for them as well. Ask God to forgive them and show them their true beauty so they don't feel the need to flaunt false beauty for the attention and power it gives them.

When it comes to things that you encounter daily, you may need to take action. If the place you stop for coffee has magazines on display that are a problem, you may consider not going there or asking the manager to place a piece of paper over the cover so that it doesn't offend children or sensitive people. I wonder what it would be like if more Christians spoke up with store managers and said they didn't want magazines with scantily clad women in the store-front displays. What if we told convenience stores that we find it inappropriate to have "men's" magazines at the checkout counter where any child can see the images on the cover? What if we called the billboard companies and told them we found the ads on their billboards unsuitable for families and young children to view? What if we refused to rent or see movies that had nudity or sexual content? Why was it that New York had to wait for the mayor to kick out the sex shops when Christians could have done it long before then through spiritual warfare?

A friend of mine owns a Christian book and music store. A tarot reader opened a store next to his. He began to daily war in the Spirit - praying for the owner and against her devils. Within three months she and her family were born again. She changed her sign from "psychic readings" to "Jesus Saves!"

The point is this: wars are seldom won without fighting battles. We must learn when we are being attacked and how to combat the enemy when we are. We can be attacked in public or private; at times when it is convenient to stop and pray or times when it is inconvenient. But as the Spirit leads, we must learn to follow Him and gain victory in our daily circumstances.

Always remember this when fighting: first resist the devil then draw near to God. This second part is often overlooked and is the key to victory in all battles. When we only focus on the fight, the fight, rather than God, is the thing that is magnified. Most Christians are taught to fight and fight and fight but wonder why they lose and lose and lose. The victory doesn't come in the fight, but in the presence, in the Spirit.

FLEEING

There is a time in battle when we must retreat. This is also true with temptation. The Bible warns us to "Flee sexual immorality" (1 Cor. 6:18), and to "flee youthful lusts" (2 Ti. 2:22). There are times when lust may get overwhelming and the godliest thing you can do is to get away from it fast. I share this story in more detail elsewhere in this book, but on a beach one time in Europe, women started going topless. I thought to myself, "God! How would Jesus have kept His mind pure on a beach like this!?" The Holy Spirit's answer was, "Jesus would not have been on a beach like this." The moral is that you may be in situations that are so ungodly that you can't win. I've gone into stores that had so much filth for sale – everything from seductive trinkets to posters to you-name-it – that I just had to leave.

I have had days where the devil's attacks were relentless. It seemed that every 10 seconds I'd have a tempting thought or image go through my mind. No amount of prayer or attempts to "change my mind" and think about other things worked for more than a few moments. My body yearned for sexual release. My soul ties called out to me. I was in physical, spiritual and mental anguish to look at pornography. I've even had those days back-to-back for three or four days at a time. The most godly thing that I usually can do is to get out of my house, and get somewhere safe. I've gone to bed some nights four or five hours before I normally would just because the battle was too strong and I knew I wouldn't make it another 30 minutes. I had to just lie down and pray that God would let me fall asleep quickly so that I wouldn't be tempted to sin against Him any longer.

There are places where we simply will not be able to hold our own. Just as you wouldn't be able to stand strong in a strip club, there are other sexually charged environments in which you just won't be able to keep your head above water. Maybe it is a beach, or a bar, or a gym, etc. Maybe it is a place you'd normally go and there is someone dressed inappropriately. One time I was in a grocery store and a bus load of swimsuit models showed up. That was a little more than I was able to handle, so I had to get out of there. The point is that there is no set rule to "OK places." You have to know if you're in over your head.

This is the reality of our battle. Sometimes coming clean takes all our will and strength. Sometimes there are places we can't go and movies we just have to turn off. The bravest thing you can do at times is to run and hide.

I have also found that if I've had exposure that was more than I can handle, even if I did the godly thing and got out when I could, I still have to go back and get EXTRA grace to cover me. If you yielded to lust in any way in that situation, you need to repent, but grace helps you overcome the fleshly desires that arise from an over-stimulated environment. We overcome the flesh with the Spirit - and it is a gift that only comes by grace.

REPRESSION

I briefly mentioned the "normal" response that most men have to temptation and attacks is to simply push them down and repress it. I believe one of the greatest reasons we struggle in our society with pornography is because we have been conditioned to repress our natural passions. We tell ourselves we shouldn't be sexual, violent, aggressive or many of the emotions that are very natural in a man. Thus we push thoughts and emotions away and think that we've "dealt" with them. Guess what? A repressed emotion has to manifest somewhere. And in most men it manifests in pornographic and sexual fantasy. These women (and men) become the object of our passion, repressed sexual desire and aggression (yes, porn is violent – even the passive stuff is violent). We must learn how to channel our natural passions if we are to escape the damage of repressed emotion.

A good friend of mine recently went into therapy for anger, depression and many other emotional problems. I had no clue that anything was wrong with him. "That's the problem," he explained to me. You see, all of his life when something was wrong, he'd just push it down and not talk about it. He had years of unresolved anger, hurt and frustration that was starting to come to the surface. It didn't go away just because he didn't want to think about it.

Many times we hear about children that have behavioral issues and nobody can figure out why. They go into therapy and eventually the therapist uncovers an issue that they never dealt with. Other times we even hear about children developing fragmented personalities to deal with repressed issues. Only once the root is uncovered and dealt with do we see the child's behavioral issues go away.

I think in many ways, suppressing temptations and desires contributes to our "behavioral issues." Society and the devil throw images and temptations at us constantly and then tell us, "you are a dirty pig" if you think about the temptation. This is like someone shooting you over and over with a dart gun and telling you not to object or make a sound. Sooner or later, something's got to give.

Even in godly dating and marriages we train ourselves to repress natural sexual passions. Too many dating couples feel it is OK to cuddle or fool around a little. They then constantly have to fight arousal and talk themselves into not being sexually stimulated. This repressed sexuality HAS to come to the surface in some way.

Repressed sexuality continues into marriage. Men are designed to get stimulated when they are lying with their wives. Even when a man cuddles with his spouse, the natural, first response of the man is to desire his wife sexually. I cuddle with my wife, but what I don't do is repress my sexual feelings or urges. We have the power to restrain our sexuality but should not repress, suppress or pretend that it isn't there. Many men suppress this natural arousal and then wonder why their wives don't "do it for them any longer." They've spent years training themselves not to be aroused by their wives and then it actually happens for them.

There is a big difference between repression and restraint. I like to cuddle with my wife in the morning even though we don't have time to make love. As I feel her small frame next to mine and I restrain my sexuality, it always causes desire to rise up in me to love her and honor our vows, to accept no substitutes. This restraint awakens the warrior and sets me up for success whereas if I lied to my soul and repressed my sexual desires, I'd be storing up frustration and weakness that leads to a fall later. Cuddling with your spouse should lead to intimate talk, heart connection and, yes, SEX – at least when it is convenient to do so or unless you are intentionally restraining your sexual potency. The Bible says only to deprive each other with consent and for a time – then come together again (1 Cor. 7:15). If my wife knows I'm aroused and there is a good reason we can't have sex, we always set a time when we will. In that way, I know when there will be a godly outlet for that repressed passion.

A common trait shared by many of the most successful men in the world is an understanding of the link between their sexuality and their passions and power. Your sexuality is linked to your masculine power. Trainers, high level athletes and fighters from around the world have recognized this primal link for literally thousands of years. When we restrain our sexuality, we should be connecting with our inner strength on some level. "Getting violent" against the attacks of the devil should be second nature when prompted with a temptation that we must restrain (not repress).

What male passivity has done to our culture is push down nearly every normal, healthy space for sexual expression, pushed images in our face 24/7 and told us not to be aroused or stirred and told us not to be violent. Women are taught to expect their men to be "decent" and refined and cultivated and sensitive. I'm here to tell you that you need to connect with your raw, primal, sensual, powerful self. When you are sexually stirred, it should unlock an animal in you – one that will either be passionate in a godly way with your wife, or one that will be a passionate warrior against all ungodliness (while embracing sexuality as healthy and God-given).

When I was first married, my wife didn't understand why I always wanted my hands all over her. She thought I was just being crass and dirty - looking for a cheap thrill. She wasn't receptive to this kind of touch at first. She was trained by the world to think that this isn't how "men" should act around women. But she's not just a woman, she's my wife, the object of my sexual desire. The reality is that most men give and receive love with physical touch. She needed to know that this was an expression of love that NEEDED to be requited. She needed to know that to STAY attracted to her, I needed to be free to express that attraction. She needed to know that masculinity is sexual at times. (I, similarly, had PLENTY that I needed to learn about her. This is a two way street). However, now that she understands my "love language," we are able to "communicate" on that level – and let me tell you something: she LOVES when I'm a man now.

I believe that violent spiritual warfare is part of our genetic makeup just as passion and physical touch is part of our chemistry. If we repress the attacks of the devil and do not respond in kind, we bottle frustration for ourselves. If we suppress sexual stimulation, we repress passion and bottle lust for a later time. Sex and violence come packaged together. Porn is an outlet for them both. Men also love to live vicariously through movies and entertainment, which also often package sex and violence in one gratifying dose of emotional anesthesia.

You can't keep getting stimulated and do nothing about it. You need an outlet. The outlet will either be passion in the form of lust and pornography, or you can get passionate about destroying the works of the devil. Your lustful thoughts will either fuel your sin or turn into fuel that makes you fight.

"The price of freedom is eternal vigilance." (Thomas Jefferson). You are either fighting for freedom or giving up ground. Your spiritual and emotional chemistry is designed for this. You are wired for warfare. You can't afford one thought that you don't take captive or one temptation that you don't willfully and appropriately resist. So get violent. Give your soul the space to be the passionate warrior that it is designed to be. Channel sexual energy appropriately. Learn to enjoy being primal and powerful more than you enjoy the release of sexuality. Destroy the works of the devil because he wants to destroy you.

~Mighty Man Training & Application~

1. Stir yourself up and draw a line in the sand. Fervently tell your sin that you will NOT entertain it any longer and you will NOT give away any more of God's blessings.

2. The next time you see an ad or an image in the media that is supposed to stir up lust, give the devil a violent, "NO!! I recognize your attack and I will not give in." Then ask God to guard your heart and your mind.

3. When you see a woman in public dressed in such a way as to corrupt her beauty and incite lust, begin fighting in the spirit to tear down those strongholds. Reject her temptation. Pray that God forgives her. Pray that God would save her and cause her to be secure without that lust.

4. Flee if you must. If you just can't keep your head above water, know when to beat a hasty retreat. Get out of the environment and into something that allows you to think God's thoughts. Repent for letting your mind wander. Ask God to close those doors. And rehearse the things we've already learned so that you have all the tools to fight with.

5. Get FERVENT in your prayers with God. You need His help and grace more than you need your next meal – more than you need to draw your next breath. Take some time and really pour out your heart before God. Tell Him your frustrations, fears, hopes, etc. Be brutally honest with Him and with yourself! Stir yourself up to believe that He really will deliver and set you free from this. Violently pray against every lie you have believed about yourself and about God.

CHAPTER 17

Watch the Slippery Slope

COPING WITH WITHDRAWAL

In Greek Mythology, Pandora was given a great box by Zeus and was instructed to never let it open. Zeus had also given her a gift of curiosity and she was unable to restrain herself. She cracked the box just enough to peer inside. To her despair, out came all the evils of mankind before she could close the box again... The moral? It is hard to put a lid on wickedness once you open it even a crack.

When I was dating my wife, we had agreed that we would wait until we got married to have sex. What we didn't have spelled out was... everything else. And so we spent much of our relationship on a slippery slope - testing the waters. We didn't have rules about kissing, cuddling, etc. We quickly discovered a Pandora's Box - once you start down a certain path or course of action, it is harder and harder to stop and put the lid on. Time after time, kissing would lead to making out, making out would lead to some inappropriate touch, and then, not willing to go "all the way" we would find ourselves in a place of total sexual frustration. Not only that, we knew we crossed "the line."

People are always trying to find "the line." How far can I go before it is sin? This is not the attitude of a godly man. Considering that the Bible teaches that we should FLEE from lust, we must get real with the fact that we can't even go toward "the line." Eventually, my wife and I realized as a young dating couple that we had to set stricter and stricter boundaries for touch, proximity and anything that could lead to arousal. The same is true for the games we play with sin exposure.

There is no "step-down" solution for sin despite the fact that we live in a culture of carnal compromise and 5-step quick fixes. Overeaters can choose from every type of "diet" food their soul could possibly crave and think "I don't have a problem. I'm eating 'healthy' food now." Smokers can go to Lights, Ultra Lights, Menthols, patches, gum and who knows what else. Junkies can get on prescription drugs or go to Methadone clinics and step-down their addiction.

Just like a junkie will go through withdrawal, you will also crave porn as you come out of this (unless God gives you a grace that I simply didn't have). There is no such thing as Porn-Lite - half the gratification, fewer devils. It is normal as you crave porn to want to try to fool yourself with a number of "lesser evils" and think that you are getting away with something.

The problem, in my experience, is that the step-down "solutions" or "lesser evils" we play with as we go through withdrawal are a slippery slope and nothing more than a carnal solution to a carnal problem. The Bible warns that even the tiniest exposure to sin will completely work its way into your heart (1 Cor. 5:6, Ga. 5:9). Why do we think otherwise? Adam and Eve didn't have the option of taking a nibble of forbidden fruit... even a nibble would have cursed all humanity for all time. Having a little carnality is like saying, "I'll only take a little of what the devil is offering... I'll only watch this one scene in a Hollywood movie... I won't look at porn, per se." And then we expect that the devil we just agreed with will play by our rules and not later demand more of our heart than we wanted to give away.

What we looked at to salve our soul's desire can never satisfy a place that only God can fill. Because there is no REAL gratification that can be found in lust, that movie scene will open a door in your heart that will cause you to crave more. This is how the slippery slope leads to the law of escalation - you can NEVER be satisfied by something that CANNOT satisfy you! So one thing leads to another... and "innocent exposure" leads to soft-core porn, soft-core becomes hardcore, hardcore becomes perversely twisted porn, that becomes worse... and in time you are interested in things and doing things that you would have been appalled at in the past. What happened? Your heart said, "yes" to the slippery slope which has no end. To agree with something "harmless" can only grow into something worse tomorrow.

So let's get practical with the ways we open these doors. In many ways, this chapter is similar to the teaching we have read about walking in sobriety. In fact, many of the same "permissible" worldly things will be the very things we turn to again when we are trying to overcome the feelings of withdrawal. Many of the actions we take will be the same as in the sobriety chapter - but the heart issues are very different. Sobriety is about coming to the realization that there are things in the world that will open doors for lust and removing them. The slippery slope relates to the games we play and the compromise we allow with ourselves as we go through withdrawal from pornography.

FANTASY

The mind is a dangerous weapon when it is engaged in carnal and sensual thought. It is easy to continue to think along a sinful train of thought and tell yourself, "It's OK... I'm not looking at porn." This is a slippery slope of deception. You can't entertain lustful thoughts... or even thoughts that LEAD to lustful thoughts. Thoughts will come at you every day. What you do when they arrive makes a huge difference. Don't let them linger or entertain them like a long-lost-friend. The book of 2 Corinthians tells us that in order to win the war and pull down our strongholds, we need to learn to take our thoughts captive right away (vv. 10:5,6). Change what you are thinking about instantly when fantasy thoughts arise. Think about godly things - or arm yourself with personal scripture verses for these times. Make this second-nature.

There are many different types of thoughts that can be dangerous. Obviously if you remember different pornographic episodes, change your mind ASAP. But other forms of fantasy should also be nipped in the bud before they come to fruition. Don't entertain fantasies about past girlfriends or beautiful women you see in passing. Don't even fantasize about completely fictitious scenarios and people. (Some men have asked me if cartoon porn is OK because it isn't "real" people.) The lust, however, is still real. The devil it is feeding is still real. You can't afford to entertain lustful thoughts. The end result will never once be good. It ALWAYS opens doors that I didn't want open.

I've spoken about beauty. It isn't sin to see a beautiful woman and think, "Wow, God! She's beautiful." But if you allow your mind to keep thinking about her for long, you will find yourself quickly on a slippery slope.

Fantasy of any sort is a slippery slope and will trip you up at the end. It may get in "under the radar" because we aren't actively looking at porn, but it is feeding our obsession enough to make it stronger to take hold of us time and again.

INNOCENT ENTERTAINMENT

I've touched on this before, but it is worth mentioning again. We need to watch WHAT we watch and WHEN we watch it. Don't rent movies with questionable scenes or with women that we would tend to lust after. If you innocently happen to be watching something that takes a turn for the worse, be smart and turn it off - then pray immediately. There is nothing that you will be missing in the long run except more pain and heartache. If you are with your buddies watching a movie and a scene comes on that you shouldn't be watching, look at the floor, the wall, leave the room or fast-forward if you've got the remote. Remember that what is playing is an attack! Pray your way through that scene and trust that God can keep you out of harm's way.

There is no such thing as "innocent exposure." It always gets a foothold unless you actively and violently say "NO" in your heart against it and recognize it as the attack it is. Do this with accidental exposure as well. I've been innocently surfing the net and gone to a page with something on it that would be damaging. It is easy to do these days. Video sites are the worst. It seems like even if the video you want to watch is "clean," there will be related videos or banners that are no good.

I was on a video site once and clicked on an "alternate ending" to a movie I had seen and liked. The clip came up, and right next to it there was some banner ad for a dating site with all kinds of suggestive images. Foolishly I kept watching the clip while girls in my peripheral vision were shaking everything that shakes. Hours later, I had forgotten the clip, but was still remembering the banner ad. Be careful. Know how you will respond to accidental and innocent exposure before you are in the midst of a situation that will set you back into sin.

Another time, I was doing an image search. I had the browser set to filter out inappropriate content. But nevertheless, one of the images was of porn. Instantly my heart started pounding and I clicked away. But I didn't stop, pray or violently oppose those thoughts. A few minutes later I found myself hoping that there may be other images that sneak through so that I could have more "innocent" exposure. Sure enough there were other images. Where did I think all this "innocent" exposure was going to lead? To innocent behavior? Next thing I knew I had clicked on one of the links and was fully immersed in sin.

CURIOSITY AND DABBLING

There will be struggles as you come out of this. One temptation you may face is the notion that you can go to sites that don't show full nudity, but have suggestive content. There are a thousand sites out there that the world would consider OK or that aren't "pornographic" per se. There are even sites that you may be able to visit sometimes and be OK. The danger is when we are feeling like we "need a fix," as a junkie would say, and we begin to play with things that are only slightly gratifying. I've been there. Don't do it! It is a dead-end. You know exactly where it will end up. You can't look at anything suggestive and think that it will satisfy you.

A slip-up that I ran into quite often was just curiosity. This one was especially bad when I was still using an internet filtering program. I'd wonder things like, "What kind of results would I get if I searched for this or that?" I'd try to see what I could get away with to "trick" the filter. It was as if I was thinking I could blame the filter for my slip up. "If I'm not actually searching for porn, but some 'accidentally' gets through, I'm OK." Wrong. Curiosity kills.

I just had to accept the fact there is nothing new under the sun. I'll never miss anything online. There may be new girls or new videos with old girls… but in the end it is all the same-old, same-old. Once you start opening doors, they get harder and harder to close.

OLD FLINGS

For me, I'd often struggle with thoughts about one or two porn stars for days at a time. These soul ties with certain women tormented me constantly. I'd play the slippery slope game and think, "Maybe I can find some pictures of them clothed. I'm sure there are casual shots of them online." "I'll look up their profile on Wikipedia. That won't show any nudity. It will be fine..."

But once the door was opened, just seeing a picture again of an "old flame" an object of lust (without nudity) was enough to get my heart racing. From there I thought, "Maybe I'll find them on YouTube... after all, surely YouTube censors their videos... they won't 'show anything." From there I thought, "Maybe I'll do an image search for them using strict filtering." And it was all downhill from there.

In reality, I was done for when I made the first decision to look for anything. The door was already open. "A little leaven leavens the whole lump" (Gal 5:9). That means you can't have just a little sin, just a little curiosity, just a little excitement, just a little gratification. Once you go down that path, you've opened a can of worms.

I do want to say this, however: if you start down that path, stop before you go too far. It is never too late to make a right decision. Repent for what you've allowed in and ask God to close those doors.

I'd say it is a good idea to even get rid of photos you may have of old girlfriends - especially if you had sexual encounters with them. If you are like most men, many of the "fond memories" we have of old flings are sexual. We can't think about them without stirring up lust.

DREAMS

What you dream about at night is important. It reveals what your heart really longs for. Dreams also open doors. Have you ever noticed that if you had a night with horrible dreams, you are likely to struggle more the next day? That is because you have opened doors in your sleep that produce a slippery slope. It is a good idea to regularly ask God to bless your sleep and your dreams. If you do remember having had ungodly dreams, recognize that a door may be open and ask God to shut it and help you fight any temptations that may arise later in the day.

SELF-GRATIFICATION

One of the most difficult scenarios when you are trying to come out of sexual addiction are the times when you are legitimately aroused with no godly solution. Sometimes you will just be "in the mood." That is a fact of life. It is difficult enough fighting the spiritual battle of coming clean from sin without an added physical struggle.

It is tempting at times when we just can't take any more to think, "I'll just masturbate and think about non-sexual thoughts." Even if that were possible, (the Bible doesn't really give any teaching on masturbation apart from lust, so you may escape on a technicality) the reality is that self-gratification is another slippery slope. I've played that game before. "Just don't think about women... or porn... or body parts... just get the job done... read the back of the shampoo bottle, you'll be fine." This is the type of mind game I'd play. I don't think I ever once continued to think about shampoo ingredients or kept my mind completely innocent of stray thoughts while masturbating. There would always be a moment when I would stray.

The Bible says, *"Walk in the Spirit, and you shall not fulfill the lust of the flesh"* (Gal 5:16). The only real solution is to learn to rely on God. Gratification of the flesh, even without porn, is a fleshly solution to a fleshly problem.

I suppose some would argue that masturbation doesn't make any new bonds or expose you to porn. But it is still a carnal solution to a carnal problem. That which is not of faith is sin. Better to avoid this altogether. Your escape will come more swiftly.

SO CALLED "PROPER" SELF-GRATIFICATION

Another tempting "slippery slope" is the notion that you can think about your wife and masturbate. I've attempted this many times, thinking that I could somehow do it without slipping into lust. However, I quickly learned that this was another carnal solution to my problem of carnality.

157

If you think you can play this slippery slope game and win, think again. You have better odds trying to go to the casino and beat the house. Most of the time, what happens is our mind wanders to other objects of lust or we tend to start objectifying our wife and thinking about her just as we would any of our other areas of fixation or fantasy. God designed sexual intimacy with our wives to be just that: intimate.

Even if our wives have given us permission to do this, and we were able to keep our mind totally centered on her and how much we love her and cherish our marriage bed and times of intimacy, and we were able to not objectify her in any way, this "solution" still runs contrary to the ultimate aim of being able to overcome the desires of the flesh by walking in the Spirit. The goal is still to train our flesh against using carnal solutions to carnal temptations - so this "solution" runs contrary to our ultimate goal. God wants us to learn to direct our hearts into Him. The reality is that masturbation and fantasy are never going to produce a godly outcome.

It seems like when someone finds out that I do Christian purity coaching, the next words out of their mouth are always, "What do you think about...?" It seems that people always want to find out "how far" they can go toward sin and still be "OK." People want to find some authority outside their own conscience to tell them that sin is OK, as if on the Day of Judgment, they will get a pass because so and so said it wasn't sin. If your mindset is *how close* you can get to sin, I hate to break it to you, you are *already* sinning. Let's rather think about how close we can get to God.

Perhaps the only scenario that I've been asked about that stumped me and I thought could *possibly* be OK (if the heart is true intimacy and love) is when couples have jobs or situations that take them apart for long periods of time. For these couples, talking on the phone together or video-chatting with each other online while they "self-service" becomes a part of their "long-distance intimacy." In a case such as this, I find it hard to be dogmatic, given that the Bible has no teaching on masturbation (especially in this scenario that is a product of modern technology). To those in this situation, I'd only caution that you bring God into the picture. If you can envision Him enjoying you enjoying each other as He does with conventional intimacy, I really don't have a problem with that as expression of love making – as long as love is at its heart. Monitor your thoughts and heart; and if you find it too easy to slip into selfish, lustful fantasy, you shouldn't practice this as a form of "intimacy" with your spouse.

GET LUST OUT OF YOUR MARRIAGE!

Lust is an emotion from the devil and should never be introduced into marriage. This may come as revelation for a number of men out there, but your wife is not supposed to make you feel like a porn star makes you feel.

I often hear men say that sex isn't as good when you are married. I personally believe that sex in marriage is supposed to be better than in the world - but there is a different dynamic operating - love vs. lust.

If a couple was having sex before marriage, there was inevitably an element of lust involved. Once you are married, lust is taken out of the picture and the marriage bed becomes holy and sanctified. Any man hoping that his wife will stir up those old, familiar feelings of lust and carnality is in for a rude awakening. This is a hard teaching and takes spiritual discernment. It came more naturally for my wife and I because we were both virgins on our wedding night. We never knew "unholy" intercourse; but I knew the feeling that lust had in my soul from years of struggle with pornography. Therefore, when thoughts or temptations would arise wherein we could introduce lust into the bedroom, we had a heightened sensitivity to its effects.

Never confuse lust with passion. Many think that lust is just a term that applies to sex when you are "really into it." Lust is a devil, a spirit. Passion and really passionate sex are godly. But you can't have holy, lustful sex. Some men who have trained their souls through lust are tempted to think, "My wife doesn't turn me on anymore." To that person, I say, learn to love your wife and erase all memory of lust and your wife will begin to arouse you again. Accept no substitutes for your wife. Don't listen to what the world says is beautiful. Beauty truly is in the eye of the beholder and your body's own neurochemistry during intercourse will literally rewrite your definition of beauty if you'll allow it. When you learn how to truly make love to your wife, it will stir up great passion and make for a wonderful sex life.

Many men, however, never get over the lie that they are supposed to feel lust for their wives. They try to reintroduce lust into the marriage bed in a variety of ways: role playing, fantasy, dirty talk, exhibitionism and other such "bedroom aids". I would strongly advise to NEVER bring these into your private life with your wife. They misinterpret the Bible's teaching that the marriage bed is holy as though it means you can never sin while having sex with your wife. Some men even try to watch pornography with their spouses or fantasize about other women when they are with their wife. Again, NEVER do this. You will ultimately destroy your intimacy. You can't have sex with your wife and think about someone else. That is just using your wife to masturbate instead of your hand. You can't make love to someone if you are pretending they are someone else; and unless you are expressing real love toward that person in all of their God-given beauty and uniqueness, you are using them for lustful self-gratification rather than making love. This doesn't mean you can't enjoy sex or enjoy the pleasure it brings. It simply means there is someone else involved in the equation. When both people are putting the other person first, everyone wins.

Sex in marriage should be wonderful. Be adventurous. But avoid perversion and fantasy and anything that arouses lust as though your life depends on it. Proper and godly love is designed to reinforce both partners in their masculinity and femininity. You should be appreciating the beauty of your wife when you make love to her. She should make you feel like a man and reinforce your manly strength. This is the give-and-take that God designed in the marriage bed.

FULFILLMENT

Many men feel or remember the sensations and strength of lust and begin to believe the lie that their wife can't fulfill them. My sex life was never bad, but I believed that lie also for a while. Gradually, as I walked out of lust and pornography addiction, I overcame these lies and God began to really bless my sex life with my wife. But you must take the first step and trust that God will cover you and bless you.

I believe this will also hold true for single men. Single men also are subject to the lie that they have "sexual needs" that can only be met through self-gratification. I believe that if you put God first, He will honor that decision.

Some men may be called to stay single. Paul was - and for those in that situation, God gives a specific, abundant grace for the single life. I am convinced that the fulfillment of seeing our calling come to pass in God is more gratifying than the passing gratification that an orgasm could give.

Part of our true freedom is exposing the lies that say, "I'm not going to have my needs met." We can be subconsciously driven by these lies. Don't play the slippery slope. We must make a clean break from sexual temptation until we are truly free.

GETTING BACK ON TRACK

In my experience, the most important thing to do after you've played on the slippery slope is to get back to grace. If you've peeked into "Pandora's Box" it will have an effect on your soul. You will have opened doors that ONLY God can close.

I've frequently quoted the scripture from Galatians 5, "Walk in the Spirit and you won't carry out the desires of the flesh." When you even go near a fleshly desire, it only stirs up greater fleshly desire that lingers in your mind and imagination. At these times, I believe we need a greater measure of grace than we would normally have just so we can get back to an even keel.

All the other principles that we've learned will also apply, but remember, it all comes back to grace. We can't puff ourselves up in the flesh and overcome the flesh. We must always fight the flesh with the Spirit - and that is a gift from God.

~Mighty Man Training & Application~

Withdrawal is not pleasant to go through. But trust me, there is no step-down solution that will make it easier. We MUST press through. We can't play with "innocent" lust or we will just open doors that will lead us right back into full-blown struggle again.

It does get easier. Really. And the end result is worth it. Therefore settle the fact that there will be things you've looked at and thoughts you've entertained that can't be a part of your life any longer.

Think about the slippery-slope games you've played in the past. Repent for those as well and make the decision right now to be vigilant and fight any small amount of temptation you encounter into your life.

If you've been playing the slippery slope game, repent, know that it only has one end, and get the grace to get back to your right mind. Ask God to help you plan how you will avoid the slippery slope that leads to a fall. Ask Him to expose the lies that have made you justify these things as "harmless" or acceptable when you know they will lead to something worse.

"I have made a covenant with my eyes; Why then should I look upon a young woman?
-        Job 31:1

CHAPTER 18

Falling... and Getting Back up Again

For a righteous man may fall seven times And rise again.
- Proverbs 24:16

I've been there. I understand how it feels. It is a horrible thing to want to do what is right, to hate your sin, to do everything you know how to do to get it out of your life... and then fall again. It is disappointing. Frustrating. Demoralizing. It is easy to feel like a total failure and think you are starting back at square-one. When you are in the gutter, it is easy to want to stay in the gutter and wallow a little. But we have to get back up again. That's life.

I've said it before, my journey in didn't happen overnight and my journey out didn't either. I can't tell you the number of times I've thought, "That was the last time." And nearly every time, I've believed myself. And every time I found out I was wrong, there was a lot of painful heartache, self-disappointment, regret, frustration and every other emotion you can imagine.

I'm sure you've wished you could just push "reset" and make it as though you'd never sinned. And I'm sure, like me, you've wished you could win the war without fighting the battles. This sin doesn't go down without a fight. I wish I knew a magic prayer that you could pray and the struggle would go away. I have learned, however, that the struggle makes you stronger. I wish

I had a quick fix that would make quitting cold-turkey easy. These desires are normal reactions to how demoralizing it can be to fall.

It is bizarre to hate your sin but keep running back to it and not understand why. So let me say, I can sympathize with anyone who is so saddened and crushed by their failures.

ONE STEP AT A TIME

If you haven't "arrived" it isn't the end of the world. Guess what? Even if you totally conquer this, you'll still have other things for God to work on. We are all a work-in-progress... so the goal is progress, not perfection. Remember our foundational lessons about grace and love. You are God's workmanship and He knows your weaknesses better than you do. He never sits back in His throne thinking, "Wow! I didn't see that one coming." He never looks at you and says, "They just sinned bigger than My grace and love will cover." If you'll take an attitude that says, "I'm going to get up, learn from that one and not fall into the same trap again," you are on your way to freedom.

I don't want to say that sin is OK - but I also want to be real. I didn't start this journey and win every single battle. Quite to the contrary. At first I'd mess up practically every day. Over time I noticed that the mess-ups would come less and less frequently. That was encouraging. I'd go for a couple days, then a week, then a couple weeks, then a month. I went from a total addict - unable to count the number of times I'd blow it in any given week, to looking back and realizing that I could count the number of slips in a year on one hand. It was like I was a wild colt on a long rope and God was just taking up the slack and reeling me into Himself little by little. When a fall would make me feel like a total failure, I looked at the big picture and I could see that God was perfecting the things that concern me. That fact gave me the strength to stir myself up even more and get back on track.

Wherever you are in your struggle, even if it is at the beginning and you are still messing up regularly, just the fact that you are reading this and looking for answers means you are further along than you were yesterday. You may not have beaten your giants yet, but if you've asked God to help you do it, He is already working in you to bring you out of this. I know it doesn't feel that way after a slip, but it is true. No matter how far along you are in your journey out, a slip feels like you are back and starting at ground zero. But I learned this is a lie from the enemy to keep you from learning from your mistake.

You aren't perfect yet. Let me know when you get there and I'll take a page out of your book. In the meanwhile, we have to ask for forgiveness, forgive ourselves, refresh our minds and learn how our falls can make us stronger when we get back up.

HOW TO GET BACK UP...

For a righteous man may fall seven times And rise again. - Proverbs 24:16

Think about the verse above for a minute... "a righteous man may fall..." Aren't you glad the Bible DOESN'T say, "a righteous man will never fall..." or "a righteous man has one shot to get it right"? God knows our weaknesses and our falls before they happen. They didn't change His mind about you beforehand. He still decided you were worth dying to save no matter how many times you'd let Him down.

The hallmark of a righteous man is not that he doesn't fall – we all will. The real virtue, the acid test of true character is how you pick yourself back up after a fall. And today is as good a day as any to start to fall forward, not back and learn from your mistakes.

In 2 Corinthians 7:11 we read about the attitudes of godly repentance: *For observe this very thing, that you sorrowed in a godly manner: What diligence it produced in you, what clearing of yourselves, what indignation, what fear (of the Lord), what vehement desire, what zeal, what vindication! In all things you proved yourselves to be clear in this matter.*

The devil wants you to wallow in your sin and sorrow after you fall. If he can get you to do that, he can get you to continue in sin. Don't follow your sin with more sinful attitudes! The time right after you sin is critical. Let your heart run to God to find His grace and love and let your attitude be that of what we just read: zeal, indignation, vehement desire, diligence to come right. A fall can be fuel for future victory if you learn from your mistake. So let us learn how to fall forward and not back.

Falling forward is all about learning from your mistakes. Most of this book was written while I was still struggling horribly and even messing up.

What I learned to do was to sit with God after each fall, receive His love and ask His wisdom: what went wrong? Where did I open the door? What do I have to change to not let the enemy win that same battle again in the future? Then lesson after lesson, time after time, I learned to shut door after door. You may have some open doors and lessons to learn that I did not. This attitude is how you will learn to shut those doors and find your freedom.

DON'T THROW THE BABY OUT WITH THE BATH WATER

Just because you messed up doesn't mean the lessons that you previously applied don't work. It also doesn't mean you are back where you started if you learn and grow. The reason there are as many chapters and lessons as we find in this book is because we are complex beings. Each lesson is an area in which the devil can get access to our heart. He will try to exploit every weakness in order to get you to sin. This is why learning to walk in the Spirit is so important. If it is just you vs. the devil, you'll lose every time. But the Spirit of the Lord in you gives you the victory over anything that comes your way. The Spirit of the Lord shows you where you have open doors, how to close them, how to guard your heart and how to walk in the truths we've learned so that you have no space for the enemy when he comes at you again and again.

The other blessing of walking in the Spirit is that you can instantly get back on your feet after a fall because of amazing grace and recognize that your standing with God didn't change because your are righteous because of Christ's works, not your own. Apart from this truth, I always found that after a fall I was MOST easily tempted again. This is because I'd already empowered that enemy and agreed with its lies. It is like when a shark smells blood in the water. They know their prey is wounded and they attack with fervor. Therefore, we must stir ourselves up and run to God through grace if we are to get back into God's territory.

So fall forward with God. Learn from your mistake. Expose the lies. Close the door that opened and rehearse the lessons we've learned so that all access the devil may have to your heart can be shut down. Use the Training & Application portion of this chapter as a checklist to quickly refresh the tools we've already learned. We must be ready with all of these tactics because the enemy will change his tactics constantly to tempt you in the areas you are most weak.

~Mighty Man Training & Application~

The time after a fall is critical. We must quickly repent and close the doors so that we don't continue into a downward spiral. Here is a quick guide to get back on track.

1. **Repent:** This is a no-brainer. Ask God to forgive you and cleanse you from all unrighteousness. Remember what godly repentance looks like. Don't wallow in guilt – wallowing and condemnation proves you are still trusting in YOUR works - real repentance is a power shift from your strength to God's. Ask Him to restore you and set you back on the path. Petition His help cleansing your mind of the mental pictures you may have had and cleanse your soul from any soul-ties to the people and perversions you may have seen. Finally, ask Him to deliver you from any demonic influence that may want to exploit your weakness.

2. **Remember the law of grace:** Only God's protection, power and revelation will lead you out of this - not your own strength. We are usually the weakest after a fall. There is also usually an area of our pride and sense of achievement that gets bruised. This means these are the times when we need the MOST grace. It is only by God's grace that you will get free from this. Ask God for the grace and strength to not go back to your sin.

3. **Remember the law of love:** Remember God's love for you didn't change with this episode. He wants you to run to Him and learn His unfailing love. He's your Father and He understands. He still loves you as much as Jesus!

4. **Mentally prepare for the next struggle:** It is usually very difficult again right after a fall. Prepare your heart to fight. Know that temptations will come again. How will you react when they do?

5. **Take control of your thoughts:** Since the devil likes to kick you when you are down, you will probably have to recognize these thoughts and take them captive frequently. Use the principles from Chapter 13, Change Your Mind.

6. **Sober up:** If there was an open door that you didn't close, repent and close it. If you just got careless, repent and put on a sober mind. Remember, the enemy doesn't take temptation vacations.

7. **Employ the Fear of the Lord:** Any time we sin, we exalt our needs over the commands of God. There are consequences to sin. Turn before you open doors.

8. **Recharge your vision:** Remember all the reasons you want to beat this sin and think of how it will feel when you have. Put these visions as a belt of truth around your waist.

9. **Make the devil pay:** If you remember the people you were lusting after, remember to forgive them and pray for them. Make your weakness a strength.

10. **Find your inner mighty man:** Remember to stir yourself up and shake off any complacent cobwebs. You are in this for your life. Get violent against future attacks.

11. **Avoid slippery slopes:** Was your fall related to compromise? If so, repent. Now you know what to watch out for next time so you won't fall for the same trick twice.

12. **Fall forward:** Was your area of weakness unrelated to any of these lessons? Learn from your mistake. Ask God what the open door was for you this time. Repent and move on. Don't let the same temptation take you down twice.

YOU ARE ALMOST THERE

If you can get to the place where you are doing these things regularly, you will be ready to move on to lessons of the heart and finding your true freedom.

It may take time before this is second nature for you. But hang in there. It will happen for you.

~ Part IV ~
Finding Freedom

We have laid the foundations. We have learned tactics... tools that can help us win battles when we are tempted. But if you are like me, the more you fight the more you realize you need REAL freedom - heart change. The more you fight, the more you also realize how dependant you are upon God for His deep healing and presence. We don't want just sin management - we need a real solution.

This is the attitude that brings us to the place of humility - a place where we yearn to sit at the Father's feet and allow His presence to change us from the inside-out.

These lessons that follow may take time and reflection to learn. Tactics are things that YOU can do (through God's grace and strength), but heart change is tougher because only GOD can do it in you. You will need to give yourself time to pray through each chapter. The more time you spend in God's presence, the more you will become like Him who you behold. If you want heart change, you MUST spend time every day with God - only then will you drown out the myriad of worldly influences that bombard you throughout the rest of your 24 hour day.

There is nothing greater than when you realize that you are not the same person today that you were a year or a month ago. This is what we have been yearning for all along... so let's begin...

CHAPTER 19
All In All

ALLOWING GOD TO FILL THE VOIDS IN YOUR HEART

I was having one of those weeks... nondescript. Work felt like I was just "going through the motions." Prayer felt like I was talking to the ceiling. I felt like a robot. I didn't have the desire to do anything, eating anything, pray anything, read anything or watch anything. One night for lack of anything more interesting, I decided to watch TV. Nothing was on, per se, except this show about exotic cars. I like cars, but cars are often dressed up with sexy women and this show was no exception – not busty babes in bikinis or anything "over the top", but nevertheless, a number of women in dresses too small, showing too much cleavage as they "innocently" demonstrated the cars' features – one of the enemy's classic attacks - seduction and sensuality in a classy package that flies under the radar. I recognized that the show wasn't innocent, but I made a poor choice and decided to watch the show anyway.

The next day I was doing some research on the internet and a link came up that looked intriguing. It was not a link that I should have clicked. But I did. It wasn't porn or anything like that, but it was sensual content under the guise of "socially acceptable and innocent." It didn't occur to me that I was sliding on the slippery slope I had started on the night before. (I should have recognized and followed my own teaching). I had opened a door with the car show and I was desensitized to the battle for my soul. After looking at that site, I found myself battling again like I hadn't in a long time. I hadn't had a real battle for my soul in months. I thought I was over that type of temptation (that's pride - we are never so spiritual that we are immune to sin). One thing led to another and I blew it. I still didn't realize that the enemy had come in the night prior.

Afterward I was repenting and praying and asking God how and why I was so oblivious to the slippery slope and how I could repent and close the doors. Suddenly a light came on and I remembered the night before and the car show. I realized that I had opened the door then and my struggle and lack of willpower was due to that cause-and-effect. So then the question became, "Why did I let my guard down the night before?"

God's answer took me by surprise, "You need some excitement, some passion in your life." I knew the thoughts couldn't have been mine. I was not thinking anything along those lines and I certainly never would have thought that God would say something so... practical... so normal. Honestly, the thought almost seemed like worldly heresy to me at first that God would tell me to have more excitement in my life.

As I contemplated this revelation, I realized that my view of God and Christianity had been tainted – or at least one-sided. I love church and worship. Why then did I have this mindset that God was stale and boring when the Kingdom of God is righteousness, peace and joy (Ro. 14:17)? I know the scriptures teach that God sings, laughs and dances (Zeph. 3:17). Why do I have such a hard time picturing God doing any of those things that His Word says He does? Why did I picture God acting more like the cold, mathematical architect from the Matrix movies than like the author of abundant life and joy? In my mind, I was having a hard time getting past God being an old man with a white beard on a throne in the sky - an emotionless, logical, calculating entity.

While it is true that God is the most logical being in the universe, He is not a giant, stoic Mr. Spock. He is also the author of all emotion, love and laughter. While He is certainly the most just, wise and level-headed being – that doesn't negate His less stoic character traits. He is the liveliest being in the universe as well. Jesus was fun. The Bible tells us that He had more life and joy in Him than all of His contemporaries (Ps. 45:7, Heb. 1:9). No wonder He was a friend of sinners... people love to be around joyful people who are full of life. And didn't Jesus say that if you have seen Him, you've seen the Father – in Him the fullness of God dwells (Jn. 14:9, Col. 2:9)? If Jesus was joyful and full of life, how can the Father be any different?

As I thought about how full of life God is and how exciting the Christian life should be, but then considered how stale and bland I had felt the day before, I suddenly knew why I allowed myself to watch that TV show. My soul was starving for excitement. That isn't sin. We have a basic human need for excitement. The problem was that I didn't have the understanding that God was exciting enough to meet my needs for excitement and so the sensuality of the TV show promised to fill that void, the need for excitement. God wanted to fill my soul's void for excitement with a real life that isn't based in the world.

How many other soul needs does God want to fill but can't because His character is misrepresented in our minds? When we think about porn, it sounds fun. When we think of religion and God, it sounds boring. We need a faith shift to see things for how they really are. God wants you to come fully alive and to live an abundant life! **Only when we begin to trust God to fill ALL our needs will we stop mistaking the devil's bondage for freedom.**

FILLING ALL IN ALL

Some people may think back to high school psychology class and remember studying a big pyramid diagram called Abraham Maslow's Hierarchy of Needs. While it isn't doctrine, his idea was that every human has basic needs: biological needs, security needs, love and belongingness, self-esteem and emotional needs and a need for purpose. Without these things being full, a person will constantly be searching for something to fill those needs.

Christian evangelists will often talk about the "God shaped hole" – the place in your heart that only God can fill. The "God hole" is actually a lot bigger than you may realize. God's Word says that He actually wants to be your "All in all" – the source of all life in all areas of life (1 Cor. 15:28, Eph. 1:23). Paul prays that we would *"know the love of Christ which passes knowledge; that you may be filled with all the fullness of God (Eph. 3:19)."* Furthermore, God tells us that He gives us ALL things that pertain to life (2 Pet. 1:3). The word "life" in that passage is "zoe" in the Greek. Strong's Bible dictionary defines it as "the absolute fullness of life - life as God Himself has - both essential and ethical; the state of possessing vitality." God wants to give us ALL things that pertain to being fully alive – enjoying Him and our life to the fullest.

Do you get the impression that God wants better for than to simply give us a ticket to Heaven? God wants to be more for you than a Sunday Savior. He wants to be a big part of our lives and to be the source for every one of our needs – not just our spiritual needs. *"And my God shall supply all your need according to His riches in glory by Christ Jesus (Php. 4:19)."*

OK, now understand the implications of this concept. We run to lust and pornography, not just because we have a physical need. Truly we don't "need" sex. In fact, physical "need" is the LEAST of our struggles. Rather, we embrace lust because we have agreed with the lies of the enemy – and we agreed with those lies because they are linked to a need the devil convinced you God can't fill or to a wound he convinced you that God won't heal. **In short, lust fills a void that we have not LEARNED to let God fill.** Sometimes it is just because we don't understand God's ways. Sometimes wounds and needs are linked. Not having basic needs met, especially by a parent or guardian can leave a devastating wound in the soul. We will address heart wounds that keep us from trusting God in later chapters. But there are also legitimate, daily soul needs - needs that are core to being human and are part of our design. These needs in our hearts HAVE to be filled; and until we learn to identify them and let the life of God fill those areas, He has not become "all in all" for us. God understands our needs better than we do. He alone can give us the "life abundant" that Jesus promises.

SPOT THE COUNTERFEIT

The reason we run to porn over and over is because it promises to fill needs in our hearts that haven't been met. Only God can supply all your needs! To believe anything otherwise is to call God's Word a lie. Pornography and the way it makes us feel is just a cheap counterfeit that never truly fills the love need and subsequent heart needs that aren't being met in God. We all need to feel loved, experience intimacy, behold beauty, live with passion and purpose and the list goes on and on.

As I've explained, one such need in my heart that I was looking to fill was the need for excitement or stimulation. Did you know that God wants to be your solution for that need also as He fills your all-in-all? But often we don't think of God or "churchy" things being exciting. I remember a popular song whose chorus sings, "Only the good die young." The singer is singing to a young girl named Virginia and trying to get her to go out and enjoy the party life with him. He tells her that being good is so boring that it is like dying young. Isn't that the way so many people view Christian acts? So the devil lies and says, "I've got the life. Sensuality will fill your void for excitement." And he makes us trade the life of God for his lies and actually steals our life away piece-by-piece.

There are so many different ways that we can truly find life, passion and zeal in God. Have you ever been to a crusade or a Christian festival that was a weekend full of preaching, vibrant worship and fellowship? Don't you come away from that exhilarated? Afterward, you are usually so fired up about God that you can't wait to share what He did with all your family and friends. Often it takes weeks to "come down" from that experience. Then once life gets boring again and your walk mundane, you slip back into sin and wonder what happened to your zeal. You just didn't tend the fire and excitement of the soul to keep those embers burning. Your need for vigor and life drove you back to the counterfeit.

Do you remember what it feels like when God puts someone in your path and you witness to them or see something that you say touch them deeply and change their life? Don't you feel most alive when that happens? What about when God reveals something to you or gives you a breakthrough in your life or relationship with Him? There is nothing like that in the world that compares. How do you feel when you have seen something happen that you know could only be attributed to God, a modern day miracle? Isn't it amazing to feel you are in the center of God's will? THAT IS WHAT WE ARE DESIGNED FOR!

As wonderful as all those things are, how frequently do they happen in your day-to-day life? Christians are bored. And we wonder why we keep running to the world for life and excitement. Because we aren't living Christian lives to the full, we are shot full of holes. The devil's counterfeits will never give a satisfying solution to the needs of the soul. But neither will one experience with God give a life-long dose of life. Soul needs are like eating. You can't think about the meal you ate a week ago and wonder why you are hungry today. You must feed the need of the soul regularly or you will be tempted to go get your life from somewhere else.

Spiritual pursuits are important, but allowing God to fill the needs in your heart and desires in your soul doesn't have to be over-spiritualized either.

It doesn't mean that you have to fill your schedule with Church activities. Your relationship with God should be the first priority in building a vibrant, healthy soul. But as you spend time with God, He will show you the things that are in your heart and what you are called to do and even simply what you enjoy. Sometimes the most "spiritual" thing you can do is something you love to do. I love martial arts. Some of the most "spiritual" experiences I've had are on the mat, pitting my skills against an opponent. This feeds a part of my soul that God put there and that no amount of church can fill.

I have a friend with an amazing singing voice - truly a gift from God. He loves to go to karaoke nights at the local bar. One night he invited me to go with him. Afterward, he confided that he feels guilty for going to a bar and singing secular songs. He wasn't out getting drunk or skirt-chasing - he truly just loved to sing. However, he had such a tainted view of this gift God gave him that he assumed that it could only be pleasing to God if he sang in church. I was shocked. God doesn't care where a bird sings - He is glorified when it uses the gift of song that He gave to it. If you have a gift, yes, use it for God and bear fruit for the Kingdom and store up treasure in Heaven - but God also gives us gifts for our own enjoyment - otherwise He wouldn't wire our souls to enjoy our gifts. When an earthly father buys a bicycle for his child, he wants to hear them squeal with delight and see them ride it everywhere. If the child doesn't enjoy the bike or thinks they can only ride it to church down the street, they dishonor the father's gift.

One of the reasons that our culture generally doesn't think of spiritual things as being exciting or fun is because we've so segregated church from our passions and assumed that a calling is limited to any of the few ministries offered by our local church. Many have been forced into that mold and think that spirituality is boring because they don't love ushering, children's ministry, greeting, etc.

However, while those are things that churches emphasize, I'm sorry to say, Jesus never commanded us to do those things. The great commission tells us to "go into all the world…" Yes, meet the needs in your local church, but for MOST of us, that is not where we will find the greatest joy and our calling. When we go into all the world and start doing the things we are passionate about, we meet people with similar passions. These heart-connected friendships go deep and should almost always lead to evangelistic opportunity in the most natural, genuine way possible. So God's Kingdom can even come into "secular" areas when we are following our passions. There are people in the world that will NEVER respond to classical evangelism, never come to church or be saved unless they make a true connection with people of like passions. We need to stop leaving God at church and realize that the things that make our soul soar are part of our "spirituality" even if they aren't classically spiritual. You WILL glorify God if you cultivate the diverse passions He put in you; but NOT if you have this idea that this has to be separate from your "spiritual life." When we understand that our passions are part of our calling and bring God into them, not only will we excel greatly, but God will show us how to use these to advance the Kingdom. The awesome byproduct is that you will feel ALIVE and love your life!

AA members will tell you that they are "clean" when they aren't drinking. They'll tell you they are "clean and sober" when they are making healthy changes that build a happy, sustainable future. As you come out of this, it is important to live with passion and purpose to enjoy lasting freedom. Definitely serve in your local church. Some people do find their calling there. But if you still feel as though there is something missing in your heart - if you still have a burden to do something outside your church, pray and see what the Lord may have you do that no other person is called to. Most of the great men of faith we read about in the Bible had a relationship with God that was foremost in their life, but that fueled a calling that was far removed from synagogue life.

God is looking for passionate Christians to influence every area of society: religion, politics, business, the arts, the media, etc. If you have a passion for something, you usually don't have to look far beyond that to find your life's calling. We don't have to get so Heavenly-minded that we are no earthly good. God knows the things that our hearts need. Let Him minister to your heart by revealing them. Then live!

OTHER NEEDS WITH COUNTERFEITS

Excitement and passion are not the only needs of the soul where we look to pornography as a satanic substitute. We already discussed the human need to behold and enjoy beauty earlier in the book. Pornography becomes an idol and a spiritual counterfeit for the person who isn't allowing his heart to stand in awe of our magnificent and beautiful King of Majesty.

LOVE AND WORTH:

I think the greatest catalyst of sexual concupiscence, carnal fulfillment of yearnings, is the basic need to feel loved, valued and accepted. I have noticed the times in my life when my self-esteem is the lowest are also the times when I have the greatest urges to go look at porn.

A sad story a friend of mine told me is when he was addicted to drugs, he'd often call the same prostitute every week. She'd come and they'd talk about all kinds of things like running off together, etc. One day he asked her if she would run away with him and he realized that she had been saying all those things as "part of the act." In his mind she was giving love and worth... but her love was only worth what he was paying. Porn gives the same promise to a lot of men.

Also, pornography is often an outlet that allows you to project the way you feel onto these people you watch. If you feel worthless, you can project that onto these sex objects. If you are feeling unloved and taken for granted, you can take what you need from them. But as God fills the love needs of the heart, it gets more difficult to treat someone as a worthless object because you have worth in yourself. You will see others in the light of how you see God seeing you.

We don't think in these terms when we are looking at porn, but these emotions are as deep as the cries of our heart. Knowing WHY you are driven to look at porn is as important as knowing the reasons you want to quit. These counterfeit fulfillments are revealed as we meditate on them with God.

INTIMACY:

Intimacy and acceptance are other big counterfeits that the devil likes to offer us. It is a basic human need to be FULLY known and yet accepted. Marriage reflects this intimacy that God designed to exist between Him and us. I know that I've struggled with body image and weight issues since childhood. So for years in my marriage, I felt self-conscious during intimate times with my wife. For that reason I was guarded and not fully free to allow her to enjoy me to the full.

Pornography gives an illusion of intimacy because your fantasies don't ever judge or reject you. They are always ready to meet your needs. Once I chose to take the thoughts of shame captive with my wife, I started to enjoy our intimacy far more and the bond that pornography had with my heart became evident a as disgusting replacement for the real intimacy I was now experiencing in real life.

But the MOST amazing intimacy you can ever have is with the Maker who knows EVERYTHING about you, knows ALL your faults, and still has an incomprehensible love for you. This level of intimacy is life-changing and it is clear that God wants to be your all-in-all in this area. If you lack true intimacy in your marriage or you are single, you may have found a counterfeit in porn that will need to be replaced in the love and fellowship of God.

COMFORT:

Comfort is another need that pornography can fill as a counterfeit. People use the phrase, "he just needs some stroking" when they are referring to a person who is agitated and needs something to comfort and calm him. Many people get massages or back rubs to relieve stress. Others take hot baths. Some like a stiff drink. Porn addicts look at porn to find release and forget their problems.

Humans need comfort. You don't need to repent of that need. But the real issue is from whence you receive your comfort. Isn't the Holy Spirit called the Comforter? Don't you think that maybe God wanted to give you a comforter because He knows that we have a basic human need for comfort? He has given us ALL things that pertain to life.

SECURITY:

During a particularly tough stretch of business, I found myself struggling more than ever with pornography. But as I took notice of my emotions, I realized my struggle was daily precipitated with feelings of fear. I was afraid because business wasn't good and I didn't know what I was supposed to be doing to fix it. I was unable to control my circumstances, so I was running to something that I could control – or use to control my fears. When I was looking at porn, I wasn't afraid any longer.

There is no real security in life other than God. The most common command that is given throughout the Bible is, "Do not fear." And most of the time, the promise that goes along with that command is, "I AM with you." God doesn't want us to feel like we're ever without Him. Even if He chastens us, the Bible says it is out of love to bring us back into blessing. He doesn't forsake us through the rough times. He has promised that He will never leave you or forsake you (Heb. 13:5). He cares about what we are going through. He says that He is afflicted when we are afflicted (Isa. 63:9). He saves our tears and keeps a written record of our hurts (Ps. 56:8). His word gives countless promises about His provision and care for us. Why then do we run to our vices for strength when we are in need of security? Why do we build our homes on sinking sand instead of the Rock of Ages? This is another counterfeit.

IDENTIFYING YOUR COUNTERFEITS

I suppose the list of basic human needs and the way that pornography attempts to fill those voids could be endless and as diverse as any man's experience. In reality, nearly all sin stems from a demonic offer that causes us to place our faith in something other than God to meet our needs. We must learn to identify the things in our hearts that lead us to sin. That means taking responsibility for our own actions and failures.

So ask yourself the question, "For what needs are you trusting in things other than God for your provision?" Every time you feel tempted, ask God to reveal what is causing your temptation. What is causing you to believe in the enemy's provision in this area of your life? What are you hoping this self-gratification will do for you?

As you contemplate this, don't fall into the trap of thinking that sex is a "need." Sexual desire in the flesh isn't an actual NEED as much as it is a want. We hear a lot of buzz about a "man's needs" and I don't think that helps us when we begin to believe the lie that a man can't live without regular ejaculations. Yes, I'm a man and I know what it is like to be aroused and feel that sexual pressure in your loins. However, there are many men who prove that you can go without completely. I've known single men who haven't masturbated for years... and they don't die. The body has the ability to compensate when sexual release doesn't take place for a long time. So from a medical standpoint, we don't NEED to ejaculate. Therefore, we'll keep this as a discussion about the needs of the soul. Needs of the soul must be filled with SOMETHING or else the emptiness in that area will grow. These are the needs that God really can fill and become your All-in-all.

In what areas do you have a hard time actually believing that God can really become your all-in-all? Even as I'm writing this, I'm still struggling to believe that God can be and desires to be my source of primary excitement in life. He is going to have to heal my heart of the lies that tell me that Kingdom life is a drag. I'll need to remind myself of how it feels to be in the center of His will and set up my life in ministry and activities that put me in the path of divine encounters.

Some of you may not struggle with this area of lacking excitement. Most likely, however, there are **many** areas of the heart where you have unmet needs that contribute to the stronghold of pornography. You will need to learn to discern when it is a need of the soul causing your temptation.

~ Mighty Man Training and Application ~

This chapter has been about needs of the soul. Soul needs are essential to deal with, but are not the only cause of temptation. Remember back to what we've learned about discerning the nature of your temptations: Fleshly, spiritual or soul (emotional and mental). Temptations take place on all levels of your being. So here's a quick recap before we get into the soul needs this chapter addresses.

1. Remember its lessons about how to deal with a temptation in the flesh.

2. Spiritual Temptations usually begin as satanic options that promise to fulfill certain needs of the soul we talked about in this chapter and they escalate into perversion. Perverse temptations almost always indicate a need to enter into spiritual warfare. A soul need, however can usually be reconciled by simply breaking agreement with the false belief and gaining understanding of a godly solution. This is because a spiritual component doesn't enter in until we have made a choice (subconsciously) to fill this soul need with an ungodly solution. Spiritual warfare, the direct, prayerful opposition to activities in the spiritual realms can usually be limited to the following:

   a. A repetitive, harassing thought that you can't shake. Usually indicates something is present and trying to

put that thought there. Ask God to cast it away and begin
to meditate on godly things.

   b. Perverse thoughts should always be cast down. You should
tell their source to leave in Jesus' name and ask God to heal
your heart of those agreements.

   c. Overt attacks of lust from individuals using their bodies
as an object of lust (either in person or in media). These
are the darts of the enemy and should be treated as spiritual
attacks. Remember Chapter 16, "Get Violent".

3. Soul temptations can be segmented into the following categories:

   a. Soul ties – spiritual bonds between us and women with whom
we've had experiences.

   b. Broken heart needs – these we'll deal with later. These are
areas where we need spiritual healing whereas the issues
we've been talking about in this chapter can be resolved with
godly understanding.

   c. Legitimate soul needs. These have been the topic of this
chapter and are basic human needs that MUST be met in
one way or another.

For these areas where you have need, again, you must learn what your "hot
buttons" are. You may not have a need for excitement causing you to sin, but
you may struggle with feelings of loneliness or a need to behold beauty, etc.

1. Take a moment and ask God to help bring to mind emotions that
you feel regularly.
2. Now think if it is possible that pornography seems to offer a solution or
escape from these emotions.
3. If so, ask God to forgive you for trusting in something other than
Him for your needs.
4. Ask Him to become your All-in-all in this area of life.
5. If it is hard to believe that He actually can do this, try getting a
concordance or do an online search at a site like
www.biblegateway.com and read all the verses about this area of
your soul's need. You will very likely find many verses in which
God gives promises that He will fill these areas.
6. Take these scriptures and memorize them. Recite them daily. Ask

God to make them come to pass in your heart and give you the faith that He really is sufficient to meet ALL your needs.

7. For practical things like a need for excitement or liveliness, think how you can change your activities to be stimulated with godly solutions so that you won't trust in carnal ones.

Now take some time to plan how you can get your needs met. Your relationship with God must come first. What do you have to change to give yourself time to be alone with the Father?

Think about your passions and calling. What is something you have always wanted to do? This can be a hobby, a ministry or any objective close to your heart. What will it take to make time for that in your life? If it isn't practical now, what steps can you start taking to make it possible in the future? Moving forward in life is one of the healthiest things you can do.

CHAPTER 20

Coping Mechanisms
of the Heart

After a Bible study one night, a young man came to me and
mentioned that he was struggling - but not with lust - something worse. I got
a friend and we all went to pray. We quickly learned his struggle was more
serious than we thought. He was fighting suicidal thoughts nearly every day –
and every night he'd go into his closet and cry and think about putting a gun
in his mouth. As he was talking and we were praying, God gave us big
revelation for this big problem. He had a coping mechanism called desperation
in his heart. God even gave some insight into his family dynamic. As a child,
his best way to get attention was when he needed something. His family was
typically cold, emotionally absent and self-absorbed. But when he was sick or
in a critical situation, he'd get love and attention. He learned that to receive
love, he needed to be in a desperate state. Later in life, this coping mechanism
resurfaced in his interaction with God. He allowed himself to get to a desperate
place in order to get more of God's attention. By the grace of God, he was set
free that very night. He called me the next day with a report that for the first
time in months, he went to bed and wasn't fighting suicidal thoughts. Weeks
and years later, he was still free from this. His problem, as you see, was not
suicidal thoughts or tendencies. They were the SYMPTOM of a deeper
problem. They were the outflow of a coping mechanism hidden deep within

his heart. He wasn't responding to a need like we just read about, he was responding to a wound in the heart.

I had a different coping mechanism take root in my heart at a young age. I grew up with a strain in my relationship with my father. I felt as though I never had his approval. All the hobbies I had were the wrong hobbies. I wasn't allowed to go out for the sports that I wanted to play because he was sure I would fail at them. All my passions and career interests were the wrong career interests. Nothing was ever right or good enough for him. Rebellion became my coping mechanism. Rebellion is a hard shell we wear that says, I don't care about what you think or your laws - I'm better than all of that and you can't hurt me anymore. I saw this coping mechanism surface later in life as we will see.

People spend a lot of time treating symptoms instead of diseases. When we have a headache, it is easy to take an aspirin and forget about the headache. But when the headaches persist, we usually begin to look for the real cause and cure the problem at the root. We tend to do the same thing with spiritual diseases. When we see an alcoholic, we go to task to treat the alcoholism and overlook the reasons why that person has a predisposition to that addiction. Ten-step programs and lifelong accountability with a sponsor may help that person curb their behavior, but even the program will tell the person that they "never beat their habit" – they will always have a problem. They just learn to deal with the problem. I'm sorry, but there's more.

Pornography is a similar case study. When it becomes an issue, we go to war with it thinking that pornography is the issue. There are countless men and ministries who get up and talk about their "freedom" and how they "beat" their addiction. But when you look at what victory means to them, it is nothing more than sin management for life. Pornography addiction like any other addiction is a symptom of greater issues in play - issues of the heart.

We self-medicate our wounds with pornography or lustful addictions. They mask the pain. In the last chapter we saw how NEEDS of the heart can be filled with pornography. Now we see that WOUNDS of the heart also use pornography as their bandage - their coping mechanism.

Pornography is the outflow of a greater need. Sometimes the symptom of pornographic addiction can be treated by changing our attitudes and responses toward differing stimuli as we've already done in this book. But in many cases, we can fight and fight and fight, but something in our hearts keeps pulling us back. This is because fighting battles doesn't bring healing of the heart. Jesus came to heal the broken hearted. This is where real freedom comes from. Until the heart is healed, you can still have a predisposition to the habit. That doesn't give us a license to sin. That fact of our dependency should just wake us up to how badly we truly need God's grace to come out of this.

This is important: the degree to which a man struggles with lustful addictions is directly proportional to the size of the wound in his heart. If the wound is profound, the degree to which the soul will scream for a salve will be profound. This is good news actually. You don't have a lust problem so much as an area of the heart that God wants to heal, is able to heal and for which Christ has already purchased the healing. If you will stop putting on the band-aid, stop gratifying lust, the wound and the lies that empower lust will come screaming to the surface. That is the perfect place to be for a healing.

UNDERSTANDING COPING MECHANISMS

In one of my other books, I spend a great deal of time explaining the spiritual dynamic between insecurity, pride and the control mechanisms they create. In short, everyone has areas of insecurity in their heart – sometimes conscious, other times unconscious. An insecurity is basically a fear that doesn't have its resolve in God.

Money and financial security are common problems that illustrate the point. Many people worry about their finances. What is worry? Worry is fear. Why do we fear? We fear because we don't trust that God will provide or that we'll have to sacrifice something that we really want. The natural, human response to this is to introduce a coping mechanism into our lives that helps us manage our fears.

Most of the time, these "coping mechanisms" are agreements with demonic thoughts that turn into strongholds over time. For example, if a person fears they won't have enough money, they often become stingy with people and God. Tithes and offerings stop. Generosity with people, charities and relationships stop. Poverty creates this anti-biblical "control mode." Ironically, most of the things people do when they worry about money are the very opposite actions of what the Bible teaches about how to gain wealth. You never once find God give lessons about waiting to feel secure before you become generous. However, as people agree with the lies over time, a miserly spirit takes root in their life and corrupts them with a poverty mentality that will perpetuate the cycle of lack. God needs to heal the fears, treat the root that makes a person small. He then gives abundance in the heart through which supernatural generosity and abundant prosperity flows.

Here's another common example from relationships. A person experiences a broken heart from a failed relationship. Their response is to never fully open themselves up again so they don't get hurt like they did. The irony is that most coping mechanisms wall us off to the very attitude that is needed to overcome the insecurity and fear. God can only heal what we fully entrust Him with and let go of. I believe that most of us have coping mechanisms in place that govern our actions in regard to lust and pornography.

IDENTIFYING HEART WOUNDS

I think there is probably seldom an area for any man that carries more importance than his sexual desires. Most men would rather lose an arm or a leg than their "manhood." This is also something that carries huge potential for insecurities and inadequacies. Therefore, there are probably few other areas of our lives so potentially fertile for coping mechanisms lurking in the deep regions of our hearts.

Think about the following topics. How many men have elevated sex to a "need" and fear that it won't be fulfilled? How many men even fear that their sexual desires won't be fulfilled? As they fail to reconcile these fears in God, the devil builds wounds in the soul. Many times, the wounds we carry in the soul actually keep us from receiving the real thing that we need. This is how the devil likes to perpetuate damaging cyclical thinking. Men "hold their wives hostage" to meet their needs and desires, which actually steals the true intimacy they require to break the cycle.

How many men may feel insecurity about their appearance? How many men have wounds regarding their masculinity or the perception of their own strength, capability or confidence? As we meditate on any fears and insecurities, the enemy magnifies them and creates wounds surrounding false belief or any area of emotional pain that isn't reconciled in Christ. Do you see the difference between these issues and the needs discussed in the previous chapter? We have a NEED for love, but fear and insecurity are WOUNDS that arise when needs aren't met or when we believe the devil's lies that we won't be loved or accepted.

I believe that for most of us reading this book, there is more at work than simple animal urges causing us to be porn addicts. I believe that we have heart wounds and insecurities (possibly more than a single one) that are causing us to run back to sin over and over again.

Let's role play for a moment:

What if a man has a secret fear (conscious or unconscious) that his sexual desires can't be met in a godly way with his wife? Sexuality for a man is often the primary way he receives love. Therefore, he is in a situation where in his heart he doesn't believe that he will ever be loved the way he believes he needs to be. Since these fears probably aren't verbalized and take place subconsciously, a subconscious coping mechanism is formed. The devil says, "You can't trust God. God doesn't really care about your needs. Nobody will ever love you the way you need to be loved." So this man purposes in his heart that he will fulfill his own perceived needs because God can't or won't. He has put a wall up against God and made a trust alliance with a devil who promises to meet his needs.

Here is another scenario. What about a man who feels insecure about his body. In his heart he fears that no woman could really love him the way he is. He's sure he can't really please a woman. Even with his wife he is reserved. She says she loves him, but in his heart he thinks she really wishes he was another way – maybe 20 pounds lighter – maybe a few inches longer, etc., so when he is intimate, he is not free. His passions and desires go unrequited and his real sex life is shrouded in shame and embarrassment. Probably the way he feels about his body reflects a deep heart issue with God and he doesn't even feel free or know how to run to God for healing from these heart wounds and fears. But the devil comes along with a solution. "The women in pornography don't judge you. They want you." You can express all your passions with none of the shame there. And so he forms a coping mechanism because porn makes him feel alive and passionate.

What about the man who was hurt in relationships or by a father or someone who was supposed to love him? He decided to compartmentalize that fear and frustration and hurt. He doesn't know how to let Jesus come heal this wound, so it goes on for years. But when he looks at porn, he has an outlet for this. He can despise the women he is looking at. He can revile them and use them and abuse them. He can do all of this and use pornography as a coping mechanism for the fact that he really feels this way about himself. In his heart, there is a part of him that feels used, cast aside, worthless, angry – so he projects this onto objects of lust.

How many possible scenarios are there for the men out there reading this? The heart wounds must be healed if we are going to be free. We can fight and fight and fight, but if the heart isn't healed, we will still have a scenario set up in our heart for which porn seems to be the answer. I hope I touch on your issue in this chapter, but it would be impossible to cover them all. In the end, no matter what your insecurity and heart issue, God has to be the one to reveal it. And if He reveals it, He'll heal it.

Revelation from God is the best and only real way to identify the wounds in the soul. However, there is a trick that often works to identify your wounded areas: using your fantasies as an indicator. Have you ever fasted for any length of time? Anyone who has done serious fasting begins to fantasize about food and dream about food (I even hallucinated that I was eating a plate of buffalo wings once on an extended fast). Dreams and fantasies are the subconscious mind's way of helping us process the wounds and needs and questions we have. It is important to pay attention to your dreams and regularly ask God for wisdom. I've had many real breakthroughs in my life just from the Biblically based practice of asking God to bless my dreams and then reveal their meaning.

Sexual dreams and fantasies are a similar window into the subconscious soul. For many, if not most men, your sexual fantasies are directly linked to your wounds. I first realized this as a man was sharing his story and sexual struggles. He had two primary fantasies. He wanted to be raped and also to be pampered like a baby. This type of fantasy was totally foreign to me. I couldn't relate to this AT ALL. But as I tried to relate, I prayed, "Lord, where in the world does something like this come from?" Suddenly it clicked for me: this man's back-story was that his father was completely emotionally absent and literally hardly ever even said a word to him. He was the victim of passive abuse which birthed passive sexual fantasies in him. I realized conversely that my abuses were forms of active, aggressive abuse, so my fantasies were active and aggressive. As I've heard countless stories over the years, I've noticed this pattern emerge between active and passive abuse leading to active or passive sexual dysfunction and fantasy.

Active abuse can be physical violence, molestation, rape, verbal abuse, control, religious abuse or any other abuse where the victim is acted upon by a dominant aggressor. Passive abuses are any form of neglect or abandonment.

They usually give rise to fantasies where the individual is being acted upon rather than acting upon someone else.

Some would ask, "Why isn't the fantasy the opposite of the form of abuse?" For example, many wonder why people who have been molested often grow up to molest others. You would think that their trauma would make them want to veer as far from that as humanly possible. As we've already addressed, however, a coping mechanism is usually a pride-based form of protection against the negative feelings. So if the person, through molestation, was made to feel small, used, sexualized and dirty, they must cope with those feelings. Those feelings are still locked in the heart, but the fantasy will pridefully cope by making them feel powerful and in control. They will project the deeper emotional feelings, however, onto a sex object they can relate to. Their wound is screaming at them, but they cope with it through a prideful persona that perpetuates the cycle.

If you ask God to show you the link between your sexual fantasies and your heart wounds, you just may be amazed and discover where this sin has its roots. Because sexual fantasy is linked to wounds, the power that you perceive lust to have over you is actually not the power of lust at all, but the power of the pain the wound has inflicted in your soul. When you are dying for a fix, going out of your mind to look at porn, that isn't the power of lust, that is your wound starting to feel again. The numbness from the last fix is wearing off and your soul is trying to find resolve again.

Your lust triggers are also very likely linked to your wound. You probably don't have to search long or hard to realize that many of the things that will trigger you to seek out lust are actually just stirring up the feelings of the wound. Because you have learned to cope through lust, you suppress the feelings of the wound when they are triggered and numb the pain. When God reveals and heals your heart wounds, it will GREATLY diminish the allure that lust has for you and nullify the power that your triggers possess.

MY COPING MECHANISM REVEALED

One afternoon, I sat at my desk and struggled. I was really having a tough time that day. It had been about a month since I had messed up, but this was a rough attack. I was suddenly aware of some thoughts that caught my attention, "It's hopeless. I'll never be free. I'll never be the kind of man

God wants me to be." Immediately after thinking these things, I had another series of thoughts that almost pushed me to the edge of falling, "I'm just going to do it. I can't win anyway."

By the grace of God, I instantly recognized these thoughts as demonic. The devil was trying to sow seeds of hopelessness, discouragement and doubt into my heart. He was playing on an old, familiar feeling from my childhood. Because I had a masculinity wound, feeling like nothing I did was ever good enough, I had a fear in my heart that was keeping me susceptible to rebellion. Do you see the pendulum swing of coping revealed? My deep-seated feelings and fears that I'd never be good enough, that I'd fail, that I was disappointing were what rebellion was masking. Do you know what I would have done through lust to cope? I'd have found some image of some woman that I could despise. The truth is that I needed to deal with my own low self-worth.

There is nothing new under the sun. Hopelessness and rebellion are kissing cousins. Look at how Israel responds to Jeremiah's word from the Lord in chapter 18:12: And they said, *"That is hopeless! So we will walk according to our own plans, and we will every one obey the dictates of his evil heart."*

Most every sin is formed in fear and codified in pride. My fear of not being good enough made me secretly believe that God would reject me and I'd never be free from my sin. That caused pride to rise up and say, "If He wants me to not sin, He'll have to PROVE that He loves me and come get me out of it. I'm going to do what I know is wrong because I can't win anyway until God loves me enough to do something about it." This is what was going on in my heart.

But the good news is that the devil had overplayed his hand. His cards were finally on the table and I could see what was happening beneath the surface in me. I had to spend time allowing God to heal the old wounds of "never good enough" in order to let go of the coping mechanism of rebellion that enabled me to choose sin over what I knew to be right. It took a long time of fighting battles before I was at the point where I could "hear" this happening in my heart. I think our battles are really a lot like birth pains for the new man that is trying to emerge.

BIRTHING BREAKTHROUGH

I want to tell you something that may shock you and even sound "unbiblical" at first: God wants to heal your heart MORE than He wants you to stop sinning. In Luke 4:18, Jesus lays out the things he came to do on earth (and the order in which He presented them is important). First is salvation but second is the healing of the heart. After that He came to set the captives free. His order is both practical and theological. You can't practically be free until the heart is healed. But more than that, He is a good Father. If you ask me, a flawed, earthly father, if I'd rather have my son behave himself or be healed in his heart or physical body, the answer isn't even a question. I want the thing that is hurting him to stop first and foremost.

The Lord cares more about your soul than He does your sin. That isn't to say that God doesn't care about sin. Sin still hurts us and others, but honestly, we give the power of sin beyond that WAY too much credit. Your sin He has paid for and dealt with. God isn't mad at you. He isn't imputing your trespasses against you any longer as the Bible teaches us in 2 Corinthians 5. I can never say this too many times or in too many ways. Sin changes NOTHING between you and God. If it were any other way, then the blood of Jesus would not be sufficient to make us acceptable and to cleanse us. Either Jesus was sufficient sacrifice to deal with sin or He wasn't.

God wants you whole. You getting over sin doesn't excite God if there isn't heart healing that goes along with it because you would still be hurting and broken. If you managed to work up the willpower to never sin again, that would be fine and good – but you'd still have the same heart wounds – and those wounds would find expression elsewhere in your life. But God loves you too much to leave you broken. I personally believe that God will limit His assistance to stop sinning for this reason UNTIL your goal becomes healing and wholeness rather than sin control. Your sin should serve as a reminder that there is a cry of the heart being bandaged in an unhealthy way. You sin isn't God's primary concern – it shouldn't be yours either. This is hard for many to accept. You've been beating yourself up over sin for so long that you don't know how to live any other way let alone imagine that God isn't doing the same thing. But if you really search your Spirit in this, you'll know it is the truth because God is love not condemnation.

You can even find a measure of freedom in this understanding. When I had the revelation of this fact and changed my pursuit from sin control to the pursuit of wholeness, I was able to step back from my soul's aching for porn and say to that lie, "I really don't want you. You truly aren't what I need. I want to be free. I want my wounds healed." The women and images that I always believed had SO much power over me suddenly seemed pathetically powerless. My wound was the thing that was aching and screaming – not my sex drive. This alone was enough to make me steer clear of porn in the weeks that it took for God to really expose and heal the heart wounds.

I have a habit of doing what I call a "worldliness fast." I'll set aside a few days and remove all worldly influences so that I can get more in tune with God. I won't watch TV or movies. I don't listen to secular music or play video games or phone apps. I won't snack or go to worldly places. I love these times. I really feel like I connect with God when I do this. I once had a friend of mine make the comment that he wouldn't like this because he hates to be alone with his thoughts. I have since talked to other people who also hate to be alone with their thoughts. They go from music to TV to phone apps to something else constantly.

You have to break yourself of these behaviors. When we are alone with our thoughts, these are the times that God speaks to us, shows us things about ourselves and has the space to work things out of our lives. Quiet time is vitally important for every believer.

While I was struggling at my desk I wasn't "doing anything." I was just praying to God, trying to change my mind and employing some of the tactics we have learned in this book. If I had put on music or something, I may have missed that subtle thought process that revealed what heart issues and coping mechanisms I had in place in my life.

Now it is your turn with God. What wounds do you have that make it easier to trust porn than God? What lies have caused fears that form coping mechanisms in your heart? Only God can answer these questions and break the cycle.

DESTROYING LIES, HEALING WOUNDS

With all the talk about the power of wounds, I think it is important to mention that it isn't your wound making you sin, but rather the lies that are attached to that wound. A wound makes you hurt, not sin. But the enemy comes along and gives you a lie of how sin will help that pain. We, through our weakness and pain, agree with that lie and the lies on top of that lie (because often there is a network of lies and agreements), and the agreement "justifies us" in our own minds and empowers us in sinning.

~ Mighty Man Training and Application ~

There is no way for God to heal a heart issue without you investing in quiet time. The next time you are struggling, try something radical. Think about the amount of time you would normally waste looking at porn. Is it 20 minutes? An hour? Two hours?

Take that time that you would have thrown away and give it to God.
- Ask Him to show you things in your heart.
- Ask Him to heal areas that have been hurt.
- Ask Him what coping mechanisms you may have and what lies and fears they are based on
- Think of any specific instances in your life that hurt you. Ask Jesus to tell you what He was trying to say to you at that time. Let Him heal your heart.
- Can you relate to any of the scenarios that we laid out in this chapter? Maybe you have more than one coping mechanism or a combination of a few. If you were to sit and write out a few scenarios what would they look like?
- When you know your heart issues and coping mechanisms, repent and renounce them. Then take the time with God for Him to show you the proper way to act, think and live. His ways are better than our ways.

BREAKING FREE

This chapter is so vital to our ultimate freedom. If we can expose the fears and lies, heal the heart issues behind them and surrender these areas to God, we can sever the ties that keep us bouncing back to sin like a yo-yo.

Chapter 21

Love One and
Hate the Other

So here was my dilemma: I was walking in freedom... but dreaming in bondage. It had been longer than I could remember that I had actually looked at porn. I was still fighting temptations, but they were much less intense than before. Even the memory of most porn and porn stars had faded away. The problem was that at least one night every week or so, I would have a dream that included pornography or some type of sexual act. It seemed that the days after the dreams, I would have stronger temptations during the day also. Even though I was having victory in my battles, I still wasn't free in my heart.

I asked God to take away the dreams. I prayed each night that He'd protect me. But there I was again. Finally one morning my answer came. I rolled out of bed and just said, "God. What's the deal? Why do these dreams keep coming?" God's answer was simple but profound: you still love your sin.

Now we who are stuck in porn hate it (at least in theory). We hate the bondage, the shame, we even hate the immorality... but... when we get honest, there is a part of us that still enjoys the sin. When I got honest with that revelation I suddenly remembered all the thoughts I've had during times of struggle - the longing to look at the porn and the inner conflict. I'd think things like, "God, I wish this sin weren't wrong." "I'd love to look at porn right now." I've even thought, "I love pornography." It was true. I agreed in theory that I hated my sin. A part of my soul, however, still loved it.

Therein lays the crux of the matter. Do you really *want* to be free? This is an important and fundamental question on so many levels because until you really want to be free, all the effort in the world probably won't bring real freedom. Until you hunger more for the love of God than for the cheap substitute, you'll go for the bigger desire in the soul.

I had a lot of good carnal motivators and a measure of the fear of the Lord that was keeping me from sinning... and I'm glad. I'd rather be in that place than stuck as a hopeless addict again. But I was still doing what was right simply because it was right and I was holding fast to the "someday" when I would be glad I followed God's ways. In my heart, I still secretly wished that I could have my cake and eat it too – I wanted to do what is right AND still go look at porn whenever I wanted.

The Book of Numbers tells a story of the Israelites in the wilderness. They had been delivered from the bondage of Egypt, but were still in the wilderness. They were in a sort of limbo. They weren't slaves any longer, but they weren't in the Promised Land either... and their souls were longing for the former things: *so the children of Israel also wept again and said: "Who will give us meat to eat? "We remember the fish which we ate freely in Egypt, the cucumbers, the melons, the leeks, the onions, and the garlic (Nu. 11:5,6)"* They actually wanted to go back to Egypt because of the cravings of their souls. Sometimes I can relate a little too much to the attitude of the Israelites.

That morning of the revelation, God also laid a passage of scripture on my heart. In 1 Samuel 16, God has to rebuke Samuel. He asks, "How long will you mourn for Saul?" You see, Saul was the king that God rejected and Samuel was to anoint a new king, David, in his place. We also have to have a king-change in our hearts. A while ago I had a dream I since came to realize was significant:

I was running from a large, black, two-headed horse. It was nearly two stories tall. Its eyes were red and glowing with rage. I ran into my house and slammed the door behind me. The horse slammed against the doors and windows but could not break in. Finally, the horse grew sad and depressed. It laid down in the back yard and looked pitiful. In the dream, I began to feel sorry for the horse and desired to let it back in. I thought it would be kind and loving toward me. The most amazing part of this dream is that I knew the horse heads had names. They were called Oholah and Oholibah. Strange names right?

The names stuck with me and I decided to look them up to see if they meant anything. I had never heard those names before, but to my shock and horror, those are the names of two sisters of harlotry in Ezekiel. God gave me a dream to teach me a spiritual reality: if you love your sin, miss your sin, pity your sin, or think in your heart it will love or serve you, you will open a door to a powerful devil that will rule over and torment you.

Jesus says, *"No one can serve two masters; either he will hate the one and love the other, or he will be loyal to one and despise the other (Mt. 6:24)."*

You cannot serve God and love sin. You have to serve God and choose to love His ways above all your sin and cravings of the heart. *"Love the Lord your God with all your heart, all your soul and all your mind and all your strength (Mk. 12:30)."* I loved the Lord. I was putting all my effort and energy into doing what was right… but I wasn't happy about it. When tempted, my attitude was more of, "I'll do what is right because I have to." Or I'll do what is right because I don't want to give the devil space. But my attitude was not, "God I love your law. I love doing what is right! I love the freedom in you!" When you are struggling, the temptation seems like freedom and the truth seems like the bondage. It was time to depose the old king of my heart and be glad about it.

Look at what David says in Psalms: *"Unless Your law had been my delight, I would then have perished in my affliction (119:2). But his DELIGHT is in the law of the Lord, And in His law he meditates day and night(1:2). I delight to do Your will, O my God, And Your law is within my heart (40:8)."*

We know (in our head) that we should be happy to do God's will and that everything He does is good. We know in our mind that sin is bondage and death. We can agree in principle that porn is damaging and despicable… but somewhere within the addict is a disconnect that keeps this truth from getting past head knowledge to something with which you agree with all your heart.

I can promise you this: this is a lesson in true freedom. When you truly love to do what is right, how will sin have any power over you? Love of sin is what keeps us running back to it. It is easy to run to what we love - hard to run from it. So how do we get to the place where it is our joy to run from sin and run to God instead of the other way around where we love to run to our sin for comfort, release, gratification and etcetera?

Getting from Head Knowledge to Heart Knowledge

It is a scary thing to come face-to-face with this dark part of our heart that really isn't willing to give up this sin. The truth for addicts is that this sin often fills a deep need that even we don't fully understand. It has been a source of release, escape, coddling and nurturing for so long that we really don't know how to envision a life without it as our go-to if the going gets tough. The good news is that heart change comes from God not from us. He isn't requiring us to be perfectly willing so much as even willing to be willing. If you are willing to be willing to let this go, then let's allow God to work through us to bring that needed heart change.

In everything, my motto is repent first. After all, if we confess our sins, God is faithful to forgive them and cleanse us from all unrighteousness (1 Jn. 1:9). When there is sin that you have walked in, it has certain rights over you. Repentance puts it (and you) under the blood of Jesus in that area so you can be set free. My first prayer that morning went something like this:

Father, help. I repent for loving my sin and hating your truth and ways. I repent for agreeing more with satan than with you. Please forgive me for this sin and by Your grace, now work in my heart to help me come right. Work in me that I should be like David and delight in your law and love to do your will. Forgive me for complaining against the truth. I now renounce all of my former ways and every demonic force associated with them. In Jesus name, Amen.

When we pray like this, we place the heart change in the only place that true heart change comes from: God's hands. You can know the truth and agree with it until you are blue in the face… but only God can heal the heart, deliver and set you free. When it comes to real freedom, there is only so much part we can play.

David poses a question in Psalm 119 and then gives us a formula for how to cleanse our heart and ways: *"How can a young man cleanse his way?… I have rejoiced in the way of Your testimonies, As much as in all riches. I will meditate on Your precepts, And contemplate Your ways. I will delight myself in Your statutes; I will not forget Your word (Ps.119:15-17)."* This Psalm gives a four-step path to heart change in God. He rejoiced in the testimonies, meditated on the truths, contemplated God's ways and finally delighted in the statutes. Let's break this passage down further.

Testimonies

The testimonies are the evidences that we see in our own and other people's lives. If you are going to love the law of the Lord, it starts with understanding the outcome. Think about the testimony that a life free from perversion and pornography has. What does that look like? Happy marriage. Staying sexually attracted to your wife. Blessing. No shame and bondage. Raising well adjusted children. The list goes on and on.

What testimonies does pornography create? Well, a couple weeks ago, another porn star suicide made the news headlines. Sad that her life ended tragically. Even more sad to think about her eternal destiny. Try Googling things like porn star suicide or porn star support groups. Many of these women and men live in constant bondage, substance abuse and low self-esteem. You don't have to look far past the glam to see the rot and decay of sin. But what about on the other side of the screen? We see testimonies of addiction in countless men. Shame. Guilt. Perversion. Escalation of the habit that either gets more and more perverse or more and more violent. Ruined callings. Disappointing marriages. And this list also goes on and on.

This is what the Bible says is the testimony of pornography: *For by means of a harlot A man is reduced to a crust of bread; And an adulteress will prey upon his precious life. Can a man take fire to his bosom, And his clothes not be burned? Can one walk on hot coals, And his feet not be seared (Pr. 6:26-28)?"* You can only play with this sin for so long before it starts to eat your life.

Think about it for a moment. What do we really love about porn when you get down to what it really stands for? Do you really love rape and violence? Do you really love using women like meat? Do you really love robbing girls of innocence? Homosexuality? Perversions? Pedophilia? Bizarre sex acts? No. Porn endorses all of these and leads people down paths to these dysfunctional lives every day. We actually hate the things porn stands for... it is just that in the stretch between Egypt and the Promised Land, sometimes meals and bondage seem better than manna and limbo. The devil is a pro at making slavery look appealing.

"The thief does not come except to steal, and to kill, and to destroy. I have come that they may have life, and that they may have it more abundantly (John 10:10)." One testimony destroys lives. God's testimonies give full lives of happiness, health and peace. I was in a wonderfully anointed worship service when this really started to sink in. I looked around the room and every face had a smile from ear to ear. God was touching and healing every heart. The Holy Spirit was bringing real joy to each person there.

God's way is the way of restoration. He loves sinners so much He died a painful death so that they could be forgiven their sins and have a life of true happiness. He takes broken people that have been victims and heals their hearts. He finds people who have had their innocence stolen and He gives purity. Every work of God is an act of love and restoration of a broken life. So what did that fact cause David to do? He meditated on the precepts, the truths learned from the testimonies.

Real and lasting happiness is what we are looking for. Look at the testimonies. Which one has a happy ending? This is a great precept or truth to start meditating on. Take a few moments. Think about your life without pornography. What will that look like? What does a truly happy life look like to you? If you can get there with porn in your life, then I don't know how you made it this far through this book. Meditate on the fact that following Him is life and giving in to your sin is death: *"I call heaven and earth as witnesses today against you, that I have set before you life and death, blessing and cursing; therefore choose life, that both you and your descendants may live (De. 30:19)."* Sin isn't a recreational activity. It is death. God's laws are not restrictions, they are life. It is hard to embrace a restriction. It is easy to embrace life. We have to develop this life and death mentality. We have to dig down deep and make the difficult decision to get this out of our lives even if there is a part that kicks and screams at the notion. The truth is that this is what we really want. We must get radical to leave no provision to gratify the part of our heart that isn't in agreement until God has His perfect work and shows us what it is about it that we really are hungry for.

Precepts and Ways:

So whereas we used to look at God's laws as restrictive or less freeing than being able to do or look at whatever we want, when we observe the end result, the testimonies of God, we realize that the end result is freedom - the opposite of what we FELT initially.

What David learned from taking the time to think about the testimonies of sin and righteousness led him to contemplate and think about God's precepts and ways. What way does God think? He thinks in terms of our happiness. His way is to show us how to be ultimately happy and truly satisfied. As we understand that God's laws are not designed to enslave us but to liberate us to happy lives, it becomes more tolerable to place our lives under His control. We give up control of our destiny and desires and place control in God's hands. This is called trust.

A team building game we played in a young singles group at church was called Trust-Fall. Someone would stand on a chair and a group of people would gather behind them. The person would have to close their eyes, fold their arms and fall backwards. The goal was to catch the person and stand them back on their feet. Many people were scared at first that the group wouldn't be able to catch them. However, once the group did it once, people would be much less afraid to do it again. It stopped being stressful and was actually fun.

We can stop fighting God when we trust Him. It was this thought process that David used to grow his love for God's laws and statutes. When you know God's ways, you will love His law. To obey the law is to choose your happiness.

Delight:

Eventually, David grew to truly delight in God's ways and laws. I love the verse where he says, "You enlarge my path under me" (Ps. 18:36). I think about the "narrow path" that leads to righteousness. It feels a bit like walking a tightrope at first. But as we realize the freedom that God's laws are actually bringing us, suddenly the narrow path begins to feel broad; the restrictions feel comfortable; we feel fully alive and fully free.

God's Word says that God works in us so that we can both **want to** and **do** His good pleasure (Php. 2:13). Every temptation you deny is the same thing as saying, "I choose to be happy and not miserable." This process of meditation and contemplation on God's ways and testimonies may take time. But as you do this, you are letting God form new agreements and you are strengthening yourself in God's ways. He can write over bad agreements of your past and write His truths and a new nature on your heart.

MEDITATION, CONTEMPLATION AND TIME

In our fast paced world, we don't often hear terms like meditation and contemplation. We don't like prolonged periods of time spent... thinking. How boring is that? We are fine taking extended periods of time to watch TV, watch sports, watch movies and any other of the myriad of amusing activities that are out there to keep us from actually thinking. Did you know that the term "amusement" comes from two other words: "a" (without) and "muse" (to think). When you put them together you get "amuse" (without-thinking). So something amusing is something designed to leave you without thinking.

Pornography is one of those amusing activities. My guess is that any one of us who have struggled with this has no problem spending countless hours "meditating" on the things we watch. So when you watch porn you are contemplating and meditating on the ways of the devil. You are agreeing and spending time reinforcing that agreement with masturbation and orgasm. Consequently, it is natural that we have come to love the ways of the devil. As Solomon writes, "as a man thinketh in his heart, so is he."

It will take some time in meditation on God's ways to retrain you in a life and death mentality when it comes to sin. I can't stress this enough: it is paramount for Christians to spend time with God. The Christian life doesn't work apart from this. To think that you can get spiritually healthy without time with God is like thinking you can eat five meals of grease, fat and lard and get physically fit and healthy. David had to meditate and contemplate the truths of God's ways and testimonies day and night. The more conscious time you take and effort you take to affirm the truth, the more it will sink in. And the deeper it goes into your heart, the easier it will be to have it ready and sharp when you are being tempted.

I began to notice a big difference even within the first twenty or thirty minutes. I was thinking about all the reasons we've already stated that porn is death. When I would be tempted, rather than think about the things I was being directly tempted with, I'd force myself to ask the question, "Where will this ultimately lead?" Porn either gets more and more violent or more and more perverse. Which of those do I love? Neither. God's ways make us more and more pure, more and more content, more and more happy, etc.

Eventually you will start to notice a difference when you begin to agree with God. When you see it for what it really is, porn is dark, wicked and perverted. You will start to wonder what you ever really enjoyed about it.

If you do this and meditate on God's testimonies, fall in love with His ways and trust His precepts, you will begin to delight to do His works. You will have begun a real process for heart change. We know that it is God who makes the change happen, but when we do what His Word says, He comes and backs it up with real freedom.

So what are you waiting for? Start David's process and see what God does in you.

~ Mighty Man Training and Application ~

Take time with God and follow David's formula:
"How can a young man cleanse his way?... I have rejoiced in the way of Your testimonies, As much as in all riches. I will meditate on Your precepts, And contemplate Your ways. I will delight myself in Your statutes; I will not forget Your word (Ps.119:15-17)."

Remember the Testimonies:
Think about the horrible things that porn glorifies. Think about the testimonies that porn creates in the lives of the actors and the people who watch it. You never hear, "I'm happier and better off because of Porn." Conversely, God's testimonies always end in victory.

Meditate on the Precepts:
Knowing the outcome of the testimonies, what precepts (lessons, truths, etc.) can we learn about God's laws? What do the testimonies teach us about God's ways (His character and thoughts)?

Delight in the Statutes (Laws):
The heart transformation that comes from these meditations can only result in loving the laws of God. Hallelujah! We are experiencing heart change.

CHAPTER 22
A Satisfied Soul

Rejoice with the wife of your youth. As a loving deer and a graceful doe, Let her breasts satisfy you at all times; And always be enraptured with her love.
- Proverbs 5:19

The words above were written by Solomon under the inspiration of the Holy Spirit. Do you find it interesting that a man who had nearly 1500 wives and concubines warns you to be satisfied with one woman? Solomon was given great wisdom – far greater than any man. But he had a hard time restraining his passions. Is it possible that Solomon learned this lesson in Proverbs the hard way? He, more than any other man who ever lived knows the rise and fall that takes place in the soul as you see a beautiful woman, desire her, have her and then realize that she didn't satisfy the gnawing dissatisfaction of the soul. Later in Proverbs he continues this theme, *"Hell and Destruction are never full; So the eyes of man are never satisfied (Pr. 27:20)."*

Solomon actually has a lot to teach us about the lies of dissatisfaction. The book of Ecclesiastes starts off, *"Meaningless, meaningless, everything is meaningless."* We read these words of lament and realize that Solomon spent his life trying to fill the void of dissatisfaction with the next thing... and the thing after that... and the girl after that – and none of them gave him what he was really looking for. He had the power and means to do anything he wanted, have sex with anyone he wanted and buy anything he wanted... Americans would call that "living the dream." He was even the envy of the rest of the world's "super rich-and-famous." Kings would travel the globe just to come and see how ludicrously wealthy he was. But at the end of it all, after he had tried everything his heart could desire, he came back to the wisdom that his heart knew all along but his flesh had a hard time accepting: anything done on earth that isn't done for God is utterly worthless, unsatisfying and a passing pleasure that will just leave you empty at the end.

Not much in society or people's hearts has changed since his time. We are still driven to think that worldly things can satiate our souls. When I was in advertising school, one of the rules of advertising that we learned is that a "successful" ad should 1) get someone's attention, 2) cause dissatisfaction, and 3) offer a solution to their newfound unhappiness. We were literally taught to make people unhappy and dissatisfied if we wanted to become a success in the marketing world. Society thrives on this idea: if we see it, we want it.

Consequently, humans buy into the lie that our unhappiness and fleshly longings have a solution outside of God. We are always waiting for the next big breakthrough or the next thing we believe can make us really happy. And as we gulp down this illusion over and over, we choke out our enjoyment of the good things that we already do have. We can't fully enjoy our house because it isn't our "dream" home. We don't enjoy our car because it isn't that car. And women... don't get me started. How could we *ever* be *totally* satisfied with just one when everywhere we turn there are beautiful women splashed across some piece of advertising carrying an unspoken promise, "I'm what you really want... I'm the one that will make you happy."

So we choose not individual temptations per se, we choose an ongoing lifestyle that agrees with the lie of dissatisfaction. Thus we choose not to be satisfied with our current options (whether married or single). On a subconscious level, we don't want to be satisfied with just one woman or our wife... at least not satisfied enough to avoid being enticed by the cornucopia of possibilities that we find in porn and lust.

God didn't create you to have anything and everything your heart desires. Freedom isn't the ability to do whatever you want – freedom is the ability to make good choices that will lead to ultimate happiness. Adam and Eve were the two most free humans that ever lived. The entire earth was theirs and they walked and talked openly with God. But even they couldn't do anything they wanted. God gave them one tree that they could not eat from. They needed to trust God and stay satisfied with their options.

The devil used a combination of discrediting God and also creating seeds of dissatisfaction with them. The message was "God is holding out on you. You'll be like God – better off and wiser if you sin. Trust me. Don't trust God." When Eve saw the fruit looked tasty and received those seeds of dissatisfaction, the combination of all the factors was enough to cause her to sin. Not much has changed since then. The devil still tries to discredit God, cause dissatisfaction and get us to eat "forbidden fruit."

IDENTIFYING THE HEART OF DISSATISFACTION

The voice of dissatisfaction is more subtle than the violently intense cravings of the flesh that keep you reeling as you first start to break ties with lust and pornography. It was only after walking in victory over my battles for a while that I even began to notice this chipping away at me. The reality is that it was there all along helping to fuel the lustful actions. I had learned the lessons to subdue the intense fights - this was a lesson to destroy a root issue.

I remember one of the first times I realized the power of this was while watching a movie that had a scene that had some women dancing seductively. There was no nudity or sex, but it was provocative. I remember thinking that I wanted to watch it, but knew I shouldn't. I didn't actually watch the scene, but as I looked away I remember thinking, "Can I really do this for the rest of my life?? Will I never again be able to look at enticing women? How can I live and never allow myself to look at another woman other than my wife? Think of all I'll be missing." Though I had never realized it before, these subtle thoughts had been in my heart all along causing me to feel the sting of dissatisfaction every time a new temptation presented itself.

I saw dissatisfaction entering into my heart in other ways also. I found myself thinking about certain women I had seen in porn that had really amazing and unique features. I caught myself one afternoon thinking, "Wow. If only my wife had this or that or..." Why was I thinking those thoughts? My wife is actually very beautiful. But that isn't the point. Dissatisfaction tells you that you need more, different and better. Even though I enjoy my wife immensely, I hadn't chosen to be FULLY satisfied with her; therefore the door was open in my heart to desire something other than what my wife could offer. So I would find myself sitting and thinking about what I didn't have or arousing curiosity about what I might be missing if I don't look for something to fill that void. Like Solomon, my flesh and a spirit of dissatisfaction gnawed at me and persuaded me to fancy the notion that somehow I really needed more than one woman for the rest of my life.

To break away from dissatisfaction you must choose satisfaction. That is why God tells us if we are married, "let her satisfy you at ALL TIMES (emphasis added)," and if we are single, be content to stay as you are (1 Cor. 7:8). It doesn't matter if you are desperately single or in a loveless marriage... we'll get to all of that. The bottom line is that if you open the door and decide to be dissatisfied, even 1500 wives like Solomon had can never make you satisfied – because you've subconsciously chosen a lifestyle that will put its trust in the next thing that comes along instead of enjoying and cultivating what you already have. In order to be truly happy in life, your heart has to let go of its options and choose to be satisfied. The thing in us that believes "the grass is always greener on the other side of the fence" has to go. God shall supply ALL my needs according to His riches and glory (Php. 4:19).

A SATISFYING COVENANT

God has given us a covenant that promises to give real satisfaction. David speaks of this saying, *"They are abundantly satisfied with the fullness of Your house, And You give them drink from the river of Your pleasures. For with You is the fountain of life; In Your light we see light (Ps. 36:8,9)."* David isn't talking about Heaven. Over and over he talks about being satisfied fully, *"Thus I will bless You **while I live;** I will lift up my hands in Your name. My soul shall be satisfied as with marrow and fatness, And my mouth shall praise You with joyful lips (Ps. 63:4,5)."*

Notice how many times David says, "I will" - not just in the Psalms above either. "I will" is a common theme of David's life. He made worship, praise, blessing, and satisfaction an act of will and not of emotion. David knew something of satisfaction that his son Solomon had to learn the hard way. You have to CHOOSE to be satisfied or you'll default to a state of dissatisfied unhappiness. The only way to be fully satisfied in an imperfect world is to choose to be satisfied. In heaven, satisfaction will be natural. On earth it is a virtue to cultivate.

Think about your life for a minute. Do you have clothes? Did you eat today? Do you have safe water to drink? Do you have a place to sleep tonight? Are you going to heaven? We really do have a lot to be thankful for. If God has already met so many of your needs and desires don't you think He also wants to see you sexually satisfied? Romans 8:32 says, *"He who did not spare His own Son, but delivered Him up for us all, how shall He not with Him also freely give us all things?"* God has already given you His MOST valuable thing. Everything else is small in comparison. Therefore we can confidently choose to be satisfied and know that we won't miss out on anything we need if we'll just trust Him. He says, *"No good thing will He withhold From those who walk uprightly (Ps. 84:11)."*

You have to choose by faith to accept that you can be more satisfied with what God gives you than with all the women you can take for yourself in lust and pornography. And so we must tear down the strongholds of the mind and heart that keep us believing more in our feelings than in the Word of God.

A fully satisfying, powerful life comes only by faith and costs only your illusions!

DISARMING THE ILLUSIONS OF DISSATISFACTION

I remember when I was growing up, a story made the news about a teenager who committed suicide. There was an interesting twist to this story. The young man killed himself, not because anything tragic happened in his life; he wasn't abused; he didn't break up with his girlfriend. You may remember the story: his Dungeons and Dragons character was killed… and he killed himself. He had spent hundreds of hours building up a fantasy reality and when it all came crashing down, his actual reality was in a tailspin also. He had allowed fantasy to dictate his reality.

We may think how foolish this young man was, but pornography and lust is a similar problem – it builds up an illusion that is an escape from real life. Think about it for a minute. What is pornography? It is a fantasy reality. If you allow your mind to go there, you can have any woman you want in any scenario you want as often as you want it. The same is true if you choose to lust after a woman you may see walking down the street. She's not for you in reality… but in our fantasies, anything can happen. What happens then when you snap out of your fantasy and find that your reality isn't quite that self-gratifying? How do you cope with the disappointment of what you have in real life? You could take the proper steps and begin to choose to be satisfied and make godly choices that may improve your reality – but most of us don't recognize the stronghold of covetous dissatisfaction and we choose to run back to our fantasy realities over and over again rather than make choices to improve our real life and relationships.

How will you learn to cherish what's in front of you if you are always looking at and desiring something else? The "wandering eye" will always take your eye off the prize. Many men who get married stay single in their hearts. They never stop "checking out" every woman they see. I was recently at the beach with my family for a trip. I noticed that I was doing this myself. Every time a pretty girl was around showing some skin, I just had to go and take a look. I didn't realize what damage I was doing to my soul. Later in that trip I was at a store and it had been so common to see pretty girls around every corner that I caught myself with a feeling of anticipation in my heart - actually looking forward to the next corner, hoping there'd be another girl to look over. When I realized what I was doing, I had to stop. God had already revealed that I should be choosing satisfaction and I finally had to stop and say, "Why do I even want to see another woman? I choose at this moment to be satisfied and stay satisfied with my wife." Instantly it was like a hundred pounds lifted off of me. I began to enjoy my day and appreciate the people in my life around me.

Choosing to be satisfied with my wife actually made the other women less enticing. That doesn't mean that you can't see a beautiful person and appreciate that they are beautiful. But there is a subtle difference with dissatisfaction. Dissatisfaction is always searching for something because it hasn't chosen to be satisfied. Proverbs says, *"A satisfied soul loathes the honeycomb, But to a hungry soul every bitter thing is sweet (v. 27:7)."* What good does it do any man to even allow himself to look at other women and "check them out" anyway? They aren't for you. They are ILLUSIONS and fantasy – like trying to grasp the wind. Fantasy CANNOT make you happy because you always have to come back to reality. Our "freedom" to look only creates illusions that make our realities less appealing.

Cast off your false illusions and begin to shape your realities!

OVERCOMING DISSATISFACTION AS A SINGLE MAN

It is hard to trust that God shall supply all your needs when you are single. I remember when I was a single man, I made the choice, "God first, dating second." When I actually met my wife, I was completely oblivious to the fact that she was interested in me. Later I found out that when she met me, her first impression was, "This guy has a calling and I want to follow him." My decision not to chase women made the right woman notice me. She saw something IN me because I was trying to cultivate my passions for God. In order to get my attention, she had to join every committee I was on and make it painfully obvious that she was interested in me before I finally caught on. How would my life be different if I had chosen to be a dissatisfied, skirt-chasing single and made finding a wife my primary goal? I would have been so preoccupied with finding MY best that I would have missed out on GOD's best for me.

Single men, listen to me. The Bible says not to chase women or give our strength to them. And Paul warns us to choose to not look for a spouse if we are single. Dissatisfaction can horribly affect God's plan for your life and calling. If you are the one doing the chasing, you have reversed God's plan. You are to be the spiritual leader of your family and if you find a wife who wants to be chased, you may have a hard time later getting her to follow you. You will have already established a relationship paradigm where you want to chase her instead of her following you. God created woman as a "helper" for Adam. When God brings people together, they will complement each other perfectly. If you aren't pursuing God's purposes, you don't need a helper.

Pornography is just an extension of this fixation on women. The eye that is always looking to wander from God is still seeking something. It is the heart's way of saying, "I don't trust God to provide for my needs. I'll go meet them on my terms until God comes through for me." Pornography then adds to this inordinate focus on women and makes you more dissatisfied with being single than you would have been if you had never spent time feeding your habit. It becomes a self-perpetuating cycle. The more time you spend dissatisfied, the more you compensate with pornography and then the more fixated and dissatisfied you become.

This cycle only prolongs God's timing to come through for you if you desire a spouse. If you cultivate the treasure inside you, you will cultivate the things a woman is really looking for: confidence, passion, purpose, vision, direction, calling... If you make following God a priority, you will become the type of man that God can add to. Then, if God doesn't put a woman in your path like He did for me, the day will come when He will give you the green light to go and find one with His blessing as He did for many men in the scriptures.

Let's get real about one other thing: premarital sex. The Bible calls it fornication. It is sin. Serious sin. The Bible teaches that NO fornicator will enter the kingdom of heaven (1 Cor. 6:9, Eph 5:5). You can't play with this one – but it is running rampant in Christian circles. A single friend of mine was on a Christian dating site and nearly every "Christian" man she met wouldn't date her because she absolutely wouldn't fool around before marriage.

A common argument I've heard is that single men aren't willing to risk having a wife who doesn't "satisfy" them. Don't go there men. You have to trust that the woman God has in store for you will learn to love you properly. That doesn't mean you may not have some obstacles to overcome, but as a rule of life, a blessed courtship will lead to a blessed marriage.

OVERCOMING MARITAL DISSATISFACTION

There are a number of stumbling blocks I have heard as I talk with married Christian men. A stumbling block is another way of making an excuse to choose dissatisfaction and sin over satisfaction with the wife God has given you. Men think things like, "My wife can't meet my sex needs." "My wife isn't sexual enough." "My wife doesn't 'do it' for me any longer." "I'd be OK with my wife if she'd lose 10 pounds or get a boob job, or..." Let's get back to basics. God doesn't want your excuses. His word stands: *Let her satisfy you at ALL TIMES.* "Let her." "Let" means, "choose to allow." Dissatisfaction is an act of choice and, if we tolerate it, we will create a self-perpetuating system. **Dissatisfaction will ALWAYS lead to more dissatisfaction.**

You have to break the cycle before you can make any headway in changing things in your marriage and sex life. You have to give your sexuality over to God completely if you want Him to be able to bless it. Often trust and satisfaction have areas of overlap. If you have a hard time trusting God, you won't be able to choose to be satisfied. (For those in truly unloving marriages, we need to go a little deeper than basic satisfaction issues. We will talk about this in additional depth later.)

Pornography always fuels the system of dissatisfaction. How do you think it is even remotely possible that you will grow in love and satisfaction for ONE woman if you are giving yourself a daily dose of 100 women? How will you learn to appreciate the nuances of your wife's beauty if you spend hours worshiping the beauty of others? What will happen when we finally do go back to our wife? We will inevitably compare her to all the others and find ourselves longing for more. That longing causes us to run back to the others and the cycle continues. Some men even allow themselves to fantasize about their porn idols while they have sex with their wife. How damaging to you and to her! I believe women feel and pick up on this dissatisfaction and it continuously erodes their self-esteem and belief that they can actually make their husband happy. Why should they even try to please their men if they can never satisfy them? As they believe in their heart that they can never satisfy a man (and they can't if a man is walking in dissatisfaction), they begin to accept the lies that there is something wrong with them and do everything imaginable to get more beautiful and stay beautiful. But all their efforts are like chasing the wind if a man won't choose to be satisfied with them. Conversely, some women give up the notion altogether that they can be beautiful and may even start to resent and despise beauty - resent and despise intimacy.

We MUST wake up to the vicious cycles this stronghold perpetuates. You can never be happy until you choose to be satisfied. It is never enough to have what you want, you have to want what you have. Pornography makes us think that we are missing something vital if we don't go and gratify its desires. It speaks a loud message into our hearts, "I refuse to be satisfied with one woman. I won't be content with what God has given me." "I will take matters into my own hands." It is time to break this cycle.

Will you fight for your fantasies or for your realities? Has God given you a wife? Be happy with the one you have. Are you single? Be happy and content until God gives you a wife. Don't lust after the women you see and covet them. They are either another man's wife already or may become one in the future. Don't covet and lust after the women in pornography. To choose to be free from pornography is a choice to be satisfied with your godly sexual options. Learn from Solomon. All the sexual options in the world won't make you happy.

Marriage is honorable among all, and the bed undefiled; but fornicators and adulterers God will judge. Let your conduct be without covetousness; be content with such things as you have. For He Himself has said, "I will never leave you nor forsake you (Heb. 13:4-5)."

~ Mighty Man Training and Application ~

What good has dissatisfaction ever done for you? Get rid of it now. Ask God to forgive you and help you to see it when it arises in your heart. Ask Him to give you satisfaction in your sexual options.

Single men, pursue God and trust His timing and provision. Worrying about finding a wife won't bring it any faster – probably the opposite. Choose to be satisfied today.

Married men, choose to be fully satisfied with your wife. No other woman has anything more to offer you than an illusion.

A NOTE ABOUT LOVELESS MARRIAGES

This is a tougher lesson for men who are in a marriage where their wife has not learned to meet their needs – and it is easy to sit back in rebellion and say, "God needs to bless me before I'll choose to be satisfied with her." I have fallen into this pit and there is no godly solution until you first break the chains of dissatisfaction. Early in my marriage, I had a friend who would talk about his sex life with his wife. He'd talk about how they have it every day; sometimes multiple times a day. He'd tell stories about how when they'd get home from work, they'd just leave their clothes at the door and spend the entire evening naked. And I'd think, "God, why can't my wife and I be like that?"

Maybe you are thinking, "I'd settle for once a week... every other week... etc." The reality is that some men really are in marriages that are loveless. I don't want to make sex out to be a need - it is not. Make no mistake about that. But if your primary love language is touch and that way of expression is foreign to your wife, you may indeed justifiably feel unloved. In my own marriage I had to communicate to my wife that I wanted her to express love through both touch and sex because that was my love language. I needed her to give me hugs, hold my hand, etc. Without that, she could be expressing love to me but it wouldn't "get in." I similarly had to learn to express love in a meaningful way to her because her "love language" was not touch - so I could touch her and physically express my love for her without her ever feeling loved. Even beyond this, I still had a desire to express myself through touch. She had to learn that if I was going to grope her randomly it was a healthy expression of my own soul whereas she had previously been tainted with a mindset that men who did that sort of thing were sleazy. Now I can express myself that way and she is free to enjoy it. These are just a few of the myriad of miscommunications of love needs that I had to work through in my own marriage. But I also struggled with feelings that my wife didn't give love or receive my love. Like anyone feeling this way, I didn't even know where to begin at first. I needed God to show me what I needed before I could begin to work on how to fix it. So take a deep breath. These types of things take time to work through and figure out.

God doesn't expect you to be satisfied with a "loveless" or failing marriage – but you will have to choose to trust and to be satisfied that God can work in your wife's heart and make her able to meet your needs. Depending on how far advanced this is in your marriage may determine the amount of grace you must receive to be satisfied with where you are today in this progression and love your wife with Christ's love as He heals both of your hearts.

The feeling that we are not being loved in a marriage is usually not true. Usually, a couple does love each other but doesn't know how to express it in a meaningful way. If we don't understand this, feelings of dissatisfaction and feeling unloved may build into resentment and a host of other destructive emotions. We have to remember that often our spouse may have her own wounds that keep her from responding in healthy ways to normal stimulus. Other times our own wounds and misunderstandings keep us from really knowing what we truly need or desire, making it impossible for the REAL needs to be met. Consequently our spouse may be constantly trying to meet our perceived needs and burning out because it is a bottomless pit. **I had to learn that I didn't need more sex, but for my wife to express love to me through sex.** When we actually started to make love - with love at its core, this filled my "love tank" in a way that sex ten times a day without this would not have.

To heal a loveless marriage, you will have to cultivate a level of trust where you are willing to break dissatisfaction and be content with your wife and your situation until God heals what's broken. A loveless marriage isn't a license to sin and stay dissatisfied. You must adopt a mindset almost as though you are a single man again and must court your wife until she is ready to change. You will be the one who must change first so that you can show her

God's love - only God's love can heal a wounded marriage. You must set the standard for selfless love in your home. You may feel as though you are the only one giving love for a while, but we are called to love our wives as Christ loves the church and gives Himself for us (Eph. 5:25).

We'll go into more detail on this in the Trust chapter to follow as this requires a slightly different approach than a man who has simply allowed dissatisfaction to taint his marital happiness and sexual fulfillment. For now, make the commitment to be satisfied with the fact that God is ready and willing to work through you. If you make this commitment, you can rest knowing that powerful forces for change are already in motion and you aren't "stuck" in a hopeless situation.

CHAPTER 23

Trust

GROWTH & CHANGE THROUGH SURRENDER

If you get a concordance and look up the word "trust," you will find two books of the Bible that have far more to say about the topic than any others: Job and Psalms. The ironic thing about this is that the writers of these books had more reasons not to trust God than nearly anyone else. David, who wrote most of the Psalms, and Job both endured a vast amount of trial, suffering and persecution – even though they didn't do anything to bring it upon themselves. Job lost his home, all his children, all his wealth and his health in a day. David was hunted, hated, and homeless for years with no evidence that things would ever get better. Through these trials they were faced with a choice: do you trust God even though it seems like He isn't doing anything to help you; or do you blame God and trust your own plans and provisions? Job's answer: *Though He slay me, yet will I trust Him (Job 13:15).*

We can all take a page out of their book. Most likely you don't trust God as much as you may think you do. Case in point: if you really believed that God would answer your prayers, how much more time do you think you'd spend praying? If you really believed that God would supply financially as His Word says He will, would you ever worry about money or try to get a bigger "security blanket" in the bank? If you really believed that God is your justifier, would you ever worry about what other people think and say about you or get agitated over situations with people? Would you bother to defend yourself over petty accusations? If you really believed that you could be happy and fully satisfied with one woman, would you ever look at pornography or lust after other women?

Trust plays a very large role in our full freedom over pornography. When we are struggling, it is trust in God's word and provision and character that forms the backbone for submission to Him. Trust in God will cause us to have no trust in our own provision for ourselves. Trust enables you to choose satisfaction with one woman for the rest of your life. Trust gives you the space to believe that God can heal a dysfunctional marriage. Trust enables you to be content as a single man until God provides a wife. Trust allows you to believe that you will be happier without sin than you would be with it. Strengthening your foundation of trust will unlock doors for peace, security, happiness, contentment and so many other virtues almost too numerous to count. It all comes down to trust.

I remember a story I heard about how a shepherd treats a sheep that strays. Sheep tend to be pack animals and their instinct is to stay together. So often a straying sheep does so because it fears the shepherd. When the shepherd retrieves the stray, he would have to break one of its legs. While the leg mends, the shepherd would carry the sheep everywhere and feed it by hand. The end result is that the sheep gets very attached to the shepherd and doesn't wander off ever again.

Isaiah tells us that all of us have gone astray like sheep. We have all strayed from the shepherd – and we need to learn that all of His ways are to bring us to greater peace, joy and trust. We must learn that ALL sin comes from misplaced trust. The Bible says it this way, *"that which is not of faith is sin (Ro. 14:23)."* Faith comes down to trust – do you trust God and His plan for you over your plans and schemes? Think about nearly any sin and ask, "What is the reason this has power for a person?" There may be many surface reasons, but ultimately they break down to basic fears; and fears are birthed from lack of trust and faith in God's unwavering commitment to you.

One unsung hero of scripture is just one little boy with a lunch. You may have heard the story of Jesus feeding the five thousand. (If not, here is the short version). Five thousand people in a crowd are hungry and Jesus tells the disciples to feed them. They complain that they can't possibly buy enough food for this crowd. Peter's brother mentions that one kid has a small lunch. And then Jesus uses that lunch and creates a miracle of provision. The miracle usually gets the emphasis of the story, but think about the boy for a moment. Out of all the people there, he's the only one who has a guaranteed meal. He had to trust that if he gave up a little he would get back a lot and become a part of something greater than himself. The same is true for you today.

Every act of trust dangles you over the precipice of "what if?". What if I give up my guaranteed lunch and have to go hungry? What if I give up being the god of my own sexual provision and have to do without for a while? That is a risk you have to take, but God can't and won't bless something that you haven't completely given over to him.

If you are married to your dream woman who meets your every sexual need and still struggle with pornography, you probably need to go back and read the chapter about satisfaction. There isn't much of a leap of faith you have to overcome to trust that God is going to meet your sexual needs. If you're single, there is a greater element of trust that you must have. But the greatest test of trust when it comes to sexual need is when a man is in a marriage that isn't meeting his needs and there is the fear that it never will. This is the scenario when a man really learns what is in his heart – if he will trust God fully or shrink back to defeat.

CULTIVATING TRUST TO BLESS YOUR MARRIAGE

Men, the responsibilities for our marital happiness are ultimately ours. You are the leader and love bringer in your family. That will always require personal sacrifice even if you have the "perfect wife." You will still have times when you need to love and meet her needs (not sexual) even when you don't feel like it. The Bible says, *"Husbands, love your wives, just as Christ also loved the church and gave Himself for her, that He might sanctify and cleanse her with the washing of water by the word, that He might present her to Himself a glorious church, not having spot or wrinkle or any such thing, but that she should be holy and without blemish. So husbands ought to love their own wives as their own bodies; he who loves his wife loves himself. For no one ever hated his own flesh, but nourishes and cherishes it, just as the Lord does the church (Eph. 5:25-29)."*

This is a tall order that has a few important lessons:
1. Love like Christ loved with a self-sacrificial love.
2. Cleanse her (forgive her for her faults).
3. Teach her and instruct her in love.

4. Get God's words for her - not the words you want her to hear, but what she NEEDS to hear. God gently washes away our junk with a word "in season." If you build her up without thinking about what you want in return, the Word will do its work and change her heart over time.

5. Eventually you'll reap the rewards.

Now there are some circumstances where you may need to get additional counsel and help (we'll talk more in the Mighty Man Training section about this). I can speak about the transforming power of trust and faith from experience. In the early days of my marriage, I was not thrilled with my sex life (It is no coincidence that I was deeply entrenched in porn at the time. Remember, porn only feeds dissatisfaction.). As I would cry out to God over this, God taught me a number of lessons. First, I had to let go of all bitterness against my wife and let each day be a new start for us. *"Husbands, love your wives and do not be bitter toward them (Col. 3:19)." Husbands, likewise, dwell with them with understanding, giving honor to the wife, as to the weaker vessel, and as being heirs together of the grace of life, that your prayers may not be hindered (1 Pet. 3:7).* If I wanted all of God's **blessing** on my marriage, I had to live by all of God's **laws** for my marriage and begin to fully trust that God wouldn't leave me high and dry.

If I was to hold my wife prisoner with dissatisfaction and bitterness, the Bible says I was hindering my prayers and working against myself. The Bible teaches us concerning prayer and forgiveness that what we *"bind on earth is bound in heaven."* Faith brings things into reality – good or bad. As we hold sins against people, we literally create spiritual patterns that give us exactly what we expect from them – more of the same. If you believe bad things about people, you will usually get exactly what you have faith for from them. This is why we must forgive our wives and begin to generate faith that we can be happy and satisfied. God's plan for you isn't a new wife or finding satisfaction in porn. God wants to equip you with the faith that has the power to bring deeply committed love into your marriage. Your wife is the "weaker vessel" (1 Pe. 3:7). She must be full of love from you before she can give love back. If she is full of love and confident that you have her best in mind as Christ does for you, she'll follow your lead.

When I made the decision to love my wife no matter if I was getting anything out of it or not, I was truly placing my sexual future in God's hands. I was saying, "God, I'm not trusting porn to meet my sexual desires any more, I trust that you'll enable my wife to do it however long that takes." I purposed to learn how to love my wife and meet her love needs even if she wasn't meeting mine. (I mentioned "love languages" in the last Application section. I recommend looking into a book called "The Five Love Languages" if you want to learn more about how to love your wife in a way that will be meaningful to her – your wife probably doesn't receive love the way you do, so we have as much to learn about them as they do about us.) As I began pouring love into my wife and our marriage without bitterness or resentment, I had my convictions tested. There were many nights when I had to cry out, "God, I'm the only one really loving in this marriage – it isn't fair." Every time I whined about this, He reminded me of how He patiently waits for me to return His love. Real love doesn't require a response. It loves for love's sake. If you "love" and ultimately expect something in return, the only person you are really loving is yourself.

It really didn't take long before my wife started being overwhelmed by the way I was showing love to her. She started making regular comments about how I was "the best husband in the world" or that "I was good at loving her." These realizations led her to ask me how she could love me better; how she could be a better wife. She wanted to be my dream woman because she was full of love. But if I had tried to "fix" her love language without her invitation, it would have made her resent the effort because I'd be requiring her to draw from a love tank that was already empty. Little by little, we have created a dream marriage. I really am married to the woman of my dreams and can say, "This works." This is available to every person who names the name of Christ and is willing to trust and choose to be satisfied with what God has given them. God will answer our prayers as long as we give Him something to work with and surrender our own desires.

Trust is the only real solution that opens the door for God to bring true and lasting joy, healing and satisfaction. This kind of trust doesn't happen overnight. So how do we develop and cultivate a heart that is fully surrendered to God? First, we must overcome areas of broken trust.

HEALING BROKEN TRUST

Everyone knows that you should trust God... after all, He's God, right? Most of you reading may have even said that you do trust God. Now, however, you may see some areas of fear and control and realize that you haven't trusted to the point of total surrender (remember all sin comes down to trust). Certainly we can all agree that if we totally trusted God for our sexual needs we would never run to pornography. So where did the break in trust and the problem come from?

I can't say for certain how doors of mistrust open for everyone, but I think there are some common emotions that many people share. The book of Job is a great book on this topic. I highly recommend that you read it. Job was a righteous man who goes through a time of great trials. In the midst of it all he asks many questions which reveal that he doesn't have mature trust in God. When God finally reveals Himself to Job – His greatness, His goodness, His justice, His sovereign wisdom, Job says something that I'll never forget, *"I have heard of You by the hearing of the ear, But now my eye sees You. Therefore I abhor myself, And repent in dust and ashes (Job 42:5,6)."* You can't **force** real trust. It takes a **revelation** of the heart to trust God despite life's many circumstances which cause us to question Him. Just hearing about Him in church or growing up in Sunday school can't make you trust God any more than it did for Job to have a head full of knowledge but no experience with God.

I grew up angry at God because I felt like He had given me a cruel life. I was filled with questions. "God, how can you let this happen?" "God, why don't you do something?" "Don't you care?" At times of trial it is natural to have these types of questions. Job asked many of these same questions about God's character, but we know from the beginning of the book of Job that it was the devil doing it and not God. God never does anything bad. He only has good thoughts toward us and gives good things (Jer. 29:11, Jas. 1:7, Lu. 11:13, etc.).

Many of us have come through and are going through tough times that cause us to struggle with questions about God's character. If we have not personally gone through these times, we have seen things happen like acts of terrorism, or violent crimes against people we know and see the anguish and feel the injustice. At these times we can be tempted to step back and say, "How can a good God not intervene?" But we are thinking like Job – trying to sort out natural questions with only "ear knowledge" of God's character and no personal revelation or understanding that no wicked thing can come from a Holy God… God can't give what He doesn't have.

If we don't resolve these questions in God's Word about His character, certain beliefs can creep into our hearts that affect the way we relate to God for the rest of our lives. I have seen many people react in different ways to broken trust. I think a lot of how you respond in your heart has to do with personality. Ultimately the control mechanisms result in the same thing: sin.

Read these scenarios below. They illustrate how some people's trust issues manifest in justifying sin. See if any of them strike a chord with you. Remember, trust issues don't often codify cognizantly, they are subconscious reactions and emotions.

- Some people respond to life scenarios that create deep hurt, questioning and broken trust in a **rebellious** way which says, "You hurt me. I'm going to do my own thing until you prove you love me." "Until you fix this in my life, I'm going to keep doing this."
- Other people get **resentful** which leads to retaliation – they sin to get even – "If you aren't going to be good to me, I won't be good to you."
- Other people don't take personal responsibility – they feel justified in sin because of what God did or didn't do for them – "This is Your problem. If God really wants me to stop, He should deliver me."
- Some people like to play the victim with sin – "I'm just under attacks too strong from the devil. If God wants me to stop, He'll have to do the work and make it easy for me."
- Some people have anger, bitterness or frustration under the surface and their sin is an escape. When you are angry with God in your heart, you can't run to Him for comfort. You must run somewhere else. These people will find that they can snap and say things to God in stressful situations or they may have the problem of taking God's name in vain when they are angry. This indicates unresolved anger.
  - Some individuals become aloof and live in denial from pain. They tell themselves, "It isn't so bad. Don't dwell on it. Don't burden anyone with your problems." They also get aloof to sin. "It really isn't a big problem. Sure, God's Word says not to, but it will be OK."

I have a friend who is single and really having a hard time with God. All he wants is to be married. He is ready to walk away from the faith, thinking that God has forsaken him. His comment to me is, "I've done the God thing." But I told him, "No you haven't." You see, when he's had girlfriends, he's had sex with them. He has an intense porn problem and won't give it up. Do you see some of the trust issues we saw above at work here? He thinks that just because he's gone to church and prayed a sinner's prayer, he's given God the space to work in this area of his life and God should make everything right before he has to take responsibility for his own sins and come right. Nothing could be further from the truth. Until you are willing to do what God says simply because you trust Him and because He's worthy of our obedience - even if it means a lifetime of sexual dissatisfaction – you have not given God a fair shot.

All of us cope with hurt and broken trust in different ways, but if you've had an area of broken trust with God, it will be very difficult to choose to totally surrender your sexual desires because you will feel as though He'll forsake you. You don't kiss a cobra, and you won't love and surrender to a God you don't trust. His Word tells us to love Him with ALL our heart and trust Him with all our heart. If love and trust both take all our heart – do you see how related they are? You can't have one without the other.

Just like Peter had to trust and step out on the water by faith to see a miracle, before God can start to answer prayers and do amazing things in your life, you have to surrender and heal the trust wounds of the heart. First comes healing, then comes breakthrough. *"Oh, how great is Your goodness, Which You have laid up for those who fear You, Which You have prepared for those who trust in You (Ps. 31:19)!" "He who trusts in the Lord, mercy shall surround him (Ps. 32:10)." "For the Lord God is a sun and shield; The Lord will give grace and glory; No good thing will He withhold From those who walk uprightly. O Lord of hosts, Blessed is the man who trusts in You (Ps. 84:11-12)!"* What shall we say to these promises? Let us choose to trust and see God do amazing things in our lives!

The Mighty Man Training will take us through some prayers that can help with areas of broken trust.

~ Mighty Man Training and Application ~

First, as always, we must repent and receive the grace for God to start to work in our lives in this area.

Father, forgive me for every area of my life where I have made light of your laws, run from your truth, and trusted in the lies of the enemy instead of the God who loves me and wants the best for me. I want to trust you with all my heart, especially in the area of sexual desire and satisfaction. Forgive me for trusting in pornography to meet my needs instead of waiting for your provision. Please give me the grace to change and lead me into your trust and love. In Jesus' name, Amen.

Think about the scenarios from this chapter. Do any of them sound like ways that you have responded to hurt?
- Do you tend toward rebellion and separation when hurt?
- Are you ever scornful or retaliatory – do you sometimes want to get even when someone hurts you?
- Have you taken personal responsibility for your sins? Do you realize that your porn problem is 100% your fault and not God's?
- Have you felt like you are justified in sinning until God makes it easy to stop?
- Do you ever get angry and argue with God? Do you have the problem of using His name or Jesus' name like a curse word when you are angry?
- Do you downplay things like sin and think that it really isn't a big deal? Sin is a big deal – big enough that the God of Heaven had to send His Son to die an excruciating death to pay for it.

If you can relate to any of the above ways of thinking, take a moment and repent for those sins as well.

HEALING THE WOUND

If you have trust issues, you may need to identify the areas where your heart was hurt. **ANY thought or memory that still has emotional pain associated with it is an area that has never been resolved in Jesus!** I've heard people say we shouldn't dig up the past – but when the past still causes pain in the present, it isn't past yet… did you get that?

This may take a little while as you ask Jesus to heal each painful memory. Until you do, there may be hurt and mistrust toward God in those areas that cause you to run from Him.

- Think about or ask God to remind you of one memory that still has emotional pain – stress, fear, shame, anger, etc.
- Ask God to bless this prayer and cover this memory in the atoning blood of Christ.
- Now ask for Heaven's perspective. If you were going through that same situation or if your child were going through that, what would God say to them? What would God's attitude be? As the situation plays out in your mind, picture Jesus literally there with you and ask Him to reveal His heart toward you.
- Meditate on these things for a few minutes and see if God doesn't surprise you and give you real insights that heal your heart.
- As the heart wounds are healed, it will be natural to be able to trust God more and see where you allowed the enemy to give a false strength such as anger or rebellion in these areas. This will give you the ability to choose trust in the future.

CHOOSING TO TRUST

Say the following statements aloud and let them really sink in. Think about each one and its implications.

- I will be happier with one woman if I learn to love her and allow her to satisfy me more than with a thousand apart from the will of God.
- I will believe that God's Word has only my best interests in mind and trust its truth even when I don't understand it.
- I trust that God will answer my prayers and show me how to change bad circumstances.
- I trust that pornography can never give me any fulfillment or real satisfaction. Thus I trust that God is true and the devil is a liar.

A FINAL WORD ABOUT LOVELESS MARRIAGES

If you are in a loveless marriage, remember, your wife didn't think "I want to be a bad wife" on your wedding day. She is a broken vessel just like you and the rest of us. When you are perfect before her and God, then you can demand perfection from her. Until then you must love her the way God loves you and patiently bring her one step at a time into godly love and restoration.

This can be especially difficult when married to someone who has been abused, raped, in a past dysfunctional sexual relationship or grew up in a family with extreme dysfunction. In these cases, you may feel like you are in a bit over your head. I recommend seeking out a church or ministry that offers counseling with "inner healing and deliverance" or set up counseling with Mighty Man Ministries. These types of counselors are used to dealing with problems that simple "good, godly advice" can't fix.

If your marriage is at a point of total frigidity and your wife is unwilling to even give a little, you have to put your desires on the shelf for a while and focus on loving your wife with pure, selfless love. This requires learning her love language, the way she receives love, taking time in prayer for her every day - and most importantly ask God to reveal what He is doing in her heart as you pray for her. This is the very model of "washing her by the water of the Word" we read about in Ephesians.

You must make a covenant to love your wife selflessly for life and minister only what God gives you the space to speak. This takes prayer and sensitivity. The Bible teaches us that the spirit or tone in which a word is presented is more important than the word itself. It also says that we must learn to speak a word "in season." That is to say that people aren't always ready to receive the word. You may think you know how to "fix" your wife, but even if you do have an accurate view, God has to be the one to bring the issue to a point where He can work on it.

The principles we've been learning in this book can be great tools to help your prayer life for her - seeing her trust issues, coping mechanisms, spiritual battles, etc. Just think, God is equipping you so that you can go help others!

CHAPTER 24

Virtue

THE POWER OF YOUR IDENTITY IN CHRIST

When I was a young man, before I knew the Lord, I was quite overweight... obese is probably the proper term. Needless to say, I was not terribly popular with the ladies. As a lost young man of 15 or so, that becomes a problem as all your friends start talking about their sexual experiences. I wanted these experiences also, but I was a virgin by circumstance not virgin by choice. By the time I was going into senior high, I started seeking God. He saved me out of my destructive lifestyles – including obesity. In two years I lost over 100 pounds and something interesting happened, I suddenly had a lot of young ladies interested in me.

Other than my body changing, something else had changed: God was a part of my life now, and I had decided to keep my virginity until I was married. This became a deep conviction in me. How deep? I had every opportunity that most men can dream of test this conviction: a playboy model propositioned me, I turned down threesomes with beautiful girls, girls offered me money if I would sleep with them, I was in several long term relationships with young ladies who very much would have liked to have sex with me (they all got saved eventually, though), I even found out that there was a betting pool at my school among many of the young women with the prize going to the girl that could get me in bed. What's the point? The devil tried every trick in the book to test that decision. But it went beyond a decision. Abstinence for me became more than a decision; it became a virtue.

226

A virtue is a character-foundational way of life - a part of the fabric of our identity. For me, staying a virgin until I was married was more than a choice – **it became part of how I saw myself - I was Jon, the virgin, someone waiting.** Virginity and waiting until marriage was part of what I felt made me who I was. Dogs don't meow because it isn't in their nature. Similarly, even though it is "natural" for a young man to want to have sex (and I certainly did want to), I didn't have sex because sexual purity was MORE a part of my nature in God. Godly nature was more real to me than carnal nature. My decision was fully in agreement with who I was in Christ.

It wouldn't have mattered if you stripped me down and threw me into the midst of a group of gorgeous naked women trying their best to seduce me. It would have been IMPOSSIBLE to put me in a situation where I would have slipped up in that area because I had more than a decision to stay away from sex; waiting for marriage was a virtue for me. I don't mean this figuratively – it would literally have been impossible, in every sense of the word, to tempt me to have sex before marriage. Certainly sex was tempting in the natural sense of the word, but my virtue, my identity, not my actions, dictated what I did and who I was.

Acting on impulses and temptations is an outflow of who you are. What you do flows out of identity. The Bible says about God that when we are faithless, He remains faithful; for He cannot deny Himself (2 Timothy 2:13). God doesn't ACT faithfully – He IS faithful. The attributes of God are part of who He is, not just how He acts. It is more accurate to say that "God is love" as opposed to "God is loving." If He IS love, then it follows that He acts in a loving manner. God is Pure. God doesn't behave purely – it is stronger than what He does – He IS PURE. Purity is part of the VIRTUE of God's character. And through Christ's completed work, it must become a virtue in us. You see, the Bible says that we ARE the righteousness of Christ. It doesn't say we merely have righteousness. It isn't something like car keys that can be forgotten, lost or misplaced. You are pure because you are in the pure One and He is in you. This is reality as God sees it. It must become our reality.

We have had a lot to say about the way we think and about changing our mind quickly when temptations arise. We have spoken about agreeing with God and breaking agreements with the enemy. I believe these decisions over time are tools by which we shape our personality and begin to create virtue. But virtue is a whole new level altogether and it doesn't take root in a day under normal circumstances but by the grace of God.

ADD VIRTUE

The first chapter of Second Peter begins a progression of thought in which Peter talks about our calling. He tells us to add to our faith virtue, to virtue add knowledge, etc. (Actually many of the principles in this book follow this progression.) He admonishes us that unless we do these things, we won't walk in our calling with certainty – if we do, we make our calling sure, certain, guaranteed of success.

Faith is just the starting point. When we begin this journey in Christ, we have to take God's promises and words about us on faith. We can hardly believe such radically good news that we are pure because we've struggled so much and failed so many times. It is simply a deliberate act of faith to believe, "God says I'm this, so it must be true even though I don't FEEL it." We must ADD virtue, this God-based identity to our faith. It won't happen automatically.

We must ask God to form convictions in our heart so deep that they become part of the very definition of who we are. When we begin to define ourselves as pure we will act that way. The Bible says *"To the pure all things are pure, but to those who are defiled and unbelieving nothing is pure; but even their mind and conscience are defiled. They profess to know God, but in works they deny Him, being abominable, disobedient, and disqualified for every good work"* (Titus 1:15, 16). It is important to note that this passage is NOT talking about performance-based purity (if there could even be such a thing). This passage is contrasting those who receive purity by faith with those of a sect called the "Circumcision." These Jewish believers required that you keep the law AND follow Christ.

If purity, then, is part of who you are in Christ, temptations lose the "hook" that snares us. You will still have a sex drive, but the impulse to respond to sexual stimulus in lust can be virtually eradicated and replaced by much stronger, godly desire. What if your entire understanding of yourself lined up with God's word? Say something out loud, "I AM (your name) THE PURE ONE." It almost sounds too dramatic to take seriously doesn't it? Do you have a hard time saying with conviction that you are pure? God's Word declares this about you no matter how dirty you may ever feel. So what if you actually believed this in your heart? What will happen then when the devil tries to tempt you? Don't you think that it would seem totally foreign? If I define myself as "Jon, the pure in heart, a son of God whose nature is contrary

228

to sin," don't you think that I will easily identify any stray thoughts as ones put there by the enemy and a simple thing to brush aside?

Until we have made God's opinion our self-definition, we have allowed something scary: OPTIONS. If you don't have virtue, then you haven't come to the place where you trust your new nature. That means your self-definition is still the old nature - which means you are nothing more than dirt trying to ACT pure. This is another way of saying, "I'm going to resist until the circumstances are right." And the enemy knows when a person has these back doors open in their heart - and he'll always find a way in.

Until you add virtue to your faith you will still see slipping back into sin as something that you must fight instead of a totally dead issue. I've heard it said, "You are only as faithful as your options." If sinning isn't an option for you, no matter what the situation, you won't find yourself in a position where you have to continuously fight. Once virtue has been formed in you, you'll have true victory.

THE PROBLEM IS CHOICE

Paul tells us in Romans 6 to present our bodies dead to sin and as slaves of righteousness. This is another way of saying, "Get rid of options." A slave doesn't have free will to do what he wants. If our bodies are slaves of righteousness, we don't even have a choice to sin against God; for a slave, obedience is understood to be a given. We don't like to think of ourselves as slaves, but if we don't become a slave of God by choice, our **lack of choice** will make us a slave of our desires by default. Thus we will be slaves to sin when we feel like sinning and not even be able to understand why we do it. I've been in that place for years, making bad choice after bad choice and not understanding why I did it; and not understanding why I couldn't seem to do the good I wanted to do.

Follow this logic: when a man **has not** made the choice to see his own nature as God defines it, he hasn't made the decision NOT TO sin. He may have said, "I won't sin." But you can't turn from one thing without turning to something else. There is still an open door that must be closed. Therefore sin will become an OPTION when the mood is right and the conviction wears off. But when your identity changes, your decision isn't mood or zeal or conviction based any longer. Purity is then a part of what defines you. Sin is not an option any longer.

I remember in the movie, The Matrix Reloaded, Neo goes to visit the Oracle and is struggling with the issue of choice. Her answer to him is hugely profound, "You didn't come here to make the choice. You already made your choice. You are here to understand why you made it." When we sin, we think it is some big, "new" thing that we've done. But the agreements were there all along, waiting for the opportune time to manifest. Because choosing virtue shapes your reality, the way you view your life, and the light in which you see yourself, virtue is a powerful decision that influences all future realities and decisions.

I wish that in the same way I had created a self-defining virtue about premarital sex, I would have done the same with all acts of ungodly sexual gratification. I would have saved myself a lot of pain and heartache. Don't you look forward to seeing yourself as so pure before God, that every thought of defilement is unimaginable... even laughable?

LIVING **FROM** VIRTUE

Most believers mistakenly think that Kingdom and calling works like this: first you stop sinning, then God says, "Wow. I can really use that person now! They have this 'holiness thing' down pat.", then God gives you a big anointing and calling and acceptance, and identity, etc. So these well intentioned, but misguided souls spend all their time trying to NOT live by their old nature rather than to trying TO live by their new nature.

Learning to live by the Spirit and to operate in God's Kingdom is similar to moving to another country and wanting to communicate. What good does it do to simply not speak your native language? If I, as an American, want to fit into another culture, I must do more than to simply try to NOT ACT American. I must learn to speak the language and learn the ways of the new culture. Similarly, we are strangers and foreigners in this world when God saves us and places us in His Kingdom. The goal of this book and indeed the goal of all Christianity is not to merely cause you to stop living like the world. If you eradicate the carnal mind and could stop thinking like to world, you would still have no idea how to relate to God, to the new man or to the

Kingdom. Rather, our goal must be to change our mind and start to think and live and meditate on the better things of the new nature.

If you magically become an "un-sinner," that doesn't automatically mean that you will know God's will or be excited about God's Kingdom or your calling. But if you will get excited about God's Kingdom and your calling, if you will walk in the truth and walk in the Spirit, you will not walk in sin by default. As you do these things, **sin free living becomes the byproduct of your deep walk with God and not the means to having a deep walk with God.**

You can't stop sinning by trying to stop sinning. The Bible says that simply meditating on the "nots" and "don'ts", i.e. "don't look, don't touch, don't taste, etc." may APPEAR wise or godly but has NO VALUE against the indulgence of the flesh (Col. 2:23). This is so different from what is being taught in most circles. Christianity has been losing the battle against lust because it is telling men, "Don't look, don't touch", trying to hype them up with tactics and emotional appeals rather than teach them how to walk in the Spirit. Walking in the Spirit, walking in the truth, living from virtue, regarding yourself according to your heavenly identity, these are all the same thing – but importantly, applying these principles is the way the Bible teaches us to overcome sin. Any other self-willed, self-empowering method is only as strong as the willpower of the flesh. Despite this, most of the Christian world is trying to figure out a way to make sin management work using external motivators and self-will. God's desire has always been to cause you to fall hopelessly and irrevocably in love with Him. It isn't God's plan to strengthen your willpower, so why has this become the focus of Christianity. Why has religion created this treadmill of faulty thinking that supposes the way to overcome is to stir up more and greater willpower, hype up resolve and zeal to a higher fervor than sexual temptation, use filters and accountability for when your willpower fails, and/or somehow get so "spiritual" that temptation is no longer tempting?

You will always have a sex drive. The carnal mind will always be the enemy of God and the Spiritual mind. Your willpower and zeal will always fluctuate. Therefore, the way the Kingdom works is by empowering you to change your mind – to live by a higher principle altogether.

So many men feel like they are really doing something BIG for God by not sinning. This just shows that they are trying to stop sinning without living from the new nature. Their focus is still on the old thing – IT is magnified rather than God. When you change your mind, you are focused on new things and the old things become smaller. This is how and why Paul says, I count all things as dung compared to the excellence of knowing God and His calling (Php. 3:8). People probably looked at Paul and said, "Wow! Look at all that he's *sacrificing* for God." His response is like mine: No! Stop looking at earthly things. Stop setting your mind on carnal things. Look at the Spiritual things that God has done and set before you. Look at who you are in the Spirit. Look at where we can go in Christ. Become who you are. Then the "sacrifice" of not sinning is joyfully replaced with the eager expectation of things to come.

When tempted, stop looking at it as this "big thing" that you must overcome or this huge temptation. You are dead to that thing. Count it as small, pathetic, worthless and, here's the important part, immediately change your mind to spiritual things: your nature, calling, destiny. Let THESE be the big things. The more you "fight sin" the more you magnify it. Fighting a dead thing doesn't take a lot of effort – in fact, it isn't a fight at all. If you are fighting and fighting, you are doing it wrong. Real victory doesn't come from fighting something bad, but from embracing something better. Get a vision for yourself, your life, your walk with God, the Kingdom and your calling that you absolutely fall in love with – let these be magnified in your heart; set them before you and find that leaving sin behind becomes a small sacrifice.

LIVING UNDER HEAVENLY REALITY

Holiness is our new reality and must stay our new reality. You are not a sinner! You never will be one again, EVEN IF YOU SIN. The entire book of First John is about this phenomena and he says something shocking: "Whoever has been born of God does not sin, for His seed remains in him; and he cannot sin, because he has been born of God" (v. 3:9). John recognizes that, yes, we still sin (v.1:10), but tells us that we can't ever again be sinners. We FEEL like sinners when we sin, but this isn't an emotion that we can allow the place to define us. This new reality is greater than what feels real in our emotions. We may feel tarnished and dirty, but in reality, we are pure. But that purity must flow out of our spirit and change our souls (mind and emotional makeup).

Understand this: you have all the character of God in your spirit when you are born of the Spirit, but that reality does you no good unless you allow it to have its work on your soul. Paul prayed that Christ would be formed in you (Gal 4:19). He was praying for believers who already had Christ in their spirit.

He was praying that the virtue of Christ would come out of their spirit and be formed in their hearts. Virtue is a spiritual reality for you. But you must make it a personal reality in order for it to affect your life's decisions.

I have said and have heard people say, "I'm just a sinner saved by grace." Why is it so easy to identify with that old nature? You aren't a sinner any longer! The Bible calls you a saint. Will you still sin in various ways? Yes, but as Paul tells us in Romans 7, that is merely dead sin living in you and being worked out of you by a greater force: the Living Christ in you who is forming living virtue in you. Why should we allow our ongoing process of sanctification from sins to affect our enjoyment of the reality of our positional perfectedness through God's perfect Spirit residing within us?

We can thank God for the fact that He has sanctified us and made us pure. Pray that the spiritual reality of our purity and virtue would become a practical reality for us in our souls. That we would put on the Breastplate of Righteousness and no longer identify with our old nature, but be fully conformed to the virtue of our new nature in Christ, our Lord.

Throughout the entire New Testament, this concept of putting off the old dead man and putting on the new man is a powerful theme. I often used to just glance over those passages, thinking that maybe they were just trying to say, "Don't sin…" They are so much more profound than that. Let's look at a few:

"that you put off, concerning your former conduct, the old man which grows corrupt according to the deceitful lusts, and be renewed in the spirit of your mind, and that you put on the new man which was created according to God, in true righteousness and holiness (Eph. 4:22-24)."

"Do not lie to one another, since you have put off the old man with his deeds, and have put on the new man who is renewed in knowledge according to the image of Him who created him (Col. 3:9,10)."

"But put on the Lord Jesus Christ, and make no provision for the flesh, to fulfill its lusts (Ro. 13:14)."

"Stand therefore, having girded your waist with truth, having put on the breastplate of righteousness (Eph. 6:14)."

This idea of "putting on" our true identity is so powerful and prevalent in the New Testament. God is VERY concerned with more than just your salvation, but your IDENTITY transformation – and this is the key to it. You can see from these passages that when we put on our true nature and identity, it removes all place for the devil (Eph. 4:27) and is how we make no provision for our flesh. It is the first step to learning how to walk in the Spirit – we deny all carnal, fleshly, worldly opinions and cause our only opinion of ourselves and reality to be what God says about us.

I love the understanding this truth gives to the Ephesians 6 passage about putting on the armor of God. He tells us that we are girded with truth if we have put on the breastplate of righteousness. The breastplate for a knight would have their crest emblazoned on it so that others would know who they are and what family or kingdom they hail from. This whole idea of being girded with truth and the breastplate of righteousness has everything to do with your identity. This is where we start to be powerful and dangerous in the Spirit. This truth is what makes all the other armor of God work properly. The truth of your identity is one of the most important spiritual principles you can EVER learn. It will literally change your life if you lay hold of this and begin to walk in the Spirit by putting on the new man.

This transcends even this topic of lust but goes without saying that if we don't have our "reality" based in this world, then worldly things won't have their appeal. If we walk in the Spirit, we won't carry out the desires of the flesh.

The reality of your righteous identity in Christ as a son of God puts you into right relationship with God. When you understand that you are a full son, your spiritual highs and lows will become a thing of the past. Even if you sin, you'll realize that your position and privilege with God is not affected in the least. When a man is in right relationship with God, the love of God can begin to flow and affect every area of life.

This is the key to learning to truly love and accept yourself. If you try to love yourself based on worldly standards, you can never truly find love and worth; for there will always be flaws and other people more "lovable" than you. All self-acceptance and love based on worldly things is a lie based in pride – a counterfeit love that satan gives to steal the riches of true love. But when you understand that God formed you, knew you and called you from before the foundation of the world, as the Bible says, and restored you in Christ to the perfection of your original design, suddenly you begin to understand your value in a whole new light. Anyone can love themselves and swell with gratitude unto God when you begin to grasp this truth.

As we begin to understand just how settled the issue of sin is with God, it frees us to go to the next level of fellowship with Him. Until this point, the focus of life for most Christians is little more than sin management and trying to figure out how to get God to bless us. But when we understand that we ARE blessed already and there is no blessing that can be given that hasn't been given; and when we understand that our sin isn't keeping us from blessing but our lack of walking in the Spirit, where our blessings reside, then there is nothing left but to say, "**God, wow! I've had it backward all along. I have nothing left but to live to love you because You have handled all the rest!**" This is where eternal life abundant truly begins and mortal, **unsatisfying life of strife and struggle ends.**

Mighty man, you are better than sin. It isn't your nature. It never was. You are not a sinner. You are a son of God, created in His image. Put on the new man until your spiritual identity becomes your only identity.

Christianity will again see revival fire that changes the world when we stop trying to become righteous enough to believe that God can use little old us and start to simply let God use us as we are the righteousness of Christ. How differently would you live, believe and pray if you truly accepted and believed that you are as righteous as Christ, as beloved by God as Christ and that you partake of the same inheritance as Christ? When that becomes reality for a believer, you'll stop waiting around for God to do something for you and you'll start to say, "God what can I do for You, seeing that you've given me EVERYTHING?" When Christianity gets a hold of this truth, how can anything BUT personal and worldwide revival explode?

~ Mighty Man Training and Application ~

What are some of Heaven's Realities for our lives? Read these scriptures about who you really are after you are saved. For each one, make it a declaration over your life and take a moment to reflect on the fact that this is the real you.

Declarations of Virtue

"I am the Temple of God." - 1 Corinthians 3:16
"I am a son of God." - Galatians 3:26
"I am no longer a slave." - Galatians 4:7
"I am light to the world." - Ephesians 5:8
"I am complete in Christ". - Colossians 2:10
"I am a son of the light. I am NOT a son of darkness." - 1 Th. 5:5
"I am strong. I have overcome the wicked one." - 1 John 2:14

Take a moment to really contemplate the ludicrous reality of these identity statements. For example, you are the Temple of the Living God! Most Christians are trying to get their friends to come to church... But the Heavenly tabernacle is IN YOU! You carry the presence and fullness of God with you wherever you go! The only thing keeping you from walking in the fullness of that reality is your perception of reality - your virtue.

You ARE a light to the world. Take a moment and picture that one. The world is dark until you walk into the room. Aren't these spiritual realities fantastic! The Bible is full of realities about us that should just blow our minds! No wonder it breaks God's heart when we get so entrenched in sin - we are living so far below how He designed us and below what we have been given in Christ.

Sometimes it doesn't seem like these declarations are true when we first start to say them. My advice is to rehearse the truth until you believe it. Really, we have rehearsed lies until we have believed them. Time to turn the tables, believe and start to live as we truly are.

CHAPTER 25

Matters of the Heart

THE HIGHEST IDEAL

I write about matters of the heart here at the end, not because they are the least important lessons – rather they are the most important. They are, however, the most difficult lessons to learn. Things on the surface are easy to see, but the heart is deep. We have spent a lot of time talking about things like the Fear of the Lord. These lessons have their place initially, but they are just a starting point. That is why the Bible calls lessons like these "the beginning of wisdom." Learning these lessons can help you walk in wisdom at first, but God wants us to learn His heart and come into a loving relationship with Him. Do you really want to be motivated not to sin because of fear of loss or consequences for the rest of your life? God doesn't want you to stay in that place either.

God's plan was never to have servants or slaves, but sons and daughters - people with whom He could share His heart. *"No longer do I call you servants, for a servant does not know what his master is doing; but I have called you friends, for all things that I heard from My Father I have made known to you (John 15:15).*

This relationship is what I was hungry for my whole life. These matters of the heart were the lessons I learned last, but truly wanted the most. But all along, God was preparing my heart to live from love by filling me with His love for me. You can't give what you don't have. From the beginning I wanted to live by a higher ideal, but didn't have the capacity. I wanted real freedom, not "sin management," but didn't even know what that looked like. I wanted to love and serve God with my whole heart - to be at a place where nobody could change my mind or put me in a situation where I would sin against the One who saved me and who loves me.

God, through this process that we've read, restored a broken man and taught me what real freedom is. He restored my soul's confidence that I was loved, He showed me that I have all the acceptance from Him I can ever receive, God caused me to realize my perfect righteousness – all these things for which I was striving for so long were already mine. As I no longer was crushed under the weight and rebellion of feeling like I could never please God, that I could never live up to His "expectations"; when I began to realize that I have no blessings to "earn" that haven't already been freely given through Christ; when all these things came together in my soul, I changed. **There was nothing left for me to do for God but to simply love Him.**

UNBROKEN FELLOWSHIP

It happened one night: I hadn't been messing up or anything that I knew of, but I was just talking to God as I got ready to go to sleep. My thought was, "God, I don't know that I'm very good at loving You, but I'd like to be better at it." An old familiar scripture came to mind, *"If you love me, keep My commandments (John 14:15)."* I had heard this scripture a hundred times before and it never brought freedom. It always seemed like just another commandment. Something I had to do to "keep God happy."

There was something different about it this time, though. God was about to show me His heart in this scripture. Instead of this passage bringing condemnation, it seemed softer, more personal and intimate. And then another phrase from this same chapter in John came to my mind, "Abide in Me." Then another, "As the Father loves me, I love you." "Abide in Me." Suddenly these verses came flooding into my mind and it was as though God was saying, "Stay with me. I love you. Don't break fellowship. Abide in Me. Let my words abide in you. If you keep My commandments, you will abide in My love (Selections from John 14 and 15)."

Suddenly all these scriptures took on all new meaning and life for me. These weren't the words of a commanding God who expects us to do what He tells us to...or else. They were the pleas of the Lover of My Soul who understands that sin separates us from His fellowship. This was not "new information" to me. I academically understood that sin separates us from God. I comprehended the phenomenon that Jesus came to forgive sin and bring us back into fellowship because "God so loved the world..." However, what I was learning about the nature of God at this moment was more than academic knowledge.

It seemed almost as though I was hearing the compassionate pleas of a love-sick lover, the Song of Songs God we read about in Solomon's account. It was as if God was saying, "I love you too much to see you run to your idols. I want so much to meet the needs you think you'll find there. I love you enough to die for you. I live for you even to this day. If it were possible, I'd even die for you again and again. I love you so much. Stay with Me. Abide in Me. Keep My commandments so that we can stay connected. I love you. I love you."

The love I was experiencing from God in that moment was overwhelming. In an instant, all of the "obligation" I had always felt to get it right and be "a good Christian" suddenly melted away. All along I had wanted to get it right and even to show God that I loved Him, but wanting to love and loving are not the same thing at all. All the wanting, earnest desires and sense of obligation I had ever possessed suddenly now seemed so cheap in comparison to the power of this love. All my motivating fears of missing out on my calling or God punishing me for my sin became vomitously vile and petty when standing before the love of my Creator who wants to make me His treasure and friend.

Suddenly the thought of grieving the Holy Spirit and breaking God's heart entered my awareness on a whole new level. The thought of turning my back on His love seemed unthinkable. The cheapness of what the devil offered me in porn was detestable compared to this love. I had something new worth fighting for and to fight with: unbroken fellowship with the Lord of Love.

At the same time, in the presence of such a love as this, I was painfully aware of my complete inability to return this love. I felt a bit too much like Peter at the revelation of his Lord, *"Depart from me, for I am a sinful man, O Lord!"* (Luke 5:8). God's love was too big to wrap my head around. It was all I wanted, but it was so deep it was frightening to be a sinful man in its presence. How could God really love me like I am? How could I accept this love knowing that I would just blow it again and again a hundred times and a hundred ways sometime in the future?

God's love was so big and my love so small that I couldn't return it, earn it, keep it undefiled or even understand it. The things I'd seen and done over and over that broke His heart... how could He possibly love me as though it had never happened? "This love defies reality," I thought. Suddenly, God corrected me, "No. My love DEFINES REALITY." His love started speaking truths to my heart that began to heal wounds I didn't even know existed - and God says these same truths to you now: "You are good. You are a good son. You make Me proud. You make Me happy. I love you. You are the apple of My eye. You are precious in My sight. You remind Me of Me (you are made in My image). (Take a moment to meditate on these truths. What else does God say to you?) Despite all my fears and failures, I am the object of God's love - a love so big it defines reality and reshapes the way I see myself.

In the presence of such love, I began to understand one of the deepest wounds in my heart, one of the things that drove me away from God is the fact that in my heart I love Him more than anything in the world, knew that He loved me with this radical love, and yet I feared that my meager, pathetic love offerings were so shallow and selfish compared to His love that it made me run FROM Him rather than run to Him. Yet how do we grow in love? As we receive what He yearns to give and is giving, we can reciprocate.

The God of creation loves me enough to die for me. He didn't and will never stop loving me with that same intensity of love that took Him to the cross. He loves me just as much today as He did that day. He loves you just that much too. He isn't sitting in heaven waiting for you to come right. He doesn't get a power trip when people stop sinning – He wants them to stop sinning so that they can experience more of His love, so that the selfishness of sin doesn't steal love from others. It is all for love. He doesn't want slaves. He wants sons, friends and intimate relationships with the children He died for. He wants to see us free from our bondage more than we do. But it is for LOVE'S SAKE that He can't allow you to get free with other idols in our hearts. He wants us to love ourselves, but not for some self-derived reasons, not for our performance, not for worldly measures.

I spent so much time beating myself up about this sin that I just assumed God must feel the say way about me that I do. But I encountered a love so big that night, it changed me forever. While the sin management tactics I had learned are all true, they are fundamentally flawed, their truths trumped by higher truth. I'm free because the Lord loves ME; and the Lord doesn't love me *because* I'm free. THIS is the truth that makes everything else work, the truth that empowers all other truths. I had tried and tried and tried and failed and failed and failed using all the other tactics I had learned from Christianity because my heart had never really aligned with the Lord of Love.

The purpose of Christianity and of Christ coming to die for sin isn't for sin's sake but for love's sake. The purpose of it all comes down to love and so that we can love in return.

FUNDAMENTALLY FLAWED USUAL TACTICS

For a long time, I always knew there was something wrong with the "usual tactics." I had some "success" with cyber sitters and web filtering tools, but I knew that they weren't making me free. There are all kinds of tactics that men employ to stop sinning, but they leave us wanting more from ourselves and life. Even the lessons in this book are cheap substitutes for true freedom if we don't get to the place where we only need one single motivator: love. Protecting the love between us and God, living for love... this is the highest ideal. This is the thing that David caught a glimpse of and kept chasing his whole life. This is the cry of my heart now: that God would, in His grace, lead my heart to deeper and deeper love.

All other motivators pale in comparison to being willing to fight for love. I may not have always been able to verbalize it, but in my heart I always wanted to be able to say, "I did it all for love." I wanted a deep love for my Father to be the only reason I needed – my only concern: to give Him what He deserves and paid so dearly to give me.

I hope the lessons we've learned prior to this helped you win your battles. But I hope more than anything they left you hungry for more intimacy with your loving Father. I hope they lead you to this ideal, because if there is anything else in your heart, any other reason you want to be free beyond loving God, those reasons are selfish – merely doing it for yourself.

You see, when we motivate ourselves through things like fear of financial loss, loss of our calling, rejection by God or man, desire to have better marital intimacy, desire to be a leader, or ANY other desire, the truth is we are pursuing "godliness" for self-interested reasons. In the final analysis selfish motivators can't keep you from self-serving sin. Lust and sexual gratification is just one worldly thing we use to keep ourselves feeling OK and secure. So we replace one form of worldly, self-centered concupiscence with another form of worldly, self-centered concupiscence. We just tell ourselves it is in the name of God or right-and-wrong (so that we feel better about ourselves). Apart from love, this is the fundamental flaw with all the "usual tactics" we've studied in this book or that we find in other books on this subject.

I think these tactics will only take a person so far, but not bring the real freedom that we desire in our hearts. There is a level of freedom that can only be found when we let go of a self-lived life and give it up to God. Herein lays the crux of the matter: ugly self. Everything I had tried up until that point was done for self. It takes a revelation of the love of God to break a man of that.

BEING TRANSFORMED IN LOVE

As I think about what happened that evening, it all started with a simple statement, "God, I don't think I'm very good at loving You, but I'd like to be better." There is no "magic prayer," no formula that gets us more of God's love. However, I think the, simple humility and vulnerability of that moment put me in a place to better receive God's love. It was all about God, not about what I was doing for Him. I knew my complete inability to love God with any measure of how He loves me. I knew the only way I could even love God at all is according to His work of love bearing fruit that enables me to love Him. So in that statement, we find a few revelations: all love comes from God and God alone. He alone is Love and is the source of it all. We can't bring anything to the table. The plight of all vain religion is for man to do something that will earn himself favor or audience with God.

When we run to Him, knowing our absolute poverty and inability to bring ANYTHING to the table, we are counting on nothing but His love - that is faith. Faith pleases God. Therefore, it is by faith working through love alone that we enter into intimacy and the presence of God.

It is so fundamental to human nature to want to find some reason to value ourselves. It is no wonder coming to this place of vulnerability before God is so foreign to us. We have so many things in life that we try to attach to ourselves to add self-worth. We are always asking people what they do for a living. We are always rehearsing what we do to sound better when people ask us. We like to dress certain ways so that people know what we are all about. We like to drive certain vehicles so that people can see us the way we want to be seen. But everything we do and everything we have is just baggage that keeps us from real intimacy with God. Intimacy, real intimacy, is full acceptance in the presence of full exposure when all of our baggage is gone.

We so often run to God with our baggage blessing list: bless my business, bless my family, bless my ministry, bless all the things that I take identity from so that they can grow larger and give my identity a more firm foundation. Thus we exhaust our words and quiet-time with things that God already wanted to do and planned to bless and add unto us if we had just sought first the Kingdome and His righteousness. So we miss the real purpose of our quiet time: to work through those things and get to a real place of vulnerability with God where He can express Himself to us and through us.

God pronounced David to be king, but then allowed him to go through a wilderness time in which he lost any thought that he, himself was great. By the time David became king, he was so established as a lover of God and so rooted in God's love for him, that he didn't care if he was a king or a cave dweller for the rest of his life – his identity and self-value was not based in anything title or material value this world could offer.

Your job, family, ministry, finances, religious activity, state of sin or anything that you could add to this list will never make God love you more. He is waiting for just little you, stripped of all life's identity markers, to come naked into His presence, realizing that you have no reason to be there other than by His invitation. And when you are in that place, it is easy to want to search for something, some act, some gift to give him... but find nothing that He wants or needs. It is normal to want to run from that place of real acceptance because you know that you will, by your actions and sinfulness, soon trample upon that love. But then you come back to rest because His love is bigger than all of that... and in the light of that vast love and acceptance, all you can do is say, "I love you" back to the creator who just birthed that gift of love in you. It is the most simple and the most profound truth of the universe: God loves you. And it is from that place that all your freedom and victory shall flow.

THE RISE OF THE MIGHTY MEN OF VALOR

It is God's plan for you to be a mighty man. But do you know WHY God gives might? *"That He would grant you, according to the riches of His glory, to* **be strengthened with might through His Spirit** *in the inner man, that Christ may* *dwell in your hearts through faith; that you, **being rooted and grounded in love,** may be able to comprehend with all the saints what is the width and length and depth and height **to know the love of Christ which passes knowledge**; that you may be filled with all the fullness of God. Now to Him who is able to do exceedingly abundantly above all that we ask or think, **according to the power that works in us,**"* (Eph. 3:16-20, emphasis added). The reason God strengthens you with might is to know the LOVE of Christ. Love, furthermore, is the POWER that works in us and through us. Becoming a mighty man isn't what you think when you are a boy. To become mighty is to become like Christ, full of love and grace.

If you will set your heart to live for love, God will give you might. Why is this might essential? Because it takes sacrifice to love. It takes might to love your wife and be faithful to her. It takes might to love the Lord with all your heart, soul, mind and strength. It takes might to stir up your spirit when your flesh is crying out. It takes might to love the person being objectified for lust and to rise above that and see them as an object of God's love. It takes the might of God for self to die. It takes the might of God to be love as He is love. But nevertheless, all these things are worth it for the glorious, matchless prize of knowing this God who loves us so richly. There is nothing else that truly satisfies in this life. Love will change your life. Love will change your walk. Love will change the world. God is love; and love is the power of God.

Men throughout history fight for many reasons. They fight for money. They fight for glory. They fight for women. They fight for ideals. They fight in the name of God. But a real Mighty Man fights FOR the love of God and FROM the love of God. We fight for it - to protect the precious love that was worth the life of the spotless Lamb of God. We fight from it because a love that great is our most pure and true source of strength. To fight for the love of God, that He should receive the reward for His sacrificial love toward us is the only true freedom.

Every other motivation will only enslave us once again to powerless, selfish lifestyles. However, when love becomes your motivator... watch out devil. When I think about temptations in light of the people I love, my wife, children, God, the same attack that used to entice me now enrages me and fills my soul with righteous zeal. I don't see temptations as something appealing to me any longer when living for love because I'm not at the center, thinking about only me and I. God and others are my center. So when I think about that same temptation coming against my sons, for example, I see it for what it is: a destroyer, a deceiver, a defiler, a devil. When I see temptation that way, I want to cut the head off of ever devil that would dare to ensnare my sons in this same trap that bound me for so long.

When you live for love, you begin to connect with God's heart of love for you even more. As angry as I get thinking about how sin would defile my beautiful, pure sons, this is how God feels about me. This understanding helps us understand why God directs His wrath, vengeance, anger and hatred toward sin (all Biblical truths). Being transformed in love gives you the ability to connect with God's protective love over you in a whole new way.

Apart from this, a man is just a knight without a quest. As you connect with this love, it transforms your life and calling form being a passive, pointless self-pursuit to a passionate warrior's cry. Your home, church and friendships are filled with those who need someone strengthened with God's might and power to love radically. Love brings true freedom, true purpose, true calling.

"Who the Son sets free is free indeed." This is the heart's cry of a true mighty man. It is for freedom and unbroken fellowship that you have been set free. Go after this, seek this, hunger and thirst for this until it is your possession. We cannot settle for surface solutions. Sin management is not true freedom. Only from this place of true freedom can we also bring out our brethren into the true light. You can't pull someone into the light if you are still in darkness. But you can be used mightily by if you are a warrior of love and might.

So Stand Strong. Confident. Powerful. Ready to free the captives of this world and show them a Father who loves them beyond all comprehension. Ready to show them a better way.

We are God's army of mighty men in our generation. If we do not stand and fight for what is right, who will stand in our place? If you do not take your stand today, then when? Let us be ready to fight, wearing the full armor of God. We stand firm with the belt of truth, knowing the truth of who we are in Christ and knowing what is at stake for us and for other men. We bear not the stains of sin, but the breastplate of righteousness - fully secure in our identity as purified princes with the cross emblazoned on our chests shining forth its light. We are ready and mightily equipped with this gospel of love, poised to snatch men from the path of destruction and teach them the highest ideal. We take up our shields of faith, not faltering at the devil's accusations and lies that seek to drag us back to carnal dead life and identity; knowing that God will lead us into victory and call us to great things; not fearing what this world throws at us, but knowing that we have already overcome the world through Christ. We are steadfast in the joy of our salvation; guarding our minds; knowing that it is by grace we stand. Yes, we are dangerous, equipped with the sword of the Spirit - sharp and ready in our hands; able to slay devils, free captives, cut new paths for our family, and make history in our generation.

I call to the Davids. I shout to the Samsons. The mighty men who may have fallen to the weakness of the flesh, but who overcome and go on to change the world by the power that dwells in them. "Strengthen yourself in the Lord and in the power of His might." The Spirit that formed the world dwells in you. We are not weak. We shall not lose. Our God is with us and is for us.

It is time for the Mighty Men to go forth in victory and in true freedom.

Go with God.

Going Deeper

As you read through the Mighty Man Manual, you may have come across some areas where you feel like you need more information or could use more help. We stand with you in this fight and to see God work to perfect what concerns you. Contact Mighty Man Ministries for more information on any of the following topics at info@mightymanministries or call 1-800-664-8713.

Workbook:

Some readers may require a little more structure or want more teaching on many of the main points. The 8-week Freedom Workbook can provide both. It provides a plan that helps you walk out each of the milestone steps in your healing as well as provides additional teaching and thought provoking questions that help you really get to the heart of each issue. This is a great tool whether in a group setting or working through alone.

- If you are involved in a men's group or attend a church where you think it would be helpful to start a group, we provide a teacher's guide, group discounts and a dedicated coach to help guide your group through the course. If you want to start a group, don't wait until you are "perfect" to start – start today! The added accountability and support may be just what you and your men's group brothers need.

Additional teaching:

If you were reading and didn't understand any of the topics, we invite you to write to our ministry for additional teaching and clarification. Common questions are about (but not limited to) any of the following:

- Soul ties
- Spiritual warfare
- Curses in the New Covenant
- Spiritual Contracts for those previously involved in the occult
- And much more

Get Fired Up! Retreats, Conferences & Workshops

Jon Snyder is available to teach at your church or ministry event. Event formats and topics can be customized to meet the needs of your body and those in attendance. No matter the topic, you and your congregation will be blessed by the dynamic teaching and timely word from the Lord that Jon Brings. Contact our ministry for more information and references.

Topics may include:
- Christian destiny and calling
- Developing your identity in Christ
- The Gospel of grace
- Men's purity
- Teen purity and abstinence
- Teen destiny and calling
- Marriage

Minister & Ministry Equipping

Too often we hear of moral falls among ministers and church leaders. The devastation this causes personally and corporately is vast and heartbreaking. Our ministry can support your ministry with coaching and equipping either following such an order or hopefully before. Many times what ministers need is to hear the life-changing teaching that Jon brings to change the course of their struggle before it is too late.

We invite you to contact our ministry to get more information about how we can work with your leadership on the following levels:
- One-on-one coaching
- Core leadership equipping
- Seminars for all ministry and small group leaders

Coaching and Counseling

Do you need to work through some of these serious issues with someone who has been through it? Jon Snyder is available on a case-by-case basis for purity and marriage coaching. We also work with a network of licensed counselors and coaches across the country who are familiar with our unique approach to seeing God bring forth freedom. Contact our ministry today for more information. We will get back to you right away.

School Assemblies and Lectures

If your Christian middle school or high school or college would like to have Jon Snyder speak on any of the following topics, please contact our ministry for more information.

-   Christian destiny and calling
-   Developing your identity in Christ
-   Purity and/or abstinence

Your Input is Valued!

If you have feedback or a testimonial of what God has done, please take a moment to bless our ministry by writing to us.

Become a Support Partner

If this teaching has been a blessing to you, please consider supporting Mighty Man Ministries and sow a seed for another man or family's freedom. You can make a onetime donation or sign up for regular monthly donations safely and easily online at www.mightymanministries.com. We need your help and support to take this direly needed message to more men. Thank you!

Contact Mighty Man Ministries for more information on any of these topics at info@mightymanministries or call 1-800-664-8713.

Made in the USA
Coppell, TX
17 June 2021

57625286R00144